A Useless Guide to the Pacific Crest Trail

By

Joel (Mojave) Clark

ISBN987-0-6151-9579-7

Special Thanks to the City of Irvine, on whose punch clock I spent hours writing this Useless Guide.

Introduction

I carry the curse of being a light sleeper, which is why one of my few pet peeves in life is to be needlessly awakened after I have already fallen peacefully asleep. Tonight, my first night on the Pacific Crest Trail—one of the longest continuous trails in the world, I am awoken by my trail partner yelling the following: "Joel, there's a bear!!"

My traveling companion Matt laid beside me, zipped up tight in his goose-down Marmot bag beneath our green tarp tent—a thin rain tapping at the nylon. But there was no bear. I knew from the moment I was jarred awake that Matt was mistaken in thinking that there was some midnight bear outside of our tent; moreover, that there were any bears at all that lived in the arid sage and chaparral area of California, six miles from the Mexican border.

"What are you talking about?" I moaned into the jacket I employed as a pillow.

"Uh, mm, nothing," was the response from Matt, already half asleep just seconds after his outburst. He had mistaken my snoring for a bear. It would be hours before I successfully fell asleep again.

I had met Matt during the summer of 2000 on a college field biology trip in the Sierra Nevada Mountains. Within the first week of the outing I noticed a couple students poking fun at him for some reason. My heart went out to the guy—the odd ball—that kid who didn't quite fit in for some reason. I had always been a sucker for the eccentric outcasts. And that is how I was introduced to Matt.

I followed him outside of camp to a clearing in the forest where he field-tested his new GPS device, holding it up in the air, furrowing his brow at the screen, and rejoicing at each new satellite connection. Matt comes from a military family and had lived in three different countries and a dozen different states by the time he graduated high school. I envied his cosmopolitan upbringing. He had lived all over the country, and the world. What knowledge and interpersonal cultivation he must have gained, given his introduction to so many different peoples and cultures. The mountains were also his home, as he had grown up in a family that loved to backpack—particularly in the Sierra Nevada Mountains of California. His heart is itinerant, his feet itchy, and his aspirations lost in wanderlust.

When the idea of hiking the length of California, Oregon, and Washington—roughly 2, 658 trail miles—took root in my head one day, I knew that out of all my friends, Matt would be the one best suited to join me on such a walk.

After our initial introduction on the field biology trip back in 2000, I saw him seldom except when we organized backpacking excursions every now and then. And it was on a trip to Zion National Park where I introduced the idea of thru-hiking the Pacific Crest Trail to Matt. The conversation that spawned such a monumental journey was quite short—almost anti-climactic.

"Have you heard of the Pacific Crest Trail?" I asked him one day as we sat around our camp, loomed over by giant Cottonwoods swishing in the wind.

"No, what is it?"

"It's a trail that runs from the border of Mexico and California, to Canada. It goes through California, Oregon, and Washington."

"Really? Does it go through the Sierras?"

"Yeah! It meets up with two hundred miles of the John Muir Trail. We should do it."

"Yeah, we should."

There is an adage I heard frequently on the Pacific Crest Trail, an adage most likely uttered from the lips of every long-distance hiker, whether they are hiking the Pacific Crest Trail, the Appalachian Trail, or some other ridiculously long trail. The saying quite simply is, Hike Your Own Hike. Yes, hike your own hike. When I heard this for the first time I thought—how nice—hike your own hike. That's right. La-de-da, weee! Here we go, hiking our own hike down the trail together—just me, and my hiking buddy—hiking our own hike, together…well, for five months together, actually. Hike your own hike…meaning…meaning what exactly?

This adage was assuredly coined by a hiker long before my time, who found himself inextricably bound to a less-than-stellar hiking companion, day and night, week after week, for any number of months. Perhaps the hiker who first coined 'Hike Your Own Hike' had planned a thru-hike of the Pacific Crest Trail with an acquaintance—a hiking buddy; they each pitched in, planning individual portions of the trail, divvied up what equipment each should purchase for the whole, filled their re-supply boxes together, then, one auspicious day, they took those exciting first couple steps of their journey together. Days turned to weeks, weeks turned to months—all day and all night with the same person—through hot and cold, wet and dry. Suffice to say, they came to know the deepest content of each other's personalities through good times and especially through trying times, discovering that their personalities mixed like oil and water. Perhaps one friend rose early each morning while the other slept late; one arose in a good mood, while the other rose silently and befouled. Perhaps one person had a carefree personality while the other obsessed over trivial matters; one hiked fast, one hiked slow, and so on. Would they survive over two thousand miles without quitting or murdering each other?

One thing is for certain: at the end of it all, one of the two, while talking with this person or that person about his trek across America, ended each conversation by admonishing, "Hike your *own* hike." For that is the logical conclusion, the logical summation of his experience of being inseparable with a two-thousand-mile wet blanket. Hike your own hike…he said it; people heard it—realizing the wisdom, depth, and implications of the four words, and repeated it enough to where it reached my ears in April of 2006, at the beginning of my thru-hike of the Pacific Crest Trail with a hiking buddy of my own…

On April 26th, 2006, my friends Paul and Maddie drove Matt and me down to the southern terminus of the Pacific Crest Trail, just south of the windsock border town of Campo. The time was four p.m. when we arrived. I spotted the Pacific Crest Trail monument—a bunch of wooden posts of various heights clustered together atop a low rise. It stood some twenty feet from the international boundary with Mexico—the boundary being a tall green metal wall built of runway panels and stretching for miles in both directions. Minutemen were camped out in RV's about every quarter mile along the border. The RV closest to us was resplendent with all the pro-American bumper stickers one would expect to find on the vehicle of a minuteman. *Welcome to California. Now go home!* And so on.

Paul took the perfunctory picture of Matt and me posing next to wooden monument. I was wearing my Columbia nylon shorts, a capilene long-sleeve hiking shirt, two-layered running socks, trail running shoes, my ultra-light Gossamer Gear backpack full of water and all the food I'd need between here and our first re-supply point seven days later at Warner Springs. I was all set. The whole of last year spent researching, planning, and carefully selecting equipment had come down to this day, this moment, this minute, standing by the multi-tiered wooden trail monument, ready to spend the next five months hiking through rain, heat, snow, deserts, mountains and whatever else I could not even imagine.

I should have been excited standing there, smiling for the photograph. But a bitter wind taunted the brim of my straw hat. It penetrated my long-sleeve capilene hiking shirt leaving me cold and leaving me longing to dive back inside of my warm vehicle so that I could go back home, go back to work, and continue on in life like everyone else. In my final days before the trip, I had been so busy with moving everything out of my apartment, organizing our twenty-seven re-supply boxes, and trying to spend time with my girlfriend and friends—and family, that I had forgotten to mentally prepare myself for a five month backpacking trip. And now, as I stood there, shaking in the cold wind, I began to freak out. From where I stood on the small rise at the marker, I looked north to Hauser Mountain and the flanks of the Lagunas, and thought about the fact that 2,658 miles lay between the finish line and me. Was I really doing this?! I thought about all the snow in the Sierras that we would have to slog through, the swift creeks we would have to ford, the mountains we would climb, harsh weather, bears, mountain lions, rattlesnakes…I stopped my brain from running away from me and applied my business mind—my stress management. I had spent the last two years of my professional life opening branch offices for an advertising company. When faced with a big challenge at work, full of logistics, I would simply work hard, manage my time wisely, and take one day at a time. I learned that I could not open a branch office in one day, nor could I hike from Mexico to Canada in one day.

Paul and Maddie drove off in my car, leaving me standing like a scarecrow out in the cold on some shrubby hill. My beloved car—my comfort blanket, which took me to the gym, to nice restaurants, to my beloved girlfriend's house, was gone out of reach, leaving me with two feet. But my ability to survive the next five months without quitting would be based on my ability to adapt, to change, to adjust to my environment. I would have to find happiness when I had every reason to be bitter and angry. Through weather, bugs, and physical pain, I had to stay solid. I realized that there would be hardships ahead; thus, I made a mental resolution not to let unfortunate situations affect my attitude and my treatment of others—especially my trail partner Matt. Having grown up backpacking nearly every year of his life since the age of fourteen, Matt had a clear advantage over me. He had battled cold weather, endured swarms of mosquitoes, conquered Mt. Whitney in the High Sierras, backpacked the Swiss Alps, and all with an average of fifty pounds on his back. And he still testified to enjoying backpacking more than anything. As for myself, I had accrued three backpacking trips in my life, none of which were any longer than three days.

"Ready?" I asked Matt.

"Ready," he said.

We looked around; the wind whipped my pant legs.

"So, where's the trail?" I asked. There seemed to be a starburst of trails running off in every direction from the trail monument.

"I'm not sure," he said, pulling out the trail guide.

Wednesday, April 26th 2006

8:00 pm

Desert Bears

As I sit on the ground in the darkness of a cool night, Matt fumbling around in the tarp tent, I wonder if we will make it all the way to Canada. I wonder if we will finish. Within this past year of research and preparation for the hike, I would frequently imagine myself falling so in love with being footloose in the outdoors that I would abandon civilization altogether and simply keep on ramblin' around America, long after the trail is accomplished. I had just quit my executive level job in the corporate environment after six years of servitude, and this initial taste of complete freedom could quickly become an intoxicating elixir. What reason did I have to come back to Orange County afterwards? I had grown up there, watching the fields paved over by parking lots, watching the traffic worsen year after year. I had traveled frequently for work, and pleasure, observing many beautiful places I'd rather plant my feet. So why go back to Orange County? Why stop anywhere? Why not simply catch out on a freight train and ride her until she stops? What could possibly stop me?

Three weeks ago, I fell in love with a girl. Yes, three weeks before I would leave civilization for five months, and possibly for the rest of my life, I fall hopelessly in love. Meadow and I have grown quite attached to one another in the short time we have spent together. Our personalities seem to fit together like lock and key. She is quickly becoming a great friend and a wonderful lover. A mutual acquaintance of ours had introduced us over sushi one night in Corona Del Mar; we have seen each other nearly every night since then. But tonight is my first night without Meadow. Tonight I will crawl beneath the tent behind me and sleep on the cold earth next to Matt. Tonight, instead of feeling the gentle breath of my beloved on my neck, I will hear Matt exclaim that there is a Bear outside of the tent…in the desert.

My last night with Meadow was a most intimate affair. This morning I was tired. I should not have drunk so much wine last night. But it is dark now and I am well. Frogs sing in nearby Campo creek—a gentle wind rustles the brown rushes. A family of hikers nearby grew silent in their tents long ago. Matt lies in draperies of nylon beneath our tarp tent. A few specks of rain hit this page as I write. I may as well turn in. Good night.

"Joel, there's a BEAR!!!"

Thursday, April 27th 2006

6:21 pm

Ray Way

Tonight's dinner was pasta with smoked salmon—a dehydrated meal from the culinary artisans of Backpackers Pantry. It was delicious! Matt calculated that we hiked about fifteen miles today, coming to rest at the Morena Lake campground where, this weekend, is the Pacific Crest Trail kick-off party, identified by its ridiculous acronym ADZPCTKO: Annual Day Zero Pacific Crest Trail Kick Off. Due to my own lack of research beforehand, I was not familiar with the kick-off, and upon seeing a banner at the campground displaying ADZPCTKO, I mistook it for a Russian word identifying some cultural event at the campground.

Tomorrow and Saturday is free breakfast and dinner for thru-hikers, as well as speeches and informational meetings detailing trail conditions and water sources throughout Southern California. The campground is busy tonight but nowhere near full. Matt and I have chosen not to engage in all the festivities this weekend but rather hike out tomorrow, figuring that we would rather be ahead of the crowd to heighten our wilderness experience, and also to ensure that there is still water at the caches when we get there. It is a selfish decision; but this is survival.

Hiking today brought us through some low mountains covered in large manzanita, ribbonwood, scrub oak, and other low-lying bushes. The weather stayed bleak all day—always threatening rain, but never raining beyond a slight sprinkle. The clouds hung low like white sheets moving on a clothesline. They brushed the tops of the mountains with wet petticoats, leaving everything covered with a thick salivation of dew. We paused for lunch near the summit of one peak and found ourselves considerably wet and chilled, though not a drop of rain fell.

Due I suppose to the late winter rains this year, everywhere the mountains are green and kaleidoscopes of wildflowers paintbrush the mountain flanks. The yuccas are in bloom—their tall stalks pierce the low-hanging clouds. Matt stopped to take a picture of a highway far down below us. "We should take a picture of every road we pass on the trail," he said resolutely. I said okay. That was the first and last road he ever took a picture of.

Matt and I passed some hikers today—played leapfrog with others. One kid attached himself to us, regaling us with mindless chatter for much of the day. His trail name is Sleeping Beauty, from Virginia. I asked him how he had made it from the airport down to the border. He explained dejectedly he had paid a taxi over a hundred dollars to drive him to Campo. I also inquired how he earned his trail name, Sleeping Beauty. He was dubbed Sleeping Beauty while hiking the Appalachian Trail. Evidently, Sleeping Beauty is such a heavy sleeper that after trying to wake him repeatedly every morning, his friends finally discovered that the quickest way to get him up was to roll his body from the door of the shelters, sending him free-falling several feet to the dirt below. He was much bruised by the end of that trip.

Matt barraged him with a series of technical hiking questions as he has done with everyone along the trail so far. "What's your base weight?" "How many liters of water are you carrying through the desert areas?" "What's your entry date into the Sierras?" "How many re-supply boxes do you have?" Sleeping Beauty generally shrugged his shoulders having no answer to any of these questions, which highlighted the fact that he had not done much planning for the hike. But to Sleeping Beauty's credit, his carefree attitude and spontaneity was relieving; he approached life the way in which I tried to approach life as well. Matt on the other hand, in careful preparation for the trip, had put together a five-tabbed Excel spreadsheet with macros. He had integrated the phases of the moon with our schedule so that we would know when the best time to night-hike would be. He had also integrated all the major celestial meteor showers into our itinerary so that we would know when to watch the night sky, and when not to watch the night sky. Our hiking schedule was not broken up by weeks, nor was it broken up by re-supply points. Our itinerary was broken down by day, listing where we would camp every single night of the trip.

Within our year of preparation for the trip, Matt had introduced me to Ray Jardine's Pacific Crest Trail Hikers Handbook. Ray Jardine is the guru of ultra-light backpacking. The hypothesis of "Ray Way" is this: the modern hiker's backpack could easily be reduced in weight from the traditional fifty pounds, down to around twenty pounds, thereby increasing the number of miles one could hike per day, while decreasing the chance of injury due to an unnecessarily heavy backpack. I found many of the methods in Jardine's book to be helpful in reducing my pack weight. But a lot of what he suggested simply came down to the question of how much inconvenience does the hiker want to endure in exchange for a lighter backpack, and I didn't subscribe to all of Ray's suggestions.

For Matt though, ultra-light backpacking was a religious epiphany. I could imagine that after hiking for years with a heavy pack, Matt must have felt born-again after his conversion to ultra-light. Suddenly he was backpacking with a base-weight of ten to fifteen pounds. And in his excitement, he promulgated the tenets of ultra-light backpacking to everyone he came across on the trail. He seemed to expect that everyone shared the same enthusiasm over the religion of ultra-light which he did. Every now and then, Matt would find another believer to excitedly share weight-cutting tactics with along the trail. For the most part, I found that the thru-hikers I met along the trail had found ways to cut their pack weight down to a sensible burden, while not suffering too much inconvenience in the process.

Matt graduated college with a degree in math. Before we started our trip, he worked in San Antonio as an actuary pricing homeowner's insurance. He is analytical, precise, and intense, and does not speak with any of the common slang and phrases that come from the mouth of so many of his contemporaries. When he speaks, he speaks precisely and concisely like a scientist giving a lecture on molecular biology. Though he was a math major, he has a wide vocabulary, frequently spicing his sentences with obscure words sometimes sounding contrived and precocious. Each morning Matt mentally calculates the important mileage markers for the day: how many miles to our first water, how many miles to a good place to camp at the end of the day, how many miles to our re-supply point six days away.

Hiking today, our first full day on the trail, was good. All my running and working out in the gym has left me well prepared. My feet however are suffering and will need some time to adjust to the newer shoes and the added weight of my pack. My first blister developed today, on my right heel. After discovering the blister, I immediately dressed it with foot tape and borrowed some nylons from Matt. The blister did not cause me discomfort today. But the sheer tenderness of the bottoms of my feet in general is leaving me practically incapacitated here at the end of the day. I sit here eating our salmon pasta on a picnic bench, daring not to get up. I hope to do some quick healing tonight, or tomorrow's hike will be difficult.

We have set up our green tarp tent at campsite eighty-five, which is verily the most remote and separated campsite out of them all. As I look outside of my triangle tent picture window I see a quarter mile of green grass, punctuated with dead trees, eventually terminating at the muddy bank of Lake Morena. There are many garrulous birds, but as daylight disperses, so do the songbirds with their hymnals into the crags and elbows of the giant oaks around the campsite. A cottontail startles me, making a sudden appearance about five feet from the tarp tent. It sits there motionless, facing the lake, yet with a peripheral eye towards me. Every now and then it makes chewing sounds like its chewing dry wood. I have no idea where Matt is at the moment, but I am content to lay here on my belly, feeling the blood throbbing through my swollen footpads, listening to the frog's murky burps down at the lake, and worrying about nothing in particular; except that I have to urinate.

Friday, April 28, 2006
7:13 pm

Trail Names

Cibbets Flat campground: Matt and I hiked down the mountainside around 4:30 to have dinner and to have camp here under a big oak tree. We were famished as usual and cooked a dinner of spinach pasta with Japanese curry mix. We also added dried ginger flakes, and dried garlic flakes—one of the two endowing me with terrible gas. We only hiked around thirteen miles today due to getting a late start in the morning and enjoying too many breaks along our way.

Matt was up and out of the tent this morning before I awoke, calculating and collecting information. Finding me still asleep when he returned, he entered the tent and began crinkling a bag of corn chips near my ear, pretending that he was just situating things. I expressed to him my distaste at being awakened by the crinkling of plastic in my ear and told him never to do it again.

He took a picture of our campsite there by the lake. "How about we take a picture of every place we camp along the trail!" "Alright," I said. But that was the first picture, and last picture of our campsites he took along the trail.

The morning sky held gray, rag clouds, which chilled the air, but soon burned off to produce the much-anticipated warm spring day. The sun felt like the touch of a lost friend whose long-awaited return warms the heart.

Our late start today was to blame on the free breakfast at the PCT kick-off event at Morena Lake. I left the camp having eaten several bagels, washing it down with milk, and cranberry grape juice. Our scheduled breakfast this morning of corn meal, with no sugar, was barely palatable. The bulk of it wound up on the ground. Cornmeal was the first and last hot breakfast we ever prepared along the trail.

Matt and I keep trying to refer to each other by our trail names. Matt's trail name is Muse. I am Mojave, named after the desert I so love and have spent so much time exploring and camping.

Much like the American hobo received a road name based on a personality trait, or place of origin, most PCT hikers are given a trail name in the same manner, such as Sleeping Beauty; or a place of origin, like Bama from Alabama. It is not customary to give oneself a trail name, but we did it anyhow. Matt contemplated for days what to name himself. He entertained names such as Traveling Minstrel, Wandering Bard, and so on in that vein. He had planned on taking a small backpack guitar with him, but it never materialized. To carry around a guitar would be heresy in the ultra-light religion. Anyways, I convinced Matt that those names were too long; nobody wants to say, "Hey, what's up Traveling Minstrel!" Thus, he settled on Muse—reasoning that Muse would suggest someone who is a deep thinker; someone who enjoys discussing philosophical issues and the like. So be it.

The deep-thinking Muse took offense today though when I jested that he change his trail name to Weight Nazi, due to his continued interrogation of every hiker as to their base-weight, and unsolicited tips to strangers on ways to lessen their pack weight. He looked at me sternly. "You know, in Germany," he said, staring me square in the eyes, "calling someone a Nazi is like calling them a Fucking Asshole!"

"Well, we're not in Germany," I said. "And in America, we have funny characters like the Soup Nazi." But the whole joke had already gone over his head and down the mountain. I was sorry I had said anything.

Not too far into our hike this morning we met a spirited group of four hikers. One of the individuals went by the trail name of Squatch—a personality trait—bequeathed to him based on his fascination with the legend of Bigfoot, and his having produced a documentary on the same creature. I quickly became enamored with Squatch's intensely dry wit, and answered him in the same vein of dry humor. He carried a mini-cam in his hand and claimed to be shooting footage for a documentary on the Pacific Crest Trail. Muse and I entertained the camera for a while, answering all of Squatch's questions; then we parted ways, hoping to see each other soon.

The trail today took us through a valley of tall grass, bowing and exchanging shades of green in the breezes. A quiet mossy creek ran the length of the valley, watering the muscular oaks that leaned out of the grass here and there. We met two other thru-hikers today: Johnny Walker Red and his girlfriend, Lawn Ornament from Portland, Maine. She did not resemble any lawn ornament I have seen. They were a pleasant, soft-spoken couple—serious about their hiking. Upon learning that my name is Mojave, Lawn Ornament said, "Oh, so you're the name I've seen everywhere!" I have made it a habit to scrawl my trail name in the sand with a hiking pole every time Muse and I stopped to sit and rest.

Around four o'clock today, my feet were aching intolerably. I washed them in the cold water from a spigot at Cibbets Flat Campground, wishing for new ones. Were it not for the soreness of my feet, the hike thus far would be easy. My legs feel strong and are not tired at day's end. My lungs are mighty bellows and I never feel winded.

We did not put up the tent tonight, as there is no threat of rain. Muse has laid himself out beneath an oak tree. I have chosen the open grass behind our campsite, hoping for my first cloudless, starry night on the trail. I greatly look forward to the evening time, after dinner, when I can simply lie down and read from the New Testament, then write until the sun pulls its final ribbons of light behind the mountains to new lands.

I feel like I am eating enough. I am sleeping okay. I have a bowel movement first thing every morning. My overall mental state is sound. I am not thinking much about conveniences lost. I do not miss my car, or showers, or proper food. In my life, I have always felt like I deserve to suffer deprivations to keep me thankful for what I do have. I have always been reviled by luxury and over-convenience.

I think about my girlfriend, Meadow, and how she hates air conditioning. I turned it on in the car one day, out of consideration for her, but she made me turn it off, calling it "false air." Once upon a time, I had similarly remarked to the receptionist where I worked that air conditioning is "creating a false-environment." It is uncanny at times, the commonalities between us. I miss Meadow. I think about her all day, running certain memories through my head; all of them sweet memories—sweet as Japanese curry.

Saturday, April 29, 2006

7:25 pm

Ghost River

They say that the highest dropout rate for PCT hikers is within the first two weeks. I am not thinking of dropping out, but I do feel pretty low today. My feet are collecting blisters like a hobby, and every step I take is painful.

The first part of the day was a barren uphill climb in the hot sun. We hiked up an exposed and featureless chaparral mountainside until we were delighted to enter the first pine forest on the trail. Muse and I stopped to sit in the cool of the Jeffrey Pines and Black Oak. Blue Jays bounced about the limbs, fanning their tails and scolding us. All around, the sound of wind through pine trees; that lonesome timeless sound that makes one feel reluctantly content in deep lostness—a sound like a ghost river that still flows after the water has run dry.

No hikers passed us on the trail today. But a handful of runners came down the trail from some starting point atop Laguna Mountain. One man stopped to talk with us. He was wearing the same socks as I. Since he was the last in the race, all the other runners being ahead of him now, he divulged to us where some Gatorade was stashed off the trail two miles further up. He told us to look for the Gatorade behind a bush with a pink ribbon tied to the branch. The thought of cold Gatorade took on new level of excitement for me than it would if I was back home, sitting on a couch. Muse and I trudged off, scanning the bushes eagerly for the ribbon. We passed blue ribbons, red ribbons, orange ribbons; wait, did he say a pink ribbon? What if he actually meant this red ribbon? We just passed a red ribbon. Should we go back and check it? Haven't we hiked at least two miles already? We began searching every bush with a fluttering ribbon. No Gatorade anywhere. I was stuck with the sun-warmed water on my back. This was the first lesson learned on the PCT: Do not become exited for something until you actually see it.

The hole in my heart created by the phantom Gatorade was soon patched. The Pacific Crest Trail entered the Laguna Mountain Recreation Area where many trails crossed ours leading to campgrounds and parking lots. We found our way down a trail that led to Sunrise Highway and the Blue Jay Restaurant. The restaurant was over-decorated with every cliché Western artifact found in tourist traps across America: deer antlers, carved wooden bears, Stetsons hung on the walls, spurs and old farms tools. Regardless of the contrived feeling of the place, the cheeseburger and fries set before me was real, and I dare say my hand actually trembled a little bit as I brought it to my lips. Yes, it had been but four days since my last city meal, but it sure felt much longer than four days.

I thought about the fact that instead of *sitting* in an office for eight hours every day, I now *walk* for eight hours every day. And instead of sitting down to three-course meals three times per day, I now had one hot meal per day at a fraction of the size I am used to eating. Truly, hiking the PCT is to turn one's life upside down.

From the eastern ridge of Mount Laguna, the trail showed us to spectacular panoramas of the Anza-Borrego desert and Vallecito Valley far below, with its saw-tooth crags and palimpsests of ancient hills retreating endless into the desert strange.

Several years ago, I whiled a weekend away in the Anza-Borrego desert, alone, to collect myself after a difficult week of work. Navigating down the dirt roads in Blair Valley, I found a lonely enough location and pitched camp. While I was seated on a speckled boulder, reading quietly, my eyes fixed on a circle of stones on the ground near my tent. I had somehow failed to take notice of the ring earlier. Is that a grave? I thought to myself. I did not like the idea of camping next to a grave. There was a larger headstone at one end of the ovoid ring of stones. On the headstone was etched the following:

Blackie

1979-1993

A good dog

In the large desert silence of night, I fell peacefully asleep in my tent, some three feet from the eternal rest of Blackie, the good dog. Hours later, in a silent and windless night—a night that listened right back at you, I was awakened by a sound coming from just outside the nylon tent wall. There was no mistaking the sound—the sound of a dog's heavy panting. My eyes were thrown wide at the heavy breathing sound. Blackie? I sat up in my tent…the sound was gone; vanished just as suddenly as it had come. And there, outside of the mosquito screen window of the tent was nothing more than the creosote bushes and cholla cactus, and the eternal resting place of Blackie, the good dog.

It seems to me that a disproportionate amount of legendary tales find their homes in the deserts of the American Southwest. And were the Anza-Borrego desert transformed into an old man standing at your campfire, no shortage of legendary tales would be told to you that night.

In 1933, Louis and Myrtle Botts were camping in the Anza-Borrego desert. A strange prospector happened upon their camp one night, and gave them directions to what could be a most unusual sight not too far distant from their camp. The next day Louis and Myrtle hiked out into the desert, surely doubtful of the tall claims of the midnight prospector. But vindicated were the man's words when upon reaching Tierra Blanco Canyon, Louis and Myrtle Botts came upon the forward half of a Viking ship sticking out of the mountainside! But before the couple could return to the spot to take photographs, it is said that an earthquake caused a landslide that buried the remainder of the ship. In the 1800's legends and stories of desert stranded ships were rife in the Anza-Borrego desert environs. It was said by some that the ship seen in the desert was haunted, and could be found only on certain times of the year. And in 1878 two prospectors reported seeing a ghostly ship in full sail, floating over the extinct desert seas into the sunset!

A long time ago, the Gulf of California penetrated much further North into the present area of the Coachella Valley. In fact, the valley itself was originally supposed to be named the Conchilla valley after the numerous conch shells found in the area. But due to the unclear penmanship of the author, the Conchilla Valley went down in the books as the Coachella Valley. After the Gulf of California slowly retreated and was cut off from the sea by natural forces, it is said that a massive salt lake, Cahuilla Lake, was left behind; a lake that lingered in slow evaporation into the 16th century. It should be no surprise that many Native American legends speak of the mysterious arrival of boats up the ancient Gulf—some boats with the head of a snake, they say.

Near the present day Salton Sea is a monument erected in memorial of Pegleg Smith. Sounding more like a pirate, Pegleg's legend has it that he was an authentic desert rat who fought Indians, thieved horses, and wove many a yarn to saloon patrons while he resided in San Francisco in the late 1800's. He told of a fabulously rich gold strike he had made in the Anza-Borrego. Over the years, the location of Pegleg's lost mine has been narrowed down to the area of Tule Wash and Pole Line Road, just outside of Borrego state park. From time to time, someone crawls out of the woodwork claiming to have found old Pegleg's mine, rich with black rocks, which when the desert varnish is polished, reveal themselves to be nuggets of gold! Today, a stone pile next to Pegleg's monument gains a couple more stones each time the next hopeful prospector sets out from his monument into the hills in search of old Pegleg's lost mine. That is the tradition.

Towards the latter part of the day, to keep my blisters company, my left calf took on a dull, cramping ache. Nevertheless, we put in around seventeen miles today. Muse's feet and legs are wholly without blisters or surprise pains. I felt bad for myself, and my body that was gradually crumbling beneath me. I just do not have the years of backpacking experience that Muse has. Obviously, I had not broken in my shoes enough before starting the hike. Obviously, I had not thought about endurance training. And I hated to think that I could be the one to slow down our progress.

Towards five o'clock we were on guard to spot a specific campground listed in the trail guide. Since backcountry camping is forbidden in the Laguna Mountain Recreation Area, we are required to camp at an established campsite. But somehow we walked past the campground, and realizing we had done so, wound up crashing out on the grassy flank of a windy mountainside. As I sit here on my sleeping pad, unwilling and unable to gain my feet again due to throbbing pain, hundreds of ladybugs ascend the disturbed stocks of grass everywhere around me. They traverse my sleeping pad in angular directions, pause, and fly off on black, crepe wings.

Hiking the PCT is about being free from rules, red lights, and small print. I could care less that we are breaking the rules by camping in the backcountry. In fact, I think it ridiculous to force people into campgrounds if they would rather find some solitary respite to actually be *away* from people. But by overshooting the campground, we also overshot our chance for water and a proper toilet. I could feel Muse's mood gain gravity upon realizing that we either had to walk back to the campground, or illegally camp in the backcountry, but neither of us wanted to walk back to the campground. As the trail curved next to a road, Muse asked me what I thought would happen if we got caught camping in the backcountry.

"We won't get caught. Nobody drives around at night looking for backcountry campers."

"But what do you think would happen if we *were* caught? Think we'd go to jail?" I quickly realized that, in life, people who follow every rule to the T, do so out of an unfounded fear for the consequences of breaking them.

"We won't go to jail. Maybe they'll fine us. And if we're polite, they probably won't even fine us. But we won't get caught in the first place."

"Well, I suggest we walk off the trail as far as possible so that nobody can possibly see us from the road."

"Alright," I agreed.

We came upon a flat area a good distance away from the road.

"How about here?" I suggested.

"Mmm. I think it's still too close to the road."

I looked back and couldn't even see the road from where I stood.

I followed Muse farther as he walked up the mountain flank, following a faint and overgrown dirt road long out of use. He finally settled on the windswept mountainside from which I now write, declaring to me the awesomeness of the location. But soon after settling in to my spot on the ground, Muse rushed over to me with a new concern.

"Hey Mojave, do you think anybody is going to drive up this road tonight?"

"This road?!" I could not hide my surprise at his question. "I don't think anyone's driven up this road in a long time. It's almost completely gone."

"Maybe we should stick our trekking poles in the ground though, so that if anyone does drive up this road, they'll see it and they won't run over us."

"Well, set your poles up if you want. I'll risk getting run over tonight."

Ten minutes later, his poles were up, in crossbones fashion, a bandana attached and dancing in the wind as a warning to any traffic that might happen down a nearly extinct dirt road to nowhere.

I would like to write more tonight, but the wind is growing colder as the sun slips into the desert hills. Sleep.

Sunday, April 30, 2006

8:00 pm

Juke-Brain

My Casio Pathfinder wristwatch tells me that today is Sunday. Today does not feel like a Sunday. Normally, I would have attended the evening service at church, which incidentally ended a half hour ago at 7:30. Instead, I'm sitting in the dirt. The date, time, and days are displayed digitally on the watch face. That watch face is the last remaining artifact from my abandoned life of structure and institutions found in the city. Time, structure, institution, management—all necessary for a successful society. Our society that calls itself "free," still has its expectations, mores, and general rules by which everyone is expected to abide in order for general freedom to exist. We forego some small freedoms, knowing that the greater good is the freedom from anarchy, from confusion, from mob rule—from the animal instincts. But I am exempt from all of this now. I am society. I make the rules to govern myself. But since I trust myself, I need no governance, and since I have no occupation, nor do I depend on anyone for shelter and safekeeping, time and days are obsolete. The days of the week have no meaning to me except when I walk in to a town. If I walk in to a town on a Sunday, then the post office is closed, and I am not able to retrieve my re-supply box. But today is Sunday in the wilderness; a day suddenly denuded of any spiritual implications. Tomorrow will be the same. I will awake with the sun and walk on without the despair of having to arrive to any specific office to make any specific person content.

Who, I wonder, can say, "I hiked twenty miles on Sunday?" Well, I can say it. Today is our first twenty-miler—twenty miles being the minimum amount of daily miles that a Pacific Crest Trail hiker needs to attain in order to reach Canada before the North Cascades are buried in winter snows.

Much of our hiking today was downhill, which helps. We started off around five thousand feet, hiking through hot, barren stretches, devoid of water, and down to 3500 feet. We are currently camped by a water cistern near the dry Chariot Creek. The cistern itself is about four feet high and twenty feet in diameter. To retrieve the water, one must climb atop the cistern and push aside a metal slab to reveal an opening in which one may dunk their bottle to fill with cool, clear, water; just like the old folk song, Cool, Clear, Water. Oh and how true do those sweet lines speak to me now as I drink deeply.

All day I've faced a barren waste
Without the taste of water, cool water
Old Dan and I with throats burned dry
And souls that cry for water
Cool, clear, water

Keep a-movin, Dan, dontcha listen to him, Dan
He's a devil, not a man
He spreads the burning sand with water
Dan, can ya see that big, green tree?
Where the water's runnin' free
And it's waitin' there for me and you?

The nights are cool and I'm a fool
Each star's a pool of water
Cool water
But with the dawn I'll wake and yawn
And carry on to water
Water, water, water

Cool, clear, water

The weather at this lower elevation is considerably warmer, and I anticipate a comfortable sleep tonight in the dry air.

There is a middle-aged hiker from Central California camped near us. I introduced myself as Mojave. He smiled and said that he had seen my name scrawled in the sand several times. Johnny Walker Red and Lawn Ornament were down here at the cistern earlier, but continued on to night-hike after washing themselves and filling their water bottles.

Earlier today along the trail we came across a cache of water maintained by trail angels. The cache was a three-foot tall wooden shelf full of gallon water bottles all tethered together with string, which prevented the empty bottles from littering the trail and blowing away in the wind. In relaxation at the cache was "Pops," a hiker easily in his seventies with a bearded maw devoid of teeth, and dressed in tan pants supported by suspenders and a dirty, white, button-up shirt. Pops had a scratchy voice, like an old, dusty LP, and barely spoke above a whisper. He said he hiked six to eight miles a day and "really hoped to get to the High Sierras." I never again heard mention of Pops by anyone along trail. I hope he made it to the High Sierras.

Here at the twilight cistern, the air is still and warm—a perfect room temperature. A kangaroo rat is boldly exploring the perimeter of our camp.

As we descended in elevation today, the flora transitioned likewise and I began to see some of the same plants and flowers that I have noticed in the Mojave desert on so many of my camping trips. There is the frequent saltbush with a starburst of yellow flowers of fine fragrance. And still I pass, as I have from day one, the Ceanothus bush with bunches of tiny white flowers—flowers that emit the most memorable aroma of any to which I have been exposed. I have thought often about the fragrance over the last five days, and am content to liken the smell to sweet perfume in melted butter.

Hiking today revealed the most awe-inspiring panoramic views yet. We wound further along the eastern ridge of the Lagunas, lingering still over the Anza-Borrego desert, smugly steeped in secretive canyons and haunted dunes far below. Muse and I even spied the white peaks of the San Jacintos, still a week north of us on the trail.

The weather today was warm and breezy—not a cloud in the sky. As I walk, I think about the friends who said they want to meet me somewhere along the trail—friendly faces reaching out from the city to touch me as I pass in my world of forest and desert and mountain. I wonder if they will actually drive out to intercept me as I pass over a lonesome highway somewhere. I think about Meadow in front of her computer at work, designing belts and purses. And I think about my life, consumed in walk. My one goal: to simply walk as far as I can each day—every day.

I did not sleep well last night on the windy flank of the mountain, for the wind did not subside as it so often does after the sun sets. The wind rose and fell, swishing the grasses around me, rocking the stars in the sky. I slept intermittently, waking often when the cold wind invaded a crevasse in my sleeping bag. Late in the night, bundled deep in my bag, I woke and turned from one side to another. Some creature on the outside hissed in loud protestation of my movement—similar to the way a cat hisses in warning, but this was louder and courser. I will never know what produced such a sound, as bundled up as I was at that moment, my head cinched tight in a mummy sack. Nor did I want to chance any further movement that might aggravate the creature on the outside; that agitated, hissing creature, wandering the wind-swept mountainside in the darkness of deep midnight. No wonder campers are forbidden from camping in the backcountry.

A mélange of random songs make their way through my head as I walk for hours with nothing to hear but the sound of crunching gravel and swishing nylon shorts. Hiking the PCT is a mild form of sensory deprivation. I have no Walkman. No radio. No ipod with me to entertain my mind. And devoid of a soundtrack to listen to, my brain involuntarily queues up a perfectly random assortment of songs. Some songs make but one round, while other songs arrive daily at spontaneous moments. It is uncontrollable madness—symptoms of withdrawal from the addiction of listening to music in my car and in my room, restaurants, concerts, coffee shops. Truly, I believe listening to beautiful music to be superior to watching television. But is it really noble to be surrounded by so much music always? I can start the music in my head, but I cannot turn it off. Sometimes I hum a song I enjoy, hoping to replace the current undesirable song involuntarily queued by my juke-brain from the vast anthologies in the subconscious.

Muse and I expect to reach our first re-supply town of Warner Springs in three days, wherein we will have a full day of much needed rest. My feet are kept in constant pain by blisters and general tenderness from walking all day on rocks. I cannot understate the pain I am in come the termination of each day's march. When we find a suitable place to camp at the end of each day, I slump to the ground like I had just been shot in the head, and there I stay, hoping for no circumstances that might require me to gain my feet again until the next morning.

Things are going pretty well between Muse and me. We ask each other how we are doing throughout the day, and frequently engage in alphabet games, such as taking turns naming an animal for each letter in the alphabet, or a plant for every letter in the alphabet, or food, or movies, famous people, musical groups, countries, cities in America, foreign cities, and so on.

Nevertheless, I must write secretly of a constant and penetrating annoyance; the unnatural way in which Muse clears his throat each morning and frequently during the day is absolutely insufferable. It starts deep in his gut, sounding like he is about to puke, then erupts in a hacking noise of grotesque loudness. And this is done repeatedly in the morning, particularly after his cereal and then sporadically throughout the day. I delicately broached the subject to him the other day. To my surprise Muse said he really did not know why he clears his throat the way he does, but he would try to stop! That did not last long though as he has just cleared his throat five times in the last couple minutes.

Muse is also unnaturally cautious at times, displaying an almost phobia-like concern over marginal matters. At the end of each day he will ask me if I think it is going to rain, even if there is not a cloud in the sky. And if he does not ask about rain, Muse will ask me if I think any bears will come tonight, as if I am tracking the movement of animals in the area. Often enough, both questions are asked.

Earlier today, he practically demanded that I put on pants before drawing water from a spring with poison oak in some areas around it. I explained to him that I knew what poison oak looks like and that I would not bump in to any—which I did not. But whenever I do not respond to his authoritarian warnings, he sinks into a quiet and foul mood for an indeterminate duration of time.

Despite my complaints about him, Muse is a good guy to have along. He is a great hiker, rarely complains, and does all the mileage figuring which leaves me free to simply tramp along and concern myself with blisters and pain.

Monday, May 1, 2006

8:06 pm

Thermarest Soles

A terrible thing happened to me this morning after being unnaturally awakened by Muse, once again. In my haste to rise from the ground where I lay, I somehow put an awkward pressure on my right foot, and in the process of doing so, either pulled or tore a tendon, or a ligament, sending a pinching pain running the length of my leg. Why had I not provided my body with more time in the waking process to stretch out, loosen muscles, circulate blood?

In the early morning hours, I slept peacefully in the soft white sand of an arroyo. The time was not yet seven a.m. when I was awakened by Muse: "Five minutes, and I'm ready to hike." Muse had already eaten breakfast, done his calculations, and was hurriedly packing up his gear. Through some ceremony I had not been invited to, Muse had evidently been given the title of trail master, and had just allotted me five minutes to eat, pee, and pack up my gear. I was angry at never being allowed to wake up naturally, but I said nothing. I was angry at Muses' regimented rush every day, but I said nothing. I merely attempted to get up, and in doing so, added a pain-in-right-foot to the list of blisters, sore feet, and shin splints. Muse cleared his throat.

By noon, we had descended the mountain flanks into the infamous San Felipe Valley and Scissors Crossing renown for its capacity to be very hot, and today was no exception. Creosote bushes spiraled dendroid gray branches into the hot sky—blinding and bleached white like old lettuce. Crispy rabbit brush and glowing cholla cactus punctuated the sparkling sands, identifying this as true desert. Highway 78 ran the length of the valley—RV's glinting in the sun as they passed. I led Muse across the highway to a stand of Cottonwoods by San Felipe creek, and there we stretched out in the shade beneath the green whispering canopies. I have listened often to the voices of the cottonwoods. They whisper secrets from where they grow by water in the desert—their roots gathering deep around the water table to imbibe the precious liquid so rare and purified by miles of arid sifting mineral rock. And their jungle green canopies—antithetical to the copper stones and black lava floes from which dormant desert brush suffers rooted. I laid on my sleeping pad in the shade of the trees, no shirt, no shoes—aching feet. I listened to the trees whisper in the winds. My mind drifted.

We had planned to sit out the hotter part of the day in the shade before tackling the opposing flank of Grapevine Mountain out of

Scissors Crossing. But by 2:30, Muse grew restless and began to push and prod me enough to acquiesce to move on. I do not think he was aware that the hottest part of the day in desert climates is between about two and five p.m., after the rocks have soaked up the heat of the morning sun and begin to radiate their cache of fire back at the sky.

To alleviate the overwhelming pain in my feet, I had cut out makeshift souls from a section of Thermarest I found discarded in the bushes. The extra set of souls provided the cushioning I required as barriers against the continuous impact of my feet against the stony trail. Over the course of this last week, the traction knobs on the bottom of my shoes had peeled off, leaving the ball of my foot with that much less protection against the trail rocks jabbing into my feet.

Just before we left the Cottonwoods, a round lady with a boyish haircut and an old backpack appeared at the edge of the oases. She was easily in her fifties. We invited her to come rest, and she gladly accepted, speaking to us in what I took to be a German accent. Her name was Harriet and she divulged to us that she had been section-hiking the PCT over the last six years. I loved her spirit. She was alone, and happy with her solitude in these crumbling mountains and old deserts.

Muse and I abandoned Harriet in the shade of the Cottonwoods and set off, accompanied not far behind by another hiker, Irish, who had reclined all the while beneath the bridge over San Felipe Creek. I surmised Irish to be in his late fifties. His lips were flaking badly from sunburn, but I do not think it bothered him much. All of his exposed skin was tanned leather—a small cap protected his face. No sunglasses. He was tough as an old goat. Next to him I felt white and tender.

By the time we began climbing the ridge, the sun was in a lower trajectory in the sky, directly baking the side of Grapevine Mountain. Sweat turned brown the straw of my hat, filled the hairs of my brow and ran into my eyes. Ocotillos grew out of the mountainside, their arms pointing in contradictory directions. Loaded with three liters of water, the climb out of Scissors Crossing was slow. My feet swelled in the heat. I stopped to loosen the laces of my shoes as Irish passed us, stomping up the hot mountain.

Scorched hours later we found him encamped off the trail enjoying dinner, seated in front of his tent against the dusk sky. We continued on a bit further, where the trail led us over a ridge to a flat sandy area in a valley of scrub oak and juniper. I wanted to camp here, and night was nearly come. "I could hike another five miles," said Muse.

"But if you want to camp here, it's fine." Every time I suggested we camp for the night, Muse reluctantly stops, making sure to quote how much farther he is prepared to hike if I should decide to continue on.

Thank God today for the discarded piece of Thermarest. I run a wet towel over my toes, black from dirt. My feet are racked with pain and injury; my arms and legs, sticky from sweat. I stick them into my sleeping bag and stare up at the sky. The evening air is warm and still. It is good to be out here. And I do not complain.

Tuesday, May 2, 2006
Evening

The O.C.

Amazing! We made it to Warner Springs today; a twenty-five mile hike. And I felt every inch of it. I suffered the distance with five blisters on my right foot and one on my left foot. After lunch earlier today the rear of my left knee decided to join in on the pain, and worsened after each break I took to rest it. When we finally walked up the 1.2 miles of highway to Warner Springs Ranch, I could barely stand. In the lobby I rushed for a table upon which was complimentary coffee. Reaching to take a styrophome cup from the stack, I only managed to knock them all over. It was obvious to me that I had lost my genteel city touch—a dirt sculpture of a man. Next I capsized the cup of mixing straws all over the table. Glancing around to see if anyone was watching me, I quickly scooped the bunch of straws back into the cup with my gritty hand.

The Warner Springs hotel is a ranch style resort with individual cabin suites scattered over the green acreage. The area was once frequented by the Cahuilla Indians, and was also a stopping point along the Butterfield Stage route. All who have visited here in the past, and now the present, came to find respite and regeneration in the mineral hot springs, which presently filter down into a couple large swimming pools on the premises. I had come to do the same.

"Look!" I said to Muse as we entered our cabin. "A chair! How long has it been since we saw a chair?!" I dropped my pack and collapsed into the seat. Away went the pain. With shoes removed, I tossed my broken feet on the bed and sat there unmoved, useless, and untouchable—like a pile of junk mail on the kitchen counter. Muse was in and out of the shower in military minutes. He collected up our dirty laundry and disappeared out the cabin door to regions unknown. Gradually, I worked up the will to rise and enter the shower. For no other reason would I have moved at that moment. But I soon discovered my legs and feet in too much pain for prolonged standing. I removed the plastic liner from the trashcan and laid it across the tiles of the shower. And there I sat, naked, in an upright fetal position, my head cradled in the right angle of the wall—the hot, hot water washing off the miles of dirt and sweat. Never had a shower felt so good. Never had a shower meant so much to me. I moaned and nearly cried tears of joy and relief.

Across the highway is a restaurant in the golf-course clubhouse. Irish joined up with Muse and me as we crossed the highway together. The three of us were immediately invited to join a group of hikers already seated at a table on the patio. In all, we were GQ and his wife Switch from England, Rolling Thunder, Three-Gallon, Luigi, Irish, Muse and myself.

Warner Springs is the first re-supply point along the trail. By this time, everyone has tasted the dirt of the trail, felt the heat of the sun, and experienced pain of the feet. But spirits are high! The air here is electrified with the excitement of hikers on the adventure of a lifetime. And nowhere but The Trail have I ever felt such camaraderie with perfect strangers; strangers harkening from all over the earth.

On my right sat GQ from England. Upon learning that I was from Orange County, he asked me in an English accent, "So what, do you have like ten Mercedes back home then?"

"Ten Mercedes?" I said seriously. "No, I don't have ten Mercedes…I only have five." I knew he was going to ask me next about the television drama, The O.C.

"So you must like 'The O.C.' then?"

GQ's wife spoke excitedly. "Oh I love that show!"

"Watch it?" I said. "Why do I need to watch it? I live in it. It's shallow and superficial. That's why I'm out here."

"Well, your trail name ought to be 'The O.C.,'" proposed GQ. Everyone laughed in agreement. I laughed too. But ultimately remained, Mojave—after the desert I love.

Tomorrow is my thirtieth birthday. Tomorrow is also our first day of rest. I have no plans but to make some calls and play on the Internet. My spirit is pretty high, though my body is low. Muse and I talked in our room after dinner about slowing our pace a bit. I told him that he pushed a little too hard and that I would like to let my body adjust rightfully before we hike like that again. Muse is turning an enjoyable experience into the Trail of Tears, and he has no explanation for his drive except, "It's just the way I am." Nevertheless, I was much impressed towards the end of today as Muse took much of my gear into his pack to lighten the strain on my feet. Upon seeing my blisters for the first time while we sat in the room, he gasped in consternation, not having had any idea what kind of pain I have been walking with.

Through it all, the final miles into Warner Springs were possibly the most beautiful thus far. After cresting a hill, the trail took us into a verdant valley where the wind blew tides and shades into a sea of grasses. So taken with the spot were we that we sat and listened and felt of it. A deer bounced from one side of the valley to the next, just like out of a Wild America program. We traversed the valley, crested another hill, and were afforded yet another plain of grasses, complete with the solitary dead oak adrift in the green sea, and watercolor flotillas of wildflowers. Eventually, the trail sidled up to San Ysidro Creek and wound its way through riparian woodland of giant oaks. I would much like to hike this short section again some day, under better physical conditions.

Friday, May 5, 2006

9:34 am

Running Feather

Life here at Warner Springs has been like some kind of game show vacation: wading in the mineral pools, gourmet meals, the slow movement of the sun through the trees. Several days have passed since my last journal entry and much has happened, yet very little has happened. Yesterday I ran into Squatch again at breakfast by the golf course and he hit me up for another interview, which was done in a side room of the ranch lobby, along with T-Bird, Bama, and Nemo. Squatch remarked that I had the driest sense of humor he had come across on the trail thus far. He gave Muse and me a DVD of his previous PCT documentary "Still Walking."

Muse, Squatch, Dude, and I became embroiled in political debate over at the lodge earlier today. Both Squatch and Dude are left-of-center and reserve much vitriol for President Bush. I was pleased to see their eyes widen when, after they had thoroughly crapped on President Bush, I revealed to them that I was conservative and had voted for Bush.

Squatch was most eloquent in his response. "No way, you voted for Bush? Okay, just let me ask you one question. What the f--- is wrong with you!"

This morning at breakfast we sat with Running Feather; an older man from San Diego with many years of hiking experience. Running Feather was an ultra-orthodox priest in the religion of ultra-light hiking, and Muse sat transfixed with his teachings. "For water treatment, I use these little chlorine granules," he said, slowly touching a coffee mug to his crusty lips. "I buy these at pool supply stores." Muse asked him question after question. What kind of stove? Running Feather does not carry a stove. He explained that he hikes an average of thirty miles per day, munching almost exclusively on candy bars. Running Feather wears one pair of Speedo-like hiking shorts. When they become too dirty he takes them off, presumably standing naked at this point, washes them in a stream, puts them back on, and walks them dry. Running Feather.

Warner Springs has felt somewhat like living on a college campus: many people my age hanging out and building social networks. Many of the hikers I have met here at Warner Springs, I never saw again on the trail: Haiku, Shaggy, Nemo, Rolling Thunder. They were either ahead of me the whole time or behind—or abandoned the trail somewhere along the way. Today, I formally met Freefall, who acquired his name on the Appalachian Trail from falling down so much, and also because he sky dives. The interesting angle of Freefall is that he is a Lutheran minister. He looks to be my age and speaks with a warm, pastoral voice. I also met Bean, and her boyfriend White Lightning, who was later renamed Rabid after he was attacked by a dog and had to go to the hospital.

Muse and I have been playing a fair amount of billiards here at Warner Springs. Our games are close, but he usually wins. I did not feel like my game was up to par, probably because I am usually drinking beer when I play pool. But at dinner tonight I had two Heinekens, after which Muse challenged me to another round of pool. I won every game; several games leaving Muse with four or five balls left on the table. He gets frustrated when he loses. During our last game he was mostly watching the television in the neighboring room while I sunk balls. "I've never seen someone play so well in my life," he muttered.

Saturday May 6, 2006

8:47 pm

Lost Valley Spring

Dear Journal. I would have begun journaling earlier but Muse is afraid that there will be rain tonight, so we put up the tent in the dark. Looking up, the moon is a haloed orb behind some thin clouds that moved in at sunset. Personally, I do not think it is going to rain. Muse is just being cautious, as is his nature.

We hike about eleven miles today, about half of which was grasslands; the other half, hills. We are currently camped by Lost Valley spring and I anticipate a loud night of animal activity, as we are surrounded by oaks and sycamores, brush and sage, and lots of dark rock crevices in the crumbling schist hillsides.

This evening I have been overcome with a longing to see Meadow—enough to make me regret this trip. I want to be on vacation with Meadow right now, not the obsessive-compulsive, constantly farting Muse. But I am feeling comforted at the moment with the knowledge that I will soon spend a week with her when Muse and I leave the trail so he can attend a wedding.

Today I wore my Asics running shoes which my mother had over-nighted to me at Warner Springs. They felt loads better than the Montrails I wore the first week. However, I still acquired yet another small blister on my middle toe on one foot, and I had to tape part of my right heel due to a developing hot spot. Will the problems ever end?

My right foot still suffers from the pain of a torn something. Blisters I can deal with, but the pain in my right foot concerns me.

Sunday, May 7, 2006

7:15 pm

Ticked Off

I woke up this morning and discovered a tick on my chest. It had presumably attached itself some time during the night. Muse attempted extraction by tugging on the little bastard with tweezers, but in true tick form, it would not let go. I explained to Muse that the time-honored method of tick removal was to burn it off. We reddened the tweezer ends over the cook stove and applied the tips to the tick. The heat killed it out right, burning my chest at the same time. But removal of the tick thereafter was made easy. Now I am watching for symptoms of lime disease; so far so good.

Around eleven a.m., as Muse and I reposed in the shade of a granite boulder with some snacks, we caught wind from some passing hikers of a barbeque for hikers at Chihuahua Valley Road three miles further. Muse was up and gone in seconds. I did not see him again until I reached the barbeque at the dirt road an hour later. He had already eaten and was reclined around the grounds with about fifteen other hikers. I ate two hotdogs, an apple, handful of chips, slice of watermelon, a Budweiser, and a Pepsi. This timely barbeque was hosted by a couple of thru-hikers from a previous year. Phoenix was the name of the guy cooking. We all took some group photos and continued on.

The hike today was not particularly exciting—hot and exposed chaparral of the Bucksnort Mountains. We encountered some Coulter pines at a higher elevation, but they were all black matchsticks from a previous forest fire.

I spoke with Dude for a while on the trail about the pain in my right foot. His best guess is that my foot is pronating, meaning my foot is turning so that the outer edge of my sole is bearing my body weight. Pronating. Now I have a name for my condition, which somehow makes it less threatening.

We hiked seventeen miles today, but I actually do not feel like collapsing here where we have decided to make camp. We are at Tule Springs where a large water tank sits on a hillside. Below the tank is a spigot where gravity fed water comes out cold and clean—not to mention a hose that is run over a cottonwood branch forming a makeshift shower. Many hikers are camped here for the night. I stood beneath the shower in my shorts and lathered up; people stood around watching and waiting for their turn.

As I lie here in the darkness writing, I feel clean and well fed. Much can be said about the rare joy of feeling clean at the end of a hiking day. And I venture to say that I am happy, despite my blisters, despite my tick bite—my pronating foot! Muse, as always, is without the slightest pain, which is a blessing really. If he had anything more to worry and obsess about, I might be driven to insanity. Muse claimed some unusual fatigue today, but that is all. His biggest problem, which affects me most, is his bad gas. He farts all day, and woe unto the person who hikes close behind. Hiking behind Muse I liken to driving behind a garbage truck with a full payload. His gas smells unusually bad, and emits with dire frequency. I try to hike in the lead these days, so that I can set the pace and avoid the noxious fumes.

Monday May 8, 2006

6:28 pm

The Wolfman

On the trail, everybody is equal. We are all dirty, hungry, and thirsty; our clothes are generally the same: convertible pants, synthetic shirt, goofy hat, gaiters. It is hard to tell how some of these hikers would dress off of the trail. Some people here I would guess do not have much of a social life; thus, they take to hiking long distances by themselves, forging some trail friends along the way.

Take for example, Craig. As we all came stumping out of the mountains to the Pines-to-Palms highway today, we encountered Craig, seated beneath a white ramada at the confluence of the trail and the road. He was stocked with Sparkletts, a table full of fruit, chips and salsa, and a stove ready to whip up some self-proclaimed famous soup. Craig was waiting for us, for me, and eager to please. A pudgy man in his 40's, with a minor cleft palate, Craig was a PCT hiker from some year past and reveled in the arrival of every hiker, eager to refresh and make a new friend. Most hikers however had their hearts set on the burgers at the Paradise Café, a mile up the road. Craig watched our packs as we walked to the café—anything to help out the hikers.

Muse, Hoosier, and I sat down together. Hoosier and I ordered a Sam Adams each from the tap. Muse had lemonade. Towards the end of our meal, a willowy man in boots swept up to the counter to pay his bill. Looking at us he said, "Is there some kind a hiking convention in town or somethin'?" When he spoke, we noticed that his teeth were all sharpened to points, like those of a shark. He wore Wranglers, a cowboy shirt and a baseball style hat embroidered with the word, Native. We informed him of all the hikers walking through this time of year. "And there will be lots more comin' through," said Hoosier.

"Well, if ye want to get rid of any a them," responded the man with the pointed teeth, "send them over to my place. I'll feed 'em to my wolves."

Muse, Hoosier and I were not quite sure how to respond to this. The man drifted out the door. Days later on the trail, I was informed that I had met the Wolfman of Idyllwild, who raises wolves on his property.

Back at the trail, Craig was in busy service to a group of hikers enjoying the shade of the ramada. He had made friends. I offered to help Craig refill his water jugs. We loaded the Sparkletts bottles in the back of his station wagon and drove the mile up the to Paradise café to use the spigot on the side of the building. Sitting in a car actually felt a little foreign. Craig was happy for my help as he could not very well lift the water bottles due to spraining his back days earlier while lifting the same water bottles into the back of his truck.

I showered "dundo style" tonight in camp. To shower dundo style, I found a secluded clearing in the manzanitas, undressed, poured water on myself to get wet, lathered up with soap, and poured more water to wash off the soap. Showering dundo style can be a cold and awkward experience, but the reward of slipping clean legs into sleeping bag is enough for most any inconvenience.

A moment if I might, to write of the women encountered on the trail thus far. They are hardy lot of pioneering girls, to be sure. They seem always in a chipper mood and seem to understand perfectly well what they have gotten themselves into in undertaking this journey. Most of the girls have bodies of softball players: short and stocky, huge legs, blond hair. I am convinced that a good number of them are here to simply walk the weight off, which is possible if they stick with it. Admittedly, I need to do the same. None of the girls I have seen so far are the least bit physically attractive though. And I say this having been deprived of seeing women for about two weeks now.

I worked up a pretty good chaffing rash today. I applied Vaseline once the pain started, which helped. It seems like when one pain is conquered, another immediately takes its place. I hope to be rid of all my pains eventually, so that we can really start to hike hard every day.

Tuesday, May 9, 2006

7-ish pm

Shallow Grave

Dirt: It becomes a fact of every day life. We walk in it, sleep on it, and even eat a little bit of it. One of the many constant battles on the trail is keeping oneself clean. Without a proper shower every now and then, the battle against dirt collection is a losing one. Dirt wedges itself beneath finger and toenails to such an extent that even a proper shower will not extricate all of it. It grows increasingly difficult to stay half clean, tolerably clean. But therein lies another arena in which trail life is markedly different from city life. The focus at the termination of each hiking day is in cleaning. When there is water to spare, I poor it on myself, and shower dundo style. When water is scarce, I wipe down my arms, legs and feet with a wet towel. Either situation makes me feel better mentally and physically.

By no measure of my own dexterity, I caught my first snake today, which was sunning itself on a rock and thought not to move as I approached until I took him up. Black with yellow stripes running the length of his body, he looked to be a California Racer. After picking him up, Muse asked, "You don't think it's poisonous do you?" Well of course it is! I love picking up poisonous snakes. "No, it's not poisonous," I said.

The terrain today was a good amount of incline. We may have climbed a couple thousand feet. My feet did well, though my right foot is remarkably pained in the mornings for the first mile or so until I warm up. I keep pace with Muse and often outpace him on the inclines.

We enjoyed a nice rock and boulder show at the start of the day, then a pine forests the rest of the day. And I finally recognize where I am in the grand layout of Southern California. Our trail today traversed the eastern flanks of the Santa Rosa Mountains, which overlook the Coachella Valley. Tomorrow we will be in the San Jacintos.

We came to a saddle in the mountains today where a sign indicated "Cedar Springs" one mile down a side trail. The trail down to the spring carved an oblique angle on the barren east face of the mountain. Descending the steep, scrubby trail, I could not imagine a spring anywhere, let alone any cedars. Magically though, a rift opened on the side of the mountain, and the trail led back into a secret riparian forest of huge cedars, staring timeless across the valley and deserts beyond. Cedar Spring seemed to flow right out of a large bramble, and enough water emanated from the earth's font to give birth to a perfectly pleasant stream running the length of the old Cedar forest.

Father and son hiking team, B1 and B2 were there, enjoying the quietism of the forest. It was my turn to cook lunch and I whipped up a perfectly disgusting meal of gummy corn pasta with some kind of spice that left my mouth burning. Muse and I, despite our ever-present appetites, dug shallow graves in which to bury our failed meal.

Hiking the steep ascent on the barren mountainside back to the PCT was unpleasant. Yet I was extremely satisfied to be gazing over the Coachella Valley to the rain shadow desert mountains beyond: the Cottonwood Mountains and Eagle Mountains; for immediately over them is Joshua Tree National Park—my home away from home, my weekend escape from so many stressful work weeks. And how many times have I driven up to the Keyes viewpoint in the Little San Bernardinos only to stare west across the Coachella valley to gaze upon the very mountains upon which I currently stand! The whole experience gave me the good feeling of the immensity of the outdoors, and the insignificance of myself in comparison. Mountains, valleys; desert mountains, desert, desert, desert.

Wednesday, May 10, 2006

5:40 pm

Diseased Lizards

The trail speaks to me while I walk along, saying things like "Look at this viewpoint!" and "So you thought there wasn't enough room on this narrow mountain ledge for a trail? Well here you are and here we go!" Time and again today as we clung to the eastern face of the San Jacintos, looking down on Palm Springs, I would look at the steep ridges ahead of me and think: the trail cannot possibly go that direction. But it did, sometimes leaving the hiker a very slim margin of error. The views today were grandiose, and they came with a price. We encountered a day of steep ascents—sometimes switchbacks, sometimes crumbling inclines. And if that was not enough, just when I thought this morning, as I packed up, that I was getting an edge on the daily hiking, the trail adds another obstacle with which to wrestle: elevation. Climbing to seven thousand feet, the air became noticeably thinner. The effect was shortness of breath and more fatigue. And yet another trail difficulty emerged later in the day as we began traversing sheets of snow still lingering across the trail like unwanted relatives who do not leave after the dinner party is long over.

Earlier today, when the morning air was cool, I caught a western fence lizard. He was quite dark skinned but had some beautiful blue patches on his belly. Muse was just about to snap a picture of us together when the lizard squirmed out of my hand and darted off. "Wash your hands before you eat," cautioned Muse. "They can carry diseases." I shook my head at yet another empty admonition—another wives' tale. I grew up with pet lizards, playing with them, kissing them, eating potato chips immediately after handling them. I told Muse that what he said is not true. "Well, that's what I've heard!" he said.

Later on in the day, Muse saw me scooping some snow into my water bottle. "I would highly advise that you don't do that!" "I bet you would," I said. He turned and stomped off, incredulous that I could be so audacious, so foolish as to ignore his warnings of diseased lizards, poisonous snakes, contaminated snow. I drank the water, and it was good.

We are currently camped in Tahquitz Valley with a full moon on the rise. We are going to make our first campfire on the trail tonight. Muse and I just got into an argument over where to make the fire. Evidently, I picked a spot that he thought was too close to the tent.

Tomorrow Anju and Andrew will be hiking over Tahquitz Summit to meet us about a mile from where we are presently camped. I am looking forward to seeing familiar faces, and I am equally looking forward to the fresh food they will be bringing for lunch. Tomorrow will be a zero day in Idyllwild! I have become ravenously hungry the last couple days. I think my body has overcome the initial shock of hiking all day, everyday, and systems are returning to normal. First thing each morning upon waking, I dig a hole for my toilet. Lately, I have been adding a second bowel movement at the end of the day as well. But on a note of frustration, it shall never fail that I have to get up to urinate in the middle of the night, thus exposing myself to the bitter midnight mountain chill.

7:00 pm

I am now journaling by a pleasant campfire. We put the tent up because of some puffy dark clouds, but they seem to have passed. Our campsite is in a forest of spruce, Douglas fir, white fir, and mahogany with a loud creek flowing nearby. There is a massive, dead pine tree standing macabre as a headstone at the edge of our campsite. The pallid tree has a starburst of unusually long dead limbs tearing at the dusk sky. Who knows why a tree as large as this, and as close to a stream as this would die? But in its death it has added a palatable mystical presence—perhaps the evil spirit of Chief Tahquitz whose curse hangs in the air of an otherwise pleasant mountain forest. I am happy to be camped near this cadaverous and tentacled nightmare of a tree. We did not see many people today; just B1 and B2 from Belden, California—a quiet, but nice pair. An owl hoots from the canopies above.

Thursday, May 11, 2006

9:45 am

John Donovan

In May of 2005, sixty-year-old John Donovan mysteriously disappeared from the Pacific Crest Trail while hiking through the San Jacintos. It is generally assumed that he fell, was injured, and succumbed to a passing snowstorm.

The talk along the trail the last couple days has been the very recent discovery of John Donovan's campsite. The couple who discovered his camp had become lost in the mountains for three nights, after what was supposed to be a short day hike. After losing the trail, they followed a creek, which they hoped would lead them down from the mountain. After their third day of being lost, they were very tired and weak, but encouraged themselves by repeating the mantra, "We're going to get out of here. We're not going to die. It's not our time." The creek brought them to a dead-end gorge where they stumbled across a campsite: sleeping mat, backpack, razor, spoon, tennis shoes, and a poncho thrown in the trees for shade. But the campsite was deserted. The couple found John Donovan's identification and read his journal, the last entry eerily written exactly one year to the day the couple discovered his camp. The last journal entry was morose: a man who was lost with nobody to know to come looking for him.

The sweater and socks John Donovan left behind helped the couple survive, and with his matches they started a large signal fire and were finally rescued. The body of John Donovan has yet to be found.

I am at a loss to think of a better way to spend my morning in the mountains. Muse and I hiked up to the junction where we are to meet Anju and Andrew. The distance was but a mile, but at eight thousand feet, a mile up hill is quite strenuous for me yet. Now I sit on the ground, reclining against a rock—no shirt, no shoes, no service. Palm sized-birds flit about from ground, to branch, to rock, to streaks across the sky. The mountain forest is their home and they know it. The hilltop here is filled with the chorus of morning birds—happy to be alive, singing to God for arrival of a warm spring day.

Muse has decided to hike a mile of the PCT that we would otherwise miss by having Anju and Andrew pick us up and drive us to town. For myself, I care not that one mile out of 2700 miles goes un-walked. I am happier to have some uninterrupted silence with the birds and the mountains.

Last night, I attempted to dry by the campfire my polypropylene socks, which I had washed in the stream. I left them too close to the fire though and one of the socks melted and turned brown. I threw them both in the fire, content with the fact that I would have just five miles to hike today with one pair of dirty socks, until a new pair arrives in my re-supply box. I also left my Columbia shorts too close to the fire. They incurred a couple burn marks and holes in one of the cargo pockets. But I am pleased with these harmless scars—badges of a life in battle with the elements. Losing a pair of socks to the fire seemed to me a humorous incident; to Muse however, the sock incident was turned into a lecture on my overall carelessness, which will lead at some point, I suppose, to my eventual death on the trail. Finding no humor in the situation, my lighthearted nature quashed, Muse killed another chance to laugh at life's little inconveniences, and the evening grew quiet between us yet again. During the time when all of this burning took place, I was setting up my camera on a trekking pole to capture a true picture of our campfire with the macabre tree in the background. It was Muse's recommendation that I take such a picture; hence, I partly blame him for my burned socks.

An aerial phenomenon took place last night while we sat about the campfire. "Hey Mojave, look directly overhead," said Muse. What I saw was a silver glowing object traversing the night sky, heading from west to east. The object made no humming sound, like an airplane would, and had no blinking lights. The object also moved at a speed faster than what is normal for a plane. I would say it looked to be about the same size as Venus, when Venus is visible in the night sky. And because of its size, I found it hard to believe that I was watching the ubiquitous satellites I have seen traverse night skies many times before. The object also seemed to be self-luminescent—not reflecting the light of the sun. The object floated over the mountains and continued East towards the Mojave Desert, where it belongs—another mystery; another strange sighting; another story to take home from a weekend camping trip.

Friday, May 12, 2006

5:56 pm

Tahquitz Summit

Yesterday turned out to be anything but relaxing. The trail up and over Tahquitz Summit, which Andrew and Anju were supposed to ascend, thereby dropping down into the valley to meet us, was still blanketed with snow on the shaded east side of the mountain. Knowing Andrew and Anju would have to battle that treacherous downhill slope without trekking poles, Muse and I decided to brave the uphill climb ourselves and intercept them at the summit, which was free of snow.

Thusly, I packed up my belongings, abandoned my position of extreme recline and relaxation against the rock, and set off behind Muse for the steep, two hundred foot ascent to the summit. The climb turned out to be the scariest climb of my life thus far. The thin trail ascended along a precipitous, sloping ridge, and most of the trail was blanketed with snow, upon which if I were to lose my footing and fall, the slide would take me down hundreds, perhaps thousands of feet to sure death in the canyon below. I chose not to look down as I carefully put one foot in front of the other, kicking deep and sound pockets into the snow, alternately sinking my poles into the snow beside me. Each step was higher than the previous as we gained elevation on the ridge. I could almost hear the evil laugh of Chief Tahquitz, whose spirit the Soboba Indians believe lives atop Tahquitz Summit with a rattlesnake and a condor.

Sometimes, I wonder at the cause of my fear of heights, and the many dreams I have had of slipping off cliff ledges and falling through the empty sky. One incident that sticks out in my mind happened long ago, and appears now as a fuzzy and disjointed childhood memory. My father took me hiking at a very young age, where or when I cannot recall. I remember walking happily along a pleasant trail, my father looking down and smiling at me, his only son. My next memory is that the trail became steep, and I remember feeling the tenuous grip my little shoes had on the slippery, gravely slope. I felt at any moment like I would slide backwards and fall. I cried in mortal fear and hung onto the dirt with my hands. My father crested the slope without me, yelling triumphantly at his victory while I continued to cry, paralyzed on the crumbling hillside. I have no memory that he eventually grabbed my arm, pulling me to safety, though I am certain he eventually did. The fact that I remember the fear I experienced at that moment from so many years past, leads me to believe it the source of my slight vertigo and frequent dreams of slipping and falling.

After we crested the summit of sunny Tahquitz Peak, my tensed body unraveled from the fear and energy I exerted. I turned to a piece of rubber and slunk down into the shade to rest and wait for lunch to arrive. But the fun was not over.

Unbeknownst to us, Andrew and Anju had phoned the Ranger office ahead of time, and were aware of the impassible condition of Tahquitz Peak; thus, they had taken an alternate route to our rendezvous point—the point we had just abandoned to needlessly risk our lives ascending Tahquitz Peak.

Muse and I waited an hour past the time we were to meet them before we decided to abandon all hope of our lunch and make for Idyllwild. The trail we descended from Tahquitz Peak was not on our trail maps, and we were caused considerable stress from feeling lost, extremely hungry, and without knowledge of water sources. We eventually came across a trailhead; from there we followed a dirt road in the general direction we assumed Idyllwild to be. Through a series of run-ins with city workers who were burning brush, and residents, we eventually emerged into Idyllwild in mid-afternoon.

We found the post office before it closed. A hiker named Teflon was sitting in front of a hair salon, smoking. "Oh, you're Mojave!" he said. "Some people were looking for you up on Devil's Slide." Andrew and Anju had come up Devil's Slide: the alternate route. The mystery of the missing lunch was solved.

Dave Ledbetter is a retired citizen of Idyllwild who intercepted Muse and me in the post office parking lot. "Will you guys sign my book?" he asked. Dave had a PCT register in his car containing the signatures of all the PCT hikers whom he randomly picks up off the sidewalks of Idyllwild to ferry around to desired locations. He dropped Muse off at the Tahquitz Inn. Dave dropped me off at a clinic so I could get my right foot checked out.

I walked into the clinic at the same time as Girl Scout, a hiker my age from San Diego. He was having stomach pain. Not having had a chance to shower yet, I was sure of my odor, though immune to it myself, and felt self-conscious for subjecting the good doctor to my smell and dirt-blackened right foot. She snapped on some rubber gloves and pressed on different regions of my foot. No pain. Next they x-rayed and found no indication of fracture. The doctor finally recommended that I take three Ibuprofen three times daily with a meal to reduce pain and swelling. The doctor identified Girl Scout's stomach pain as the result of his taking Ibuprofen *without* meals. Apparently, the stuff can tear up your stomach.

As Girl Scout and I walked back down the road, Anju and Andrew pulled up alongside in their car. I was glad to see them.

Over dinner we all laughed at how we missed each other up there on the mountain, having outsmarted each other. I was about to tell them about our harrowing near-death experience ascending snow-bound Tahquitz Peak until Andrew said, "You know, I thought you guys might be waiting for us on Tahquitz Peak, so I ran up it, didn't find you there, and came back down."

"Wait," I said, hot air deflating from my head. "You went up that snowy trail, AND came back down it…without trekking poles?"

"Yeah, all I had in my hand was a bottle of water. It was fun. I slipped a couple times, but got my footing again. There's no way I would let myself fall with two thousand dollars of camera equipment in my backpack."

"I see," I said, raising a dainty blended margarita to my lips.

Anju and Andrew had run into Dude and Hoosier on Devil's Slide. "Do you guys know Mojave?" she had asked them. Hoosier slapped his knee and said, "Now what on earth would a nice couple like you want with someone like Mojave!" They laughed. Dude and Hoosier enjoyed the lunch intended for Muse and me.

Andrew and Anju said goodbye to us at the Tahquitz Inn, leaving us with the leftover snacks they had brought for us: lime flavored trail mix, Gatorade, Propel, Vitamin Water, apples, sandwiches, salami, cheese, turkey, candy bars, and other treats. I felt very grateful to have them as friends, and thank them again, whole-heartedly.

Morning in Idyllwild; I had nothing to do today but rest. After breakfast I walked to the laundromat. The owner identified me as a hiker straight away, and so we talked on such issues as snow levels, and how it was that I could afford such a trip. He was cleaning out the dryer caches as we talked. In one dryer he extracted about ten .22 gauge cartridges and a money clip on which was inscribed "The World is Mine." Listening in on our conversation, a large man doing his own laundry offered to take the .22 cartridges to feed his own rifle back home.

"You wouldn't believe the shit people leave in their pockets," the owner exclaimed to me. "I can't tell you how many times women leave lipstick in their pockets and ruin their whole load in the dryer. Then they come yelling at me like it's my fault!"

Monday, May 15, 2006

7:57 am

Haugen-Lehman

It has been several days since my last entry. The last couple days have been extremely busy and I make no apologies for my abandonment. After breakfast with Dude and Hoosier at JC's Red Kettle two days ago in Idyllwild, Muse and I hoisted our packs and were driven by Barbara at the Tahquitz Inn to the Devil's Slide trailhead. Shuttling PCT hikers to the trailhead is one of the services provided by those at the Tahquitz Inn. They even have a magnet affixed to the side of their SUV that reads

"PCT Hiker Shuttle." Idyllwild will be missed, but it was a beautiful day to begin hiking again.

We ascended the mountainside with renewed hiking acumen, overcoming day hikers who carried small daypacks or nothing at all. Our zero-day in Idyllwild had given my body great repair, and I would definitely need it for what was to come. We hiked quickly that day, nearing Fuller Ridge, which would begin the long descent out of the San Jacintos to the Ten Freeway on the scorching desert floor far below. We pushed hard and hiked until 8:00 pm. Lingering snow hid beneath the pine canopies for long stretches along the trail. We slogged through, slipping here and there in the waning light, finally pitching camp in an exposed meadow free of snow.

The next morning was cold, but we broke camp and resumed hiking at 6:40 am. While in Idyllwild, I had made arrangements with Meadow to meet us at San Gorgonio Pass at 4:00 pm on this day, and hiked quickly in an effort to meet her on time.

For the first part of the day, Muse was busy coining a trail language for us to speak so that nobody else could understand us when we talked. I participated in renaming some of our backpacking articles; then he began conjugating verbs and quizzing me as we walked along. I was done with the trail language at that point—more worried about meeting Meadow at Verbena and Tamarack at 4:00 pm. The trail descending Fuller Ridge wove back and forth in endlessly long switchbacks, the whole way providing tantalizing views of our destination far, far below. And though we could see the Ten Freeway all day in our descent, I knew it would take a long time to actually walk there.

I asked Muse if he thought we would make it by four o'clock. "Sure! I think we'll be there between two and three o'clock." I did not share in his certainty. One thing I have learned from spending time in the desert: destinations are deceptively farther away than they appear.

To make matters worse, Muse was stopping every twenty minutes to ask me for more moleskin to apply to his hotspots. Eventually, I left him with the scissors and moleskin and kept on walking, finally reaching the desert pavement where the trail intercepted a gravity-fed drinking fountain. Bean, White Lightning, Teflon, and another hiker were camped out under Tyvek tarps, waiting out the heat of the day. I drank gulps of water, and then more. Muse caught up a short time later. The time was two o'clock. We set off across the desert floor, passing the isolated, creaking community of Snow Creek, then traversed the Creosote flood plain in near hundred-degree weather. South of the Columbia River Gorge, this windswept swath of desert is the lowest point on the Pacific Crest Trail. Sweat filled my brow, ran down my face, and fell in drops from the ends of hair. The heat did not bother me so much as the thought of leaving Meadow sitting around in the middle of nowhere. In our committed hike, the entire day had been free of prolonged breaks, and felt more like a foreign legion march designed to break-in the new recruits. Finally, at 4:20, we walked beneath the Ten Freeway where sat four other hikers to whom I had no time to introduce myself. "There's water here!" one of them offered as I flashed by. "I'm alright!" I called back. They must have thought me crazy.

I stood at the deserted intersection of Tamarack and Haugen-Lehman Road. Verbena Road was nowhere in sight, nor was Meadow. Muse sat down on the curb, exhausted. I tried knocking at several cookie-cutter houses up and down the street. Nobody answered. I looked up and down the vacant street, pained under the hot desert sun. The neighborhood was deserted and looked like a small town gone bust. I flagged down a passing truck.

"Hey, do you know where Verbena is?"

"This is it," he said. "Verbena has been renamed Haugen-Lehman Road."

The man let me use his cell phone. I called Meadow who had been driving around lost for the last hour, crying. Five minutes later she pulled up to find a ragged hobo, dirty, sweaty, and smiling fondly at her.

"You probably won't want to touch me right now." I smiled at her.

"Yes, I do." She hugged and kissed me.

We drove off; the dry wind lapped my hair into curls of salt crystals.

The rest of the evening was spent stealing kisses with Meadow whenever we found ourselves alone. We whispered I love you here and there. Being with her only confirmed how much she meant to me and how wonderful of a person she is. After dinner in Palm Springs she dropped us off back at a Motel 6. We kissed goodbye several times. Today she is at work. I love Meadow.

Tuesday, May 16, 2006

2:46 PM

Goin' Out

There is an old mining town in the Mojave Desert named Dagget. It has had its share of hangings—shootings too, at the Bucket of Blood Saloon; and over the dusty streets of Dagget wandered a caste of hobos, drifters, Indians and desert rats. Every now and again, a resident of Dagget would need, for whatever reason, to visit one of the "big" cities; namely San Francisco, or Los Angeles. When it was known that a resident of Dagget was leaving for a big-city-visit, the locals would say, "he's goin' out;" suggesting of course that the big city was "out there;" suggesting also that the dusty frontier town of Dagget was "in there." I regard my new pattern of life in the same manner. For the next five months the mountains are my home, and I find myself "goin' out" for brief visits to the big city. Yet lingering around towns, however restful a town may be, is beginning to make me feel uneasy and nervous, as if the suddenness of crowds is something unnatural, something to unnerve me—something I want to get away from.

7:58 PM

The combination of a Denny's and a Motel 6 is the hallmark of dysfunctional relationships. Currently, I have a headache and my general fatigue reached a new level today. Muse felt it too, and identified the hotel room television as the source of his malaise.

"New rule," Muse suddenly said to me as we sat waiting for our food at Denny's. "No more television-watching in our hotel rooms along the way."

"What?" I said surprised. "Why do we need a rule? If we don't want to watch television, then we don't watch it. Why do we need rules?"

The waiter slid our plates of food onto the Formica table. Muse had ordered a chicken salad with a side of green beans. If you are going to eat healthy, do not start at Denny's. After a couple minutes I saw that he was perfectly dissatisfied with the meal that lay before him. He held up the menu so that I could see the photo of the salad he ordered.

"Look at this salad!" he said, tapping his finger on the picture.

I glanced between his salad and the menu. "They look the same to me."

"They're not the same! This is clearly romaine lettuce in the picture! But this," he said, indicating his own salad, "this is iceberg lettuce!"

"Is romaine healthier?" I calmly asked.

"Yes it is. Eating iceberg lettuce is like eating cardboard!"

"Oh. I like what I got." I had ordered a hamburger.

"Can I have the room key," he asked dejectedly—his gazed fixed on some faraway point.

"Are you leaving?"

"I can't take this anymore."

I put the key on the table. Muse slid from the booth, grabbed it, and was gone. I turned to watch him walking swiftly across the parking lot—shoulders hunched slightly.

Muse was in the shower when I stepped into our room. I sat down on the bed and pressed 'power' on the television remote. The television sat there quietly. Baffled, I glanced behind the TV set to find Muse had unplugged the television. Why did he unplug the television? I asked myself. Did he think that I would not be able to figure out what the problem was and simply resign myself to intense trip planning and ultra-light theory? I left the room to wander the parking lot like a cigarette butt in the wind.

Muse is a boy of extremes. He is either all in—a tightly wound ball of planning and commanding, or he is completely detached and inaccessible. For example, I was trying to find my watch earlier today, which I was certain I had placed on the nightstand between our beds. As I looked around, I asked him if he had seen it anywhere. "Nuuh," he mumbled in response, owl-eyed at the television. He was embroiled in some movie, so much so that he could not detach his attention for one nano-second to identify the watch sitting on the bed one inch from his hand.

Muse is not a multi-tasker. When he is tackling a project, the world around him ceases to exist. Nothing and nobody is more important at that moment. When he is sorting our food, the television cannot be on. Conversely, if he is watching television, he cannot do anything but watch it bug-eyed. I am his exact opposite. When I am at a task, I prefer something humming along in the background.

I admit here and now that I cannot live with this punctilious, automaton of a boy. Woe unto the future child who finds Muse as its father. Rules, regulations, and old wives' tales will be levied upon the child to the point of neurotic fear of the world and extreme pessimism, euphemized as extreme caution and protection.

Earlier today, I was flipping through the television stations and came to rest for several minutes on a movie that was just starting. I soon grew bored and changed the channel to something else at which point Muse looked over at me and said, "Turn it back to that movie or I'll sock you in the face." I left the room.

I am ready to leave this Motel 666. Muse needs the outdoors to absorb the disheveling nature of his hands. I lay my clean dinner spoon and cup on a towel on the counter to dry. The next time I enter the bathroom, the cup and spoon are laying on the disgusting sink; the towel wadded up in the corner. Muse needs the anti-biotic cream from my ditty bag, which is a small, see-through mesh bag. He dumps the entire contents on the nightstand to gain possession of the single item. I end up putting everything back in the bag. My two-liter water bottle has mysteriously disappeared. My down vest, which I hung up on a hanger, I later found in a pile on the floor. There are many people like him on this planet. It is a compliment to planet earth that she is able to absorb the dins and concussions of their lives. Sometimes, landscapes are littered and damaged for a long time by those who rearrange and leave things in a worse state as when they found them. I hate Motel 6.

I stood outside around 7:00 pm and looked towards the San Gorgonio pass with its giant wind turbines and flanks of mountains—an endless river of vehicles glimmering up and down the ten freeway. The air blowing through the pass was dirty. I had never seen the air so thick with a brown haze like this. The sun was a tan, earthenware plate hung against the sky. Something was wrong here; very, very wrong—the Denny's, the Motel 6, the brown pall of degeneration blocking out the sun; and my fatigue. This is the worst I have felt on this trip so far, health-wise. There will be blisters; there will be pains. But when there are headaches, and deep, deep tiredness, like Death is sucking out your soul through a straw, something in the air is awry. My beautiful and healthy desert air was polluted by people shuffling things around, leaving them worse than they found it.

Tomorrow my father is going to drive out here and take us away from the two-headed monster of Denny's and Motel 6, and deliver us unto the Pacific Crest Trail once again. We need to go back into the mountains immediately. Man-made conveniences are killing me softly; the zombie television steals my enchantment; the deep fryers of Denny's coagulate my veins, and dam my heart. Did you ever look around at the denizens of Denny's, or the patrons of Motel 6? They wear the scars of a life of poor decision-making—drifting about in the parking lot, hanging over the railing outside of their second-story hotel room door, watching everybody else, and waiting for something to happen. They are the other extreme; the antithesis of those with disheveling hands. These folk lead aimless lives of reckless self-indulgence and lethargy. They build nothing and suck the resources of others. Parking lots are their parks; Denny's their kitchens; Motel 6's their homes. The tendrils of their negligence wrap around me, pulling me into the gutter ash—sucking me into the oily fissures of the blacktop parking lot. I feel their carnival eyes watching me—their neediness pulling at me through these weak beige walls.

Wednesday, May 17, 2006
Noon

Rays

Yesterday morning, my parents kindly drove out to pick up Muse and me from our Motel 6 to drive us back to the trail, which was ten miles away. We arrived at the trail around 7:00 AM. A lady showed up who introduced herself as a trail angel, that is, one who helps hikers along the way, and took delight in snapping a photo of me with my parents. She asked us if we had heard about the guy who died while hiking in the Big Bear area, our next destination. We had not. I later came to find out that the man was No Way Ray who mysteriously fell down the canyon overlooking Deep Creek. This trail angel also related a story of an elderly hiker who had recently died of a heart attack on the trail. This trail angel's list of death continued. She meant well, but this was quite an inauspicious way to be sent off. My mother was unnerved.

Despite our run-in with the trail angel of death, I felt extremely energetic as we set off, and my energy continued throughout the day.

1:37 PM

We have reached some kind of campground up in the Little San Bernardino Mountains. I am extremely exhausted today and find the uphill climbs a near impossibility. Perhaps the fact that we have climbed to about seven thousand feet is the reason for some of the fatigue.

Two weeks before starting the PCT, I was camping with friends in Panamint Valley. One cool and dry night I had a dream; I dreamt of a man dressed entirely in black, with a black round-rimmed hat and round-lensed sunglasses—dark sunglasses, glacier glasses. His cheeks sucked tight to the bone; his jaw was hard tucked beneath the chin creating a masculine jaw line. The dream itself was simple; it repeated itself over and over again unnerving my sleep; this man in black who followed me around everywhere asking me the same two questions in a raspy voice: "I'm Menui; do you need anything? Will you interview me?" over and over. The voice was so clear, so forceful in my head, that upon waking in the dark of the Panamint Valley, I could hear Menui's voice echo in my head, as if fading away.

Yesterday, we forded White Water Creek where it ran through a blinding granite wash then followed Mission Creek for miles as it wound up into the mountains. The glowing desert hills rose and fell with our feet—the air tearing hot, but my body was solid, sweating to cool itself; I seemed to have boundless energy. In my rush I rounded a corner and overtook another hiker amongst the granite and gneiss alluvium whom I had not seen or met yet. He bore an umbrella aloft against the sun, and was attired entirely in black with a black round-rimmed hat and circular glacier glasses. I nodded as I passed, but momentum continued my legs past a proper introduction.

At Mission creek Muse and I stopped beneath the shade of a rambling cottonwood to make lunch. The creek was dammed with stones, forming a shallow pool into which I immediately threw my saline body.

While I was cooking, a hiker named One Feather wandered over from some unknown point and engaged us in directionless conversation. One Feather, in his mid-twenties, was hiking as far as Lake Arrowhead with his mother, Snapshot, and resembled the popularized image of what Jesus of Nazareth supposedly looked like: shoulder length brown hair; beard; white, long sleeve shirt—everything save for the one Eagle feather tied to his hair. He had the monotone speech pattern and discomforting dramatic pauses of a truly detached mind. One Feather worked as a chimney sweep in Portland, Oregon. Eventually he wandered off, claiming he was going to hunt down a rattlesnake for dinner.

Next to join us was the man in black: Ray, from Medford, Oregon. Ray was my age and exuded a demeanor of calm—not speaking unless spoken to, and always with a warm and confident smile on his tan face. He was solo hiking the Pacific Crest Trail. After having interviewed hundreds of people over the last six years of my employment, I have become ace in judging character. After a short interchange with Ray, observing his facial expressions, his measured speech, his direct answers, and his intangible aura that the world was sound, I was thoroughly convinced that he was a stand-up guy—despite his exact resemblance to Menui from my dream in the Panamint Valley.

At the moment, Muse is showering off dundo style somewhere secret. I think he is feeling as exhausted as I am. We both took a long lunch break, but here we are again, getting ready to fix dinner at 2:00 pm. He has had a rough day though. I brought him to tears earlier when I respectfully pointed out the ways in which he is annoying me. We had taken a break from walking when I told him that there are some issues I needed to bring to his attention. In an affectation of adult maturity, he nodded his head receptively and said okay. He listened and understood and could see how he was not being respectful of my belongings, meanwhile badgering me about his belongings, which were to be treated with the utmost care and caution. I also told him it was incredibly irresponsible for him to threaten to "sock me in the face" for turning the television station. "Don't you ever threaten me," I told him. "We are supposed to be friends!" We shook hands and I said no hard feelings— just some issues to be aware of. We hiked off once again. About twenty minutes later I caught up with him again at the San Bernardino Forest marker where he was in flustered tears, shifting from side to side.

"What's wrong?" I asked.

"I'm just…I'm just, really sensitive right now!" he choked. "And I don't want to have to deal with *this* right now?"

"Deal with what?" I asked, confused.

He sighed as if I was incredibly ignorant. "Deal with what?" he mocked. "I don't want to have to deal with what you just said back there!"

Annoyed with his juvenile reaction, I told him that life is not fair and that he would have to *deal* with it. Muse went on to explain how he is currently going through hard times; his grandmother is not doing so well and will probably die soon.

"Okay?" I said.

His emotions definitely had the best of him at that moment; he was not making any sense really, finally admitting to me and himself that he needed to grow up a lot more.

How many more months of this?

Dusk

I could not be more content than I am now. I am sitting in front of a stone fireplace with a warm fire lapping at hissing pine logs. Muse and I are comfortable with each other once again and towards the latter part of the day stumbled upon an old cabin in the forest—the Coon Creek Group Camp. The large cabin has a raised concrete porch attained by four steps, and a railing about the perimeter. There is a large picture window with no glass facing the porch, and front entrance with no door. Upon entering, one is greeted by a commodious brick-floored room, and tall ceiling of thick wooden rafters, creating dark corners for bats and unnamed night creatures to fester. The tall fireplace is constructed from large stones with a stone mantle, and is blackened from years of soot. There are two smaller rooms attached on either side, also with windowless frames and doorless entrances. The entire cabin is constructed of stout logs and is topped off with a corrugated tin roof. On the grounds nearby is an outhouse, which is surprisingly clean. The cabin is solid but drafty and gives one the feeling that it has been generally abandoned and gradually erased from the agendas of the Boys Scouts and camp groups. Ray joined us not long after we arrived, and finally One Feather and his mother Snapshot arrived. Muse and Ray made the best hot chocolate ever concocted along the PCT by melting a couple dark chocolate bars in with the regular hot chocolate mix, and topping it off with a Chai tea bag.

Friday, May 19, 2006
9:30 AM

Crazy Jake

I would have to peg our night spent in the log cabin at the Coon Creek Group Camp as my favorite night on the trail so far. After dark, we all sat around the tall fireplace, warming ourselves—stars shimmering in the picture window frame behind. One Feather claimed, in a low and mysterious voice that he and his mother have been followed, all the way from Campo, by someone they call Crazy Jake. According to One Feather and his mother, Crazy Jake is an elusive mountain man accompanied by an invisible dog. I listened in silence, my face warmed by the fire—dark shadows like dreams, waiting in the rafters. One-Feather continued in his monotone voice and shadowed face: "Crazy Jake is watching over us...we see the signs that he leaves behind on the trail."

"Tell them about the flash of light you saw in the Lagunas," said his mother, Snapshot. In Oriflamme Canyon of Oriflamme Mountain in the Laguna Mountains people have claimed for many years to see phantom balls of lights, or "spirit balls" moving about the mountain's East side. Old prospectors believed them to be Indian spirits guarding a ledge rich in gold. Of course, One Feather experienced the light when he was there.

"Yeah, I saw the flash of light there on the ridge...and it gave me a vision. I had a vision of twelve tribes who are going to take over all the world governments and usher in world peace for all eternity." I watched his mother nod, in full agreement of everything he said.

I laid out my sleeping arrangement on the brick floor near the fireplace that night—the crackling fire warming my head, and casting dancing shadows on the walls and up into the darkened rafters. It may have been my most restful night on the trail.

Here in Big Bear City, Muse and I had just finished breakfast at Thelma's and walked to an Internet café. I had accidentally left my wallet in our hotel room and asked Muse if I could borrow some money. My request disturbed him. He glanced off in silent thought, his eyes fixed on some distant point over my shoulder. I asked him why this was a problem when I would simply pay him back upon returning to our room. He waved his hand in the air, as if to cast off unwanted emotions. "It's insignificant," he remarked, handing me a couple bills. I am really getting sick of his possessive, bratty attitude and plan on calling him out on it from now on. Nevertheless, I was extremely proud of him yesterday as he managed to hitch us a ride on Highway 18 in to Big Bear City. A talkative man who works on trains out in Barstow drove us directly to the post office. Furthermore, Muse secured us another ride from the post office to the Motel—another Motel 6.

Good old Ray is sharing a room with us and was content to sleep on the floor last night. Today he is going to hitch back to the trail. We might leave today as well depending on my stomach, which is in turmoil, having sent me repeatedly to the bathroom this morning. There are a lot of hikers here at the motel: Starman, Teflon, Wild Thing, Guac and Blackhole, and others.

Sunday May 21, 2006

5:21 pm

Flying Rattlesnakes

I jut showered off at some creek here, northwest of the Mojave portals. Today, Muse and I began hiking at 6:45 am, needing to put away about twelve miles by noon. At noon we were to meet up with Paul where the PCT crosses highway 173. He was a little late, thinking we were somewhere else, but I borrowed a cell phone from two rednecks hauling their dirt bikes down the mountain. In short time Muse and I were sitting on lawn chairs beside the highway eating turkey and cheese sandwiches, apples, chips, chocolate chip cookies, and drinking Capri sun power drinks. I drank about five of them.

Yesterday, Saturday, was a big hiking day for us, and I turned out to be the one doing all the pushing. We put in a thirteen-hour day, hiking over twenty-five miles. Ray followed with us most of the day, but stopped at the bridge over Deep Creek to make dinner as we continued on. The PCT, as it continues high over the Deep Creek gorge, gets very narrow at times. Somewhere along this stretch is where No Way Ray fell to his death just days ahead of us perhaps.

Daylight was running out, and we kept hiking further, hoping that a campsite would avail itself. Finally, a little after eight, we reached a sturdy foot bridge and camped right there on the wooden slats, as it was the only flat area in miles. I might have had a wonderful sleep if I had not been startled awake by rain at midnight. It did not rain hard, so we stretched the tarp over the hand railings, which did well enough to protect us from the intermittent night sprinkles.

Following along Deep Creek this morning, I came across a large, banded rattlesnake after filling my water bottle at a creek. After pausing for a photo, it retreated beneath a cleft in the cliff. Muse was incredibly cautious in approaching, repeatedly asking me where the snake was. I showed him the picture of the snake on my digital camera. Muse crinkled his brow. "Is it in the air?" he asked. Not wanting to miss a perfect chance at sarcasm I answered, "Yeah, I photographed it as it was flying through the air." What the hell did he mean anyhow? Is it in the air?

We passed the famous Deep Creek Hot Springs, renown for its skinny-dippers. Skinny-dipper is always such a misleading term. Deep Creek Hot Springs should be known rather for its naked fat men, which is what I saw when we arrived, and departed just as quickly. Hikers Chai Guy and Girl Scout were there, lounging around the hot springs.

The confluence of Deep Creek and West Fork form the infamous Mojave River, which is the only west-to-east flowing river on this side of the continental divide. In ancient days, the Mojave River flowed northeast until merging with the Amargosa River, ultimately draining into Lake Manley in Death Valley. Along its backwards way, the Mojave River watered several massive prehistoric lakes: Lake Manix, which is now the dry lakes of Afton, Troy, Coyote, Harper, and Cronese; and Lake Mojave, the area which is now the dry Soda Lake and Silver Lake. These days, the Mojave River flows underground mostly, rendering the river useless to recreational activity, except where impermeable rock forces its waters to the surface. After its subterranean commute through Hesperia, Victorville, and Barstow, the river resigns itself to the alkaline sink of Soda Lake—a dry lake for all intents and purposes, though standing water is found on its surface in fluctuating seasonal amounts.

I hope Ray catches up to us eventually. He is the kind of person I need around me to act as a calming buffer between Muse and me. Ray plods along with an ultra-heavy pack, carrying his ice axe through the deserts of Southern California—not worrying about anything; just thoroughly enjoying himself. Yesterday the three of us hitched a ride together out of Big Bear City from a serious man who turned out to be a narcotics officer. He delivered us unto the trail head where sat my trekking poles, which I absentmindedly left the day before.

We made good miles during the remainder of our day; the trail north of Bertha peak ran the high ridge over Big Bear Lake amongst a forest of incense-cedar, Jeffrey pines and juniper. Ray walked behind me, regaling me with stories of his job as a long-haul trucker. "I just want to hop freight trains around America," he said at one point. I nodded my head. "Ray, you're my kind of guy."

As he was talking, the three of us tramped down Cougar Creek Trail without noticing, finally coming to a message board which informed us we had hiked two miles in the wrong direction. Ray and I burst into laughter at our stupid misfortune. I glanced over at Muse who was deathly silent, standing in his own private shaft of darkness, fuming—his gaze fixed yet again on that far off point where stood a better hiking partner; someone who never forgot his wallet—someone who never walks down the wrong trail, burns his socks in a campfire, plays with snakes, or leaves his trekking poles sitting at the trail head. On the bright side, we found running water and clean bathrooms from the Serrano campground nearby.

While we made dinner at a picnic bench, Muse mumbled, "I'm trying to let go."

He had given the sacred maps to me that day. While Ray and I walked, Muse hung far behind, like a jettisoned raft, and was generally silent and detached from conversation. I knew a "talk" was coming, and it came. While Ray was away, Muse said he was frustrated with me. He cited three circumstances as the source of his frustration, the first of which was when I accidentally left my wallet in the hotel room that morning, even though I had promptly reimbursed him when we returned to our room. I asked Muse what I *should* have done in that circumstance. He had no answer.

The next issue was the checkout time fiasco at the motel. We had not been sure if we were going to check out at noon, or stay a full day due to my stomach issues. Around ten o'clock I had told Muse I felt well enough to leave. The motel denied us a later checkout time however, so I told Muse we would have to sort our food in the hallway as the maids would be cleaning the room. He became extremely frustrated at this, listing all the tasks he had yet to do, and also that he needed to "take another shower," before we left. Ray and I were packed and ready to leave. The cleaning lady observed me placing my things in the hallway and said, "Take your time boys. I have other rooms I can clean first." So everything turned out all right. During Muse's complaint of the early-check-out fiasco, he actually turned on himself, saying, "But I guess we really weren't sure when we were going to leave because of your stomach problems."

Finally, the last of his irritation came when the narcotics officer had stopped at the post office so we could mail our bounce box. When he parked, I looked back at Muse to ask him if he wanted to take our box in. He shrugged irresolutely, so I jumped out and took the box myself, not wanting to make the officer wait. Muse explained that he was offended by my asking him if he wanted to drop off the box—as if I was inferring that it was his turn to pay. Honestly, I did not know whose turn it was to pay, which is why I asked him in the first place.

At the end of our talk, Muse reflected on the fact that he has lived alone for the past three years and is not used to having to work with people. I told him something powerful, which he agreed with and even brought up again later on down the trail. "You choose how you react to situations in life," I said. "You can get to the bottom of that hill, like we did last night, realize you have gone in the wrong direction, and laugh about it like Ray did. Or you can live your life angry and frustrated at every misfortune."

At lunch today along highway 173, Paul gave us the weather report: a storm was coming our way. Muse and I hiked a bit farther after lunch, storm clouds towering in the sky, and found a flat area in a sandy wash beside Grass Valley Creek. We put up the tent over an hour ago now, but Muse is back outside replacing the big rocks with even bigger rocks to anchor the guy lines.

When I went to wash my socks at the stream, I came across another big rattlesnake lounging on a rock. I called Muse over. Approaching cautiously, he stood behind me, and looked over my shoulder in morbid curiosity, like a frightened child at a petting zoo.

The wind is blowing in periodic tides of fierceness, and a tidal wave of massive clouds hangs precariously in the sky. I expect it to come crashing down on me at any moment. I sit here on a rock beside our tent, snapping in the wind; it sure looks and feels like something evil this way comes.

Monday May 22, 2006

5:37 PM

Silverwood Lake

I had cereal for dinner tonight at camp. We seem to have run out of fuel for our stove, which we discovered today while trying to cook mashed potatoes. We spent a good amount of time hiking along the edge of Silverwood Lake, finally coming to the Cleghorn picnic area where Ray and a hiker named Groomsman were making lunch beneath the overhang of the bathroom roof. The sky was drizzly. Ray was kind enough to let us use his homemade alcohol stove to boil our water. The mashed potatoes were great, mixed with olive oil and lemon pepper seasoning. Ray packed up and walked off with Groomsman, and I did not see them for the rest of the day. I miss Ray's company. His light-hearted spirit was a joy to be around and could make the worst situations bearable.

A hiker named Nokey was also hanging around the bathroom area. Nokey is a quiet and smiley guy in his late 20's. He is from Washington, removed from Michigan, and went to graduate school to study Library Science. I told him it is interesting that being a librarian requires that amount of education. He nodded. I told him my mother is a library technician. He nodded.

The weather today was miserable. We leapfrogged all morning with Steel Magnolia and Special 41. The storm Paul had informed us of did, in fact, visit us around midnight or after, raining consistently throughout the night. This morning began with some auspicious sunshine and broken clouds. I was foolish enough to think the storm had passed.

The first ten minutes of hiking presented us with some low, dark clouds, which made a surprise attack, sneaking over a nearby mountaintop. Though the clouds did not produce heavy rain, the constant cold wind was laced with a fine drizzle that stung my face and soaked everything nonetheless. We hiked through this nonsense for hours. The wind was particularly strong on the ridges around Silverwood Lake. Sometimes I would lean forward with my trekking poles acting as the front legs—turning myself into a four-legged creature. This I did for fear the wind would blow me off of the ridge.

I came across a wind-torn straw hat on the trail, which resembled the one I had seen Sleeping Beauty wear when we first met. I later confirmed with him that it was in fact his hat.

Muse and I were making a mad rush toward the Fifteen Freeway today, but I, dealing with a panoply of pains, decided that I did not want to push until eight o'clock or after to reach the freeway. The clouds finally broke as we crested a summit overlooking the distant Cajon Pass, and the latter half of the day turned perfectly warm. We camped at a flat area in Crowder Canyon right next to Crowder Canyon Creek.

Robert, who is Muse's cousin's boyfriend, works at the weigh-station at the Fifteen Freeway in Cajon Pass. We have been invited to stay with Robert and Christine at their house in Apple Valley, which is why we were hurrying to reach the freeway. We are close to Cajon Pass. I spied the colored string of distant freight trains threading the hills far away. And I look forward to hearing their lonesome call tonight, like a wild creature in the mountains, the last of its kind, hunted to the brink of extinction.

6:22

Letting go: The PCT forces one to let go. When you expose yourself to nature, with nothing but the contents of a backpack to your name, you learn to adjust and adapt to the vicissitudes of the raw world. In the city, we are accustomed to controlling and changing our environment. When it is cold, we turn on the heat; too hot, we turn on the air. When there is wind and rain, we retreat into our homes, turning to zombies in front of a television. For the PCT hiker there is no *inside* but for a tarp tent, which keeps out the rain, but does nothing for the temperature or the wind. And when you are hiking all day in wet wind, your shoes and socks become cold and waterlogged from overhanging bushes dumping their payloads of water into your shoes, and there is nothing at all to be done but hike on to keep yourself warmed. There is no controlling anything anymore. Mother nature is in full control and we are here to endure Her many personalities as they present themselves.

Accordingly, the PCT hiker is to remain a steady and unwavering font of positive thinking—positive energy. If you are going to complain about the weather, do not leave your house. If you are going to complain of foot pain, sit in a car and drive everywhere. But such is the lure of the outdoors for so many; the chance to be tested by hot and cold; to feel the earth in its raw existence; the opportunity to lose one's own life if careful attention is not paid; to sharpen a man into hard edges.

Muse and I were content here alone by the creek, him reading, me writing. But now six more hikers have happened upon this opportune flat area. First, Chewy and Stomper arrived. Then came Magnet and Nokey. Then Guac and Blackhole—the honeymooners from Seattle. Everyone is either settling in or cooking at the moment. They are welcome.

Wednesday May 24, 2006
10:26 AM

The Mojave

I am sitting on a back porch in the high desert—the Mojave Desert—listening to the songbirds, and the haggard ravens, watching the distant desert hills in their silent expectation that nothing important is going to happen today or any other day. The air is warm and dry. A sly breeze fidgets with the hair on my legs.

Yesterday, Muse and I slept in until the irresponsibly late hour of seven a.m. In the morning the air was crisp as lettuce, the sun a round slice of summer lemon in blue liquor. We began our hike in good spirits, Muse with long pants, long sleeve shirt, gloves, and bandana wrapped over his head and neck like Lawrence of Arabia; myself with shorts, hat, and no shirt. We paused on a crest overlooking the Cajon Pass with its flatiron granite fins stabbing at the sky—long trains thundering over the pass into and out of the Barstow classification yard.

The PCT dropped down into Lower Crowder Canyon where it followed the green creek the rest of the way to the Fifteen Freeway. Robert knocked off work at the truck weigh station and drove us over the pass and down into the Mojave where he treated us to lunch in Hesperia. Robert and Christine live on the outskirts of Apple Valley in a spacious, yet nondescript home, bearing none of the cliché accoutrements of the Southwest, which so many homes are not reluctant to display in the High Desert. A trampoline sits in the dirt backyard with a chain link fence surrounding to keep the dog, Sally, caged, lest she run freely about the desert, chasing rabbits or joining a delinquent band of coyotes.

Today is our zero day, which we are spending, in quiet anticipation of our re-supply box that should have already arrived. I am looking forward to a new pair of shoes, and Muse is in want of his Z-rest sleeping pad, after his inflatable Thermarest punctured several nights past. We have a vehicle with which we can leave to go explore the city, but I am content at the moment to do nothing but sit here on the back porch and stare out at the barren rock hillsides, tortured beneath the sun.

The Mental State

Before this journey began, I imagined myself hiking along, marveling at the beauty that surrounds. And indeed there is much beauty to be had, from a sea of tiny wildflowers to a grand vista of candy-coated mountain ranges retreating into infinity. However, the uneven and rocky condition of the trail requires the hiker to monitor the ground most frequently, allowing trees, rocks, and animals to pass unappreciated. Only when I stop to look around can I satisfy myself that the beauty that surrounds has been fully appreciated. All of this being said, I prefer to end my day and make camp several hours before the sun sets so that I can take in my surroundings to the depth of my soul, without the jarring of my steps, the focus of my eyes upon the grounds, and the filling of my ears with the crunch of gravel beneath my feet. I am finding it just as easy on foot as in a vehicle to hastily pass by the beauty of the land.

There is nothing like sundown in the Mojave—the warm air is silent and still, and waiting, as if on the verge of revealing some ancient secret; and that grand dome of sky, the first couple wind chime stars shimmering in blue black, the saw tooth hills and mountains—bats pitching in daffy angles in the air. Breathing deep my heart swells—my whole body feels as if it could take flight. I tear down a dirt road on a motorbike instead; Muse on a quad, his cousin's son on another bike, kicking dust on a dirt road retreating up into the crumbling copper hills—greasewood and cholla cactus flying past—their ridiculous forms in stunted growth across the flats.

I do not have much experience on dirt bikes—just enough to pitch one in a straight line down a deserted road. But when faced with an inclined road made uneven with lose stones and rocks jutting up through the earth, I could do nothing but lay that bike down on my own leg, the scorching exhaust pipe burning a patch of nylon pant into my tender skin while simultaneously cauterizing the wound so quickly that I should feel no pain but for the weight of the bike on my leg. We all stopped to inspect my wound and the round hole in my hiking pants. No big deal. We continued on foot up the canyon where a secret cottonwood grew against the ravages of desert sky, fed by water close below the earth. The kid told us in the old days an old man used to live up here in his shaker house. The foundation still stood, poured over the glowing rocks—rusted pipes came from the ground at odd angles, the water system gone wrong. But in the old days, the man had harnessed the spring, used the water, and lived a life of seclusion in this Indian canyon. Who was he? Why was he here? I wanted to know. Had the spring ceased to trickle from the ground forcing him to move on? Had the desert drawn shut this vein of water and opened a new gem spring in another lonesome canyon a hundred miles away? Was there only subterranean water now, feeding the deep taproot of this solitary cottonwood, living by itself in this secret canyon, like the old man of years past? But these are the secrets the reticent desert hides in its crumbling hills, secrets lost over the saline flats, and ghost lakes; secrets scrawled into desert sand by a wind-twitched creosote branch, then blown away with the afternoon winds. An owl hooted from the Cottonwood loft.

Saturday, May 27, 2006

Evening

Nitro

Muse and I just threw down camp here in the San Gabriel Mountains. A female hiker called Nitro has decided to camp in our area, which is a spectacular flat gravelly area that reminds me of the floor of the Mojave Desert. Nitro is a sarcastic, know-it-all girl who was responsible for the cooler full of soda and candy bars at highway 18 to Big Bear. She is talkative, nice, and seems very comfortable around men whom she does not know in the least.

Two days ago Muse's cousin Christine dropped us back off at Cajon Pass in the afternoon. The remainder of the day, our hike was beset with dense smog produced from the dense traffic of the Fifteen Freeway. I pushed through it with slight discomfort, while Muse seemed to suffer much more from the smog's effects. He complained considerably until we pitched camp near the top of Lytle Creek Ridge.

As a precaution, Muse hung his food up in a tree for fear of bears. He dedicated no less than fifteen minutes climbing the small oak tree beneath which we were camped. I sat on my ground pad listening as dry branches snapped—leaves, sticks, and acorns showered down on me from above as he sought out the highest reaches of the tree to secure his food. After Muse's repeated admonishment, I still slept with my food next to me. The irony of the situation was that though no bears came during the night, some lucky rodent found a completely abandoned bag of food high up in an oak tree, chewed a hole, and helped itself to all the Triscuits it could eat. I stifled my laughter in the morning.

We hiked down to the Baden-Powell trailhead where we came across Girl Scout, Chewy and Magnet around four o'clock. I asked Magnet who was smoking in the parking lot for a cigarette. He said he did not have any as he had been smoking discarded butts he found. What a spendthrift!

I was moderately tired when we decided to tackle Baden-Powell, which was another four miles of strict elevation gain through switchbacks lined with white fir and Jeffrey pine. The weather grew quite cold as we approached the summit—my left calf started to cramp. Though I was incredibly fatigued and cold, the views east and west were spectacular. A solid blanket of white clouds spread out over the land below as far as I could see, and only the mountain peaks penetrated through as if floating along a dusk ocean. We walked across a barren, exposed ridge where we found Turtle Don reclined in his sleeping bag beneath a lodgepole pine. Turtle Don, an older man, acquired his name while hiking the Appalachian Trail due to the fact that he simply walked so slowly.

Near dark we found a flat area on the leeward side of the ridge between Baden-Powell and Throop Peak, protecting us from the penetrating wind, while affording us a nice view of the sunset. Just when I thought I was alone, along came Lint, a foul-mouthed but cordial hiker of like age. He had started hiking on May eleventh, and had caught up to us already. In his hand was a bamboo staff, and his legs were tattooed with commemorations of other hikes accomplished in life.

This morning, Muse and I were still tortured by the freezing, howling wind. We packed quickly and resumed hiking at 6:15 am without breakfast, hoping to descend to warmer weather. The warmer weather never really came that day. Yet the mountain wind sculpted the glowing fog into white plumes towering up into the air like fairy castles, and gossamer sheets sliding over the ridges like ghost armies. Fog hands with dendroid fingers slowly closed in around us in a heartless sorcerer's grip. We descended into the fog ocean, pausing for breakfast at the Little Jimmy Campground. Lint caught up again and talked with us for a while.

I wore my Golite jacket all day today. The clouds were with us off and on—mostly on. At one point on the trail, there was a detour as a section was closed to protect a frog habitat. I think it was the Yellow Legged Spotted frog. As a result we found ourselves tramping three miles down the Angeles Crest Highway until re-crossing the trail at Cloudburst Summit.

My new shoes are giving me blisters after two days of use. I took scissors to my shoes in an attempt to cut away the fabric rubbing my feet. The attempt has had partial success. But I fear these ten-and-a-halfs are simply too small for my feet, which have grown larger. My toes are frequently pressed, which is very uncomfortable. Still, we hiked over twenty miles today, and though the weather remains cold tonight, it is nowhere near as cold as last night.

I am humored as I write, overhearing Muse's conversation with Nitro. He has been drilling her for about an hour on weight and equipment questions. She eventually asked him where the name "Muse" came from. He said he named himself, thinking that a Muse is someone who is musical and thoughtful. Nitro revealed to him that a Muse is what people around the Victorian ages named the spirit that gave people inspiration to do various creative things. Ultimately, he said he did not really know, and that ended the conversation. I could think of many more befitting trail names for Muse: Weight Nazi, Garbage Truck, Twenty-Questions, Over-Reactor, Calculator, Safety Boy, Miser, Wet Blanket, Anal, Romaine (lettuce), Lawrence of Arabia, Sun Screen…

Sunday, May 28, 2006

7:44 p.m.

Trail Magic

Muse is clearing his throat over and over again. The sound never ceases to be unnerving—spoiling the enchanting hush of the forest green—his loud grunt, fused with a throat clearing. We are camped in a Riparian woodland of oak, spruce and cedars with a dulcet creek trickling in deep mantillas of green. The air is almost perfectly still. Various birds sing their twilight songs in the transition time. I am exceedingly happy with the beauty found here in this little canyon. We are in the Santa Clarita area, which I usually associate with barren brown hills and brush fires. But here lies an emerald treasure of large pines, firs, cedars, and ferns, which I have not seen anywhere along the PCT until now.

I imagined that last night would be a warmer night than the previous spent on the windy ridge of Baden-Powell. When I poked my head through my sleeping bag this morning, a layer of frost sugarcoated my belongings scattered about. The blisters, courtesy of my new shoes, caused me much discomfort and discouragement when we set off today. At sulfur spring I gulped a couple Ibuprofen with my water and within a very short time my pain subsided, then was totally gone. I was so encouraged to be hiking pain free, that I took off at an aggressive pace leaving Muse tracking me most of the day.

Three circumstances of trail-magic presented themselves to us today. Descending from our mountain hollow, Muse, Nitro and I joined Dave, Becky, and Mountain Tripper at the Mill Creek Summit Ranger Station. Mountain Tripper came out of the ranger station with sodas for everyone. Muse also invaded the ranger station, and was nice enough to get us both candy bars.

After we left the ranger station, we climbed uphill for a considerable distance, finally coming to a small road atop the mountains. There were four people having a tailgate party there, one of whom was a trail runner, training for a marathon. I saw him and greeted him in my most amiable voice, hoping it would pay off. He invited me help myself to any of their food and drinks on the tailgate. The runner unfolded a chair for me, and asked Muse and I questions about our hike. I drank two Gatorades, ate salami, grapes, cheese, and Triscuits.

Near the end of our day, we came near the Big Buck Campground, which I walked a fourth mile off the trail to investigate. There were but three guys camped out peaceably in the forest with a campfire for Memorial Weekend. I struck up a conversation with them as I knew they would be keenly interested in my odyssey, as all men are, and before I knew it, I had an ice cold Heineken in my hand and a Cherry Coke in the other, which I brought back for Muse. Muse considered the soda for some time, eventually deciding that carrying the empty can was too much unnecessary weight; thus, he affixed a note to the Cherry Coke and left it on the trail for the next hiker.

Tomorrow Muse's father is going to pick us up at five o'clock from Soledad Canyon Road for a zero day in Santa Clarita. We have twenty miles to the pick up spot tomorrow.

Tuesday, May 30, 2006

8:33 AM

Grandma Eleanor

Yesterday, we put away twenty miles by two o'clock, eating up the down hill miles quickly, sometimes at a near run. Hiking downhill has a way of rattling my body to pieces. A loathsome blister on the back of my left foot necessitated my stopping several times to reapply foot tape. We began our hike down the mountain in the cool of early morning, walking in the shade of large pines and cedars. We stopped at the North Fork Saddle Ranger Station to refill water and sat down at a picnic bench to talk with Zoner from Ashland, Oregon. He was the only other hiker we encountered that day.

The air grew rapidly warmer as we traded our cool forest for the brown hillsides of Mattox Canyon, losing elevation rapidly. The trail dropped us onto a trailhead parking lot at Soledad Canyon where a group of Boy Scouts bounced around beneath a Ramada.

Muse's father, Ron, and his aunt pulled into the parking lot before long, bringing with them bread, cheese, salami, and diet Snapple. Diet? Nevertheless, the goods were much appreciated. Muse's ailing Grandmother was recently admitted to a care facility, leaving her condo in Santa Clarita unattended. After our pick-up in Soledad Canyon Muse, Ron, and I used her empty condo to clean up and do laundry.

The plan for the evening was as follows: visit Grandma at five p.m. in the care facility; at six pm, dinner with friends and family at Claim Jumper in Santa Clarita. The current time was a leisurely 3:30. I stood back and watched Muse and his father moving frantic hands to start the laundry as if every second mattered. In a flash Muse jumped into the shower, and was back out in minutes. I paced around the condo slowly, whistling a light tune to myself, and enjoyed a long thoughtful shower. When bathing was done, I stretched out on the couch for a nap. Muse and his father suddenly found themselves dumbfounded with nothing to do but sit around and wait for laundry to dry.

She laid on her back beneath the sweep of white sheets, her gaunt frame a fossil between the strata. I remembered Grandma Eleanor from a group photograph beside my father's bed years past. It was a photo of my father atop Mount Whitney and blue sky, standing with Muse's father Ron, Muse's Grandfather who has passed on, and Muse's Grandmother with whom I presently stood. No, she was not my Grandma, but she may as well have been; she was just one of those powerful ladies who became anybody's Grandmother. Grandma Eleanor had a love of the High Sierras and challenged their lonesome peaks late in life. My father has told me several times of her ritual of swimming in the nearest lake after conquering a pass in the Sierras. Therein lay Muse's deep connection with his Grandmother.

Our families have been intertwined in the forests and mountains for many years. Perhaps it was providential that Muse and I should meet in the Sierras of all places on a field biology trip several years past, both of us oblivious of our respective family's connection. And here we both were, continuing the mountain tradition—fighting with each other the whole way.

Grandma Eleanor was quick enough in mind to recognize me, despite the unshaved visage. I hugged her where she lay and she spoke deep recollections of my father and her in the old mountains—the old mountains that do not change, even as children are born, and watch their parents grow old; even as Grandparents pass away, back into the same earth from which the cold mountains rise. Memories are born, collected, and put away back into the dirt. That was the last time I would see Grandma Eleanor.

Muse, in his infinite intrigue with the paper-like scab on my leg where the bike engine had melted nylon, suggested as we sat there with his Grandmother, that I treat it with Bactracin. The black nurse handed me a sample packet, which I applied liberally to the scab. A great bubbling commenced.

Saturday June 3, 2006

12:34 pm

Paparazzi

Several interesting days have passed since my last entry. I have been both busy and lazy with my journal. As it turned out, Muse and I spent two full days at Nate's apartment in Lancaster—relaxing and playing with all our PCT photos we downloaded onto Nate's computer. The Bactracin seems to have had a chemical reaction with my nylon scab. Never have I seen such a disgusting, pussing scab on my body. I repeatedly cleaned the wound with anti-bacterial wipes, on which was left yellow and brown streaks and conglomerate blobs. My body seems to be ejecting all unwanted material through this small wound on my leg.

Everything we have eaten on the trail so far, cooked with the simplicity of hot water and stove, has been palatable (save for the corn pasta at Cedar Springs which we buried in the ground). But *with* the convenience of a proper kitchen, Muse, supplied with the extra pasta and spices we had from our re-supply box, cooked up a pot of the most offensive hodge-podge in Nate's kitchen any one of us had ever attempted to eat. Initially, I watched him in hungry anticipation as he darted back and forth from a steaming pot on the stove, adding a pinch of this, a snuff of that, too much of that green stuff, and a murderous amount of overbearing herbs and spices. Excited with his culinary prowess, Muse scooped up the first bowl, choked down several bites, and declared it mediocre. In a truer assessment, Nate declared it pretty gross. And I, hardly ever meeting a meal I did not like, declared it inedible. Muse put plastic wrap over the rest, stuck it in the refrigerator, and there it sat until the next time Nate picked us up from the trail and brought us to his apartment for a zero day. Surprised to still see it in the refrigerator, as opposed to having simply crawled away, or enveloped Nate while he slept, I disposed of the rest in the garbage and washed the dishes, which I did every time we stayed with Nate. I even hard-boiled some eggs with which I made some proper tuna fish spread that Nate appreciatively used to make a sandwich with for his lunch at work. Nate thanked me for finally throwing out Muse's culinary artistry.

On Thursday afternoon, we drove back to the Soledad Canyon trailhead, left the car there for Muse's aunt Corey to pick up later, and took up our trail once again. Turtle Don was sleeping on the bench beneath the ramada as we hiked away.

Earlier in the day, Muse and I drove ahead to the famous Saufley's hiker heaven in Agua Dulce to leave most of our gear; thusly, we slack packed ten miles to the Saufley's from Soledad Canyon, through the fins of Vasquez Rocks, free of all burdens but water and some snacks.

The Ziploc bag in which I had been carrying my digital camera had slowly and secretly split along the bottom seam. While standing in the concrete tunnel under the Antelope Valley Freeway, I snapped a couple photos and replaced the camera in the bag. The camera fell right through the hole as if I had simply dropped it into thin air, bounced several times on the concrete, and came to rest in the pleasant creek wandering harmless through Escondido Canyon. Perfect. Its life had been snuffed out.

To my surprise, because I am never carrying the maps, the trail merged into the main street into old town Agua Dulce. This is the first, and last time the trail would become the main street of any town. At the edge of Agua Dulce, we met three older hikers already in conversation on a picnic bench. They were Loper, Sunset, and Paparazzi. Sunset was from New Jersey and was a uniquely accented man—tanned face, wide-set eyes—captain Ahab beard. I was not sure to regard him as decidedly masculine or feminine or a combination of both. Either way, he struck me as an ageless wanderlust, moved by the currents of life's serendipity. The gleam in his eyes was the culmination of life experience—catching out on steam trains, touching land at exotic ports-of-call around the world. His eyes told me so. The peace on his face—that permanent sly grin when he regarded me said that I was young and had a long way to go.

Paparazzi, who turned out to be a professional photographer, joined Muse and me at the Sweetwater Café on Main Street Agua Dulce. He also told us that he tests equipment for the owner of Gossamer Gear, which is why Paparazzi had asked me earlier how I was enjoying my Gossamer Gear backpack.

Paparazzi is the squirliest, most mumblesome man I have met anywhere. Every sentence began with preamble, and ended with a maddening amount of qualifiers, "to each his own," "at least that's how I do it," "but you're probably tired of hearing about this;" or he would simply trail off into an unintelligible mess of mumbled words accompanied by shoulder shrugs and nervous chuckles with half closed eyes. I liked Paparazzi.

All day Muse had been talking about night hiking. "So how would you feel about some night hiking?" "Think you're up for any night hiking tonight?" and so forth. I kept giving him noncommittal answers because I would rather stay overnight at the Saufley's Hiker Heaven, in Agua Dulce. Muse has become woefully predictable however, and after some thought, I predicted he would want to stay at the Saufley's as well; he just didn't know it yet. So, to satiate his whimsy, and his penchant to control and plan the immediate future, I told him I would like to do some "night hiking."

We arrived at the Saufley's about a mile off the downtown stem, and let ourselves in the side gate of their yard. Their commodious backyard is set up as a respite for PCT hikers. Donna Saulfey and her husband revel in hosting hikers, and hike portions of the trail themselves each year. In the ranch-style yard are three tent barracks housing about ten cots. First come, first serve. There is a trailer parked at the edge of the yard, the bedroom of which is reserved for couples and newlyweds. There is also is a singlewide trailer with a common area, kitchen, bathroom, and a bedroom—also reserved for couples and newlyweds. Guac and Blackhole, the newlyweds from Seattle, claimed that room.

When I spied Muse over on the patio, enraptured with a classical guitar he had found, I knew "night hiking" would not be mentioned again. And it wasn't. I showered in the trailer and went to sleep on the lawn.

Monday June 5, 2006

12:19 pm

Backcountry Beer

We are in the Mojave Desert, where the sky is a hot frying pan. Muse and I have sought out some shade beneath a large jeweled Juniper tree where we have both attempted sleep. As the sun moves, our shade lessens, and feet which were once shaded suddenly grow hot; we shift closer and closer to the base of the Juniper, and the Juniper, ornamented in stars of white berries, feels loved.

We have been hiking since 5:30 this morning, in an attempt to put away as many miles before the sun should reach its zenith. The temperature hovered around eighty degrees before 8:00 am; we have been following the California aqueduct all day.

A lady who works for the water department drove by on the dirt road a while ago and informed us that we were not even on the PCT. Thinking back to the morning walk, it became clear to me that as we had been walking with our heads down to avoid the directness of the rising sun, we must have missed where the trail broke away from the dirt road and have been walking off the PCT for several miles. She told us not to worry; if we keep following the road we are on, we will eventually intersect the trail in several more miles. "You'll be walking through private property though, so don't go off the road or anything. I know the guy who owns the property, and I don't think he'll mind." That was good enough for me.

The private property started as we climbed over a swinging gate across the dirt road. There was not a building in sight, and I wondered who owned this property and for what reason. Dry, brown hills and canyons closed in and gave way as the road wound through remarkless land. Muse caught up with me with his latest precaution. "Hey Mojave, I think we should be real quiet through this section."

I glanced at him inquisitively. "Quiet? What are you talking about?"

"You know," he forced. "Just, no yelling or anything."

I strung him along further. "Why would I yell? When do I ever yell?" I knew he was picturing some crazy old desert rat with a shotgun yelling at us to get off his wastelands.

"Never mind," he responded dejectedly, sinking back behind me once again.

Several days past, we were at the Saufley's Hiker Heaven. After rising from my bed on their green lawn, Muse and I took up our packs and rejoined the trail via Mint Canyon, which led us to traverse an exposed stretch of low mountains devoid of trees or the slightest rock formation. At the crest of a hill, we came across GQ and Switch, the married couple from England, who were stretched out beneath the canopy of a lonesome tree. The heat seemed to have gotten the best of them, leaving their relationship raw. They asked us if we were heading for the Andersons, which we said we were. After leaving the Saufley's Hiker Heaven, Muse and I had been hearing tales of the Andersons—the next family who host passing hikers at their home.

We passed two water caches that day, both supplied by the Andersons. The second water cache was an unexpected wilderness luxury. On the brown leaf grounds beneath a low grove of trees just off the trail were several lounge chairs and coolers. The entrance to the hollow was guarded by a plastic skeleton hung on a branch; a pink flamingo lawn ornament greeted me as I ducked to enter. I was titillated to discover the cooler stocked with cold beer and soda. I jammed my hand deep into the icy water, bearing aloft an MGD—cold streams running down my arm. Two beers in a dehydrated body on a hot day is a superlative pain killer for weary feet. I worry not of dehydration. Muse will do that for me. Several hours after my beer, I floated along happily, head swimming, smile plastered on my face—gliding over the trail effortlessly.

We hiked twenty-three miles that day to San Fransciquito Canyon Road, hitching a ride from a young man leaving the fire station who dropped us off directly in front of the Andersons. Terry and Joe Anderson turned out to be an eccentric and carefree married couple living in a house decorated with every kind of wind chime, dangling and swirling bobble, and lawn ornament. The wooden deck in the front yard was taken hostage by motley group of dirty hikers hoisting complimentary MGD's to soak into their beards. I met and spoke with Wild Thing from Seattle who was rolling cigarettes, Dr. Jones, Hot Sister, Lucky from Ireland, and Puck Fu—a loud and deranged attention-hog, and one of the very few hikers whose personality was resoundingly discordant with the benevolent culture of the PCT. For those who paid attention to him, he led an expose there on the porch on the proper method of knocking someone out in a fistfight—injecting personal anecdotes, and furthermore demonstrating headlocks on those who sat nearest to him.

In back of the house was the "Enchanted Manzanita Forest:" a forest of large, crimson-branched manzanitas and scrub oaks that stretched back far enough that I found no fence or boundary line. After showering, Muse immediately disappeared to a decidedly private corner of the Enchanted Manzanita Forest. When I found him he simply remarked that he was enjoying some solitude, which I figured was a euphemistic statement as the present hikers at the Andersons were a smoking, drinking crowd—a bar crowd. I know he felt out of place, as there would be nobody with whom he could discuss string-theory and time travel.

For dinner Terry Anderson cooked up hotdogs and her famous taco salad. Everyone formed a buffet line and heaped piles of food onto paper plates. After dinner and four beers I found my own dayglow niche in the Enchanted Manzanita Forest, and would have slept soundly if Puck Fu had not also bedded down near me, talking to Green Tea until sometime past two a.m.

Securing a timely ride back to the trailhead from the Andersons the next morning proved difficult. They woke up late and were generally useless until enough coffee had bridged the synapses in their brains to allow linear thought. Before our departure, Joe Anderson lined up GQ, Switch, Muse and me for a picture in front of their garage on which is fixed a banner of hiker autographs. To get us to smile, the portly Terry Anderson suddenly drew up her robe and mooned us.

We hiked most of the day without crossing any hikers. Around six o'clock we came across Stomper from Quebec, who was sleeping beneath a tree with his bug bivy covering most of his body. The bottle flies and biting flies have been relentless the last couple of days. Aided by some unnamed instinct they home directly in on my festering scab, biting and further infecting the already palpitating wound. Long pants do not help, for the flies find their way right into the burn hole in my pants, which I attempted, with no permanent success, to seal with duct tape.

The landscape that day was much better than the day before, with our elevation at five thousand feet around Sawmill Mountain in the Angeles National Forest. The trail alternated between groves of large pines, spruce, and incense-cedars, and head-high bunches of manzanita and chemise. Muse stopped along the trail to gaze at the blue Tehachapi Mountains in the distance.

"We should take a picture of every mountain range we hike over!" Muse said to me with the zeal of a spectacular idea.

"No."

"Why not?"

"Just like you wanted to take a picture of every road we cross; just like you wanted to take a picture of every place we camp at night. It won't happen."

"Yeah, I guess you're right."

We came to a spring trickling down a rock face; the water flow was scarce enough to require about five minutes of patient waiting to fill a liter bottle; that with careful channeling of the water into the nozzle with free fingers. I have seen two deer this evening.

Towards dusk Muse, Stomper, and I stopped at a surprise water cache in the mountains. We watched curiously as cars kept driving by on a backcountry dirt road; we were later informed that there was a rave party that night atop the mountain. In fact, when Muse, Stomper and I stopped to camp, we could hear a distant bass booming throughout the night.

We rose at 5:30 a.m. and headed down the mountain rapidly—losing our cool groves of tree-cover once again, trading them for a burnt up mountainside of charcoaled pines and an overgrown thistle-trap trail. In the push through the scraping brush, my right gaiter was torn from my foot, and is presumably lost to the mountain.

5:00 pm

It is a warm day to be sure. Muse and I are waiting out the sun underneath a corrugated piece of metal, set up as a sun block. Nearby is a bridge over Cottonwood Creek; underneath six hikers hide out in the shade, waiting for the sun to take its heat somewhere else. I can hear Puck Fu talking loudly beneath the bridge. He has been talking nonstop for the last three hours. I suppose other people are talking as well, but I can only hear his voice, like a loud midnight drunk. Sometimes, when the wind blows this direction, I catch fragments of his exposition: "Our fucking government..." and "That's because you sit and watch TV and have no friends..."

Just on the other side of the scraggly bush near me is a dead coyote, turned mostly to bones, but for its hairy leggings. The coyote skeleton in this parched desert has formed the perfect Southwestern cliché scene. Foreigners like Stomper from Quebec must get a kick out of seeing something like that. I would take a picture, but my camera, while it turns on and makes all kinds of fun noises, cannot perform the most important task of taking photos, after the infamous drop in the concrete tunnel.

Muse's friend Nate from Lancaster, drove out to pick us up from Hiker Town along Highway 138 yesterday around three o'clock. Hiker Town is a man's property on which are built several buildings fitted with laundry, shower, a television room and general areas for relaxation. When I entered the TV room at Hiker Town, there sat Sleeping Beauty, amongst some other hikers. I had not seen him since our first stop at Warner Springs. Sleeping Beauty has been hiking with one pair of socks for the entire five hundred miles so far. They are threadbare and full of holes. Scarceness of money is the reason he wears but one pair of socks, according to him. I told Sleeping Beauty I thought I found his straw hat by Silverwood Lake, ripped apart by the storm, and he confirmed that Silverwood Lake was where he had lost it.

Yesterday evening with Nate, we all dined at El Torito in Lancaster—an incredibly satisfying meal, complete with the tableside guacamole. As hungry as I was, I could not quite finish my carnitas plate; the leftovers are currently sitting in Nate's refrigerator. Hopefully, they will still be there for the next time Nate drives out to pick us up.

This morning at Nate's, we all rose at four a.m. so he could drive us back to the trail and get himself to work on time. The morning was cold and windy as his taillights disappeared down Highway 138. I put on sandals after an hour of walking and enjoyed the relief from pain they gave my feet. We walked for miles along the California aqueduct, which started off as fenced culvert of southbound water before disappearing into a massive pipe, three-fourths of which was buried in the ground leaving a dinosaur-like spine running for miles up into the distant hills. I walked atop the elevated aqueduct spine as it lined the edge of a degenerate housing tract for miles. In the threatening morning sun I gazed down into backyards from my sky trail: fifth wheels run aground in side yards, a plastic kiddy pool with a swamp of green water, a berserk dog barking at me and tearing up the yard as I pass—half brown, half overgrown lawns. Some time later we began walking down the wrong road as mentioned earlier.

Now it is 5:30; the air has cooled significantly; some wispy clouds are setting up and most of the hikers beneath the bridge have walked off: Stomper, Sleeping Beauty, Detour, Hot Sister, Green Tea, and Puck Fu.

Tuesday June 6, 2006

8:20 pm

Cuervo

6/6/06 has been a day from hell. My feet have been hurting all day. The middle ball of my right foot is forming a gigantic callous in an effort to thwart the pain, but the pain is deep—the ache of a severely bruised bone, probably from hiking down hill too fast. It is a different pain—markedly different from the topical sting of the many blisters I have ridden out so far. This pain concerns me deeply and its continuance, I feel, could drive me off the trail.

Yesterday, we left our slant of corrugated metal around 5:30 and traversed the western edge of the Mojave, until the trail gradually rose into the foothills of the Tehachapi Mountains. We "night hiked" until ten p.m. to make up for the hours spent waiting out the sun. As the sunlight faded, and darkness crept from beneath the yuccas and rabbit brush, we descended upon Tylerhorse Creek. I could see a campfire burning in a grove of trees ahead of us. Two burros were tethered to the ground as we approached the campsite where stood Cuervo—a gray-bearded old man, but tall and wide-shouldered. Cuervo was an anachronism from the old West. Shreds of cloth served as bandanas around his forehead, beneath which were deep, hollowed eyes—his arroyoed face in shadowed relief from the campfire—silver earrings hung from his ears, his feet bedazzled in plain brown boots, and every other tooth knocked out like the target dummies of a carnival game. I was sure he had been wandering native trails in the mountains and deserts for years, accompanied by his two burros, his two dogs—one of which was half wolf; and toting along those black iron pots and skillets that presently blackened further over his campfire.

So thoroughly impressed was I by the old-world authenticity of Cuervo, I hardly noticed the other PCT hikers seated about his campfire. Cuervo resembled every of turn-of-the-century cliché image of a prospector. I have seen his ghostly black and white visage in a hundred glass cases in pioneer museums across America, labeled as the man who first discovered gold in such-and-such creek, staved off an Indian attack at fort whatever, claimed to know where the Lost Dutchman mine was before he died in the Great Whatever of wherever. We talked for a while; he said he planned on traveling as far North as the Lassen River.

Regretfully, I left Cuervo and hiked on further in the evening hours with Muse close at my heels. My new super-watted headlamp I purchased in Lancaster gave me dominion over the night-time trail as it could illuminate opposing ridges, and knock already-blind bats out of the air. We had been up since four a.m. that morning and we both felt fatigued come 9:30 p.m. It has become customary for me to be the one to suggest we stop to camp for the evening, and every evening when I suggest we do so, Muse is sure to follow with an answer such as, "Sure, we can camp if you want. *I* could hike another five or ten miles, but if you want to stop here, then that's fine." Tonight was no exception. Around ten o'clock we mutually decided to start looking for a place to bed down when a perfectly flat and clear area presented itself just off the trail. "How about this?" I asked. Muse paced the ground, giving his perfunctory analysis for flatness and absence of red ants (He has been bitten twice now and destroys with his trekking poles every red ant hill we come across).

"Looks good," he said.

I took off my pack.

"Though, I could do another two miles if you want."

I put my pack back on; "Alright, let's do another two miles." I walked off.

"Naw, wait," he said. "I'd rather stay and camp."

"I'm fine," I said. "I don't mind doing another couple miles."

"Nah." He stared down at the ground. "You called my bluff."

Just an hour ago we crossed Highway 58 to the town of Mojave; we climbed up a ridge and found a flat, but terribly windy spot in a cluster of Joshua Trees. It is nearing dark. I was in such incredible pain towards the latter half of the day up to this very moment, I had to grit my teeth and sing rhymes of encouragement to help myself continue on. Muse is aware of my pain, but the severity of it he is oblivious to; I do not like to complain about circumstances that cannot be helped. Accordingly, our current campsite, while windy, is a perfect flat area, obviously used by many hikers over the years, and I made it known to Muse that my foot pain prevents me from continuing a search for some place less windy. Muse says he is going on without me to find somewhere free of the wind, but I know he won't leave; he is "bluffing" again.

Scott Williamson passed us today at an outdoor shower and water cache. He is all the talk of the PCT this year because he is yo-yoing the trail, which is to say he is hiking from Mexico to Canada and back to Mexico. He wore simple running shorts, ankle socks, button-up shirt and a baseball style hat. He was carrying a ULA backpack. Scott averages between thirty-seven and forty miles per day. Can you imagine! Muse pummeled him with ultra-light questions, which he graciously answered, seemingly in no hurry at all. And what would be the hurry? Scott waited for me to finish showering, then stood beneath the strange outdoor shower himself. "Ahh, that feels nice," he said. Scott is known to be a humble guy and I found him to be nothing but. He walked off and we never caught up to him again.

Monday, June 19, 2006

1:57 pm

Jawbone Canyon

More than a week has passed since my last journal entry. I am starting a new notepad, having exhausted the last one with the nonsense of my life.

Muse and I started our pre-scheduled week-off-the-trail, so that he could attend an important wedding, and I could finally let my aching feet heal.

The night we got off the trail was a wondrous disaster. Muse had arranged for Nate to pick us up from where the trail crossed Jawbone Canyon Road up in the Piute Mountains. The last time we were staying at Nate's house, both of them ran their fingers over a topographical map, following Jawbone Canyon Road from the Fourteen Freeway up into the six thousand foot Piutes where the road crossed the PCT. No problem. On the specified day, Muse and I arrived at the pass several hours before Nate was scheduled to pick us up.

"This is it?" I asked, looking at the dirt road before me.

Muse stared deep into his map. "Yup, this is Jawbone Canyon Road."

"It's dirt."

"I know. The topographical map didn't tell us that."

I suddenly had a sinking feeling that Nate's car, a Saturn, would not be able to negotiate twenty miles of dirt road up into the mountains. Muse was already talking about what he wanted to order at El Torito this evening when we reached Lancaster. I told him I would start thinking about El Torito *after* I was actually in Nate's car.

We waited until four o'clock—the scheduled pick up time. Nate did not come.

The sun went down.

I played baseball with a stick and some rocks.

"So, what are our options now?" I asked.

"Well, I'm out of food so continuing on is not an option." Muse makes sure to consume all food on the last day before a re-supply point is reached. "According to the map," he continued, "if we start walking down Jawbone Canyon Road, we will reach the Fourteen Freeway in twenty-six miles. There's a BLM office there."

We waited for Nate until nine p.m.; nothing but darkness arrived. Depressed beyond measure, we filled our water to capacity at Robin Bird Spring, and began walking down the dirt road, hoping for some sign of a house, a car—anything along the way wherein we might contact the civilized world for help. After several miles we came to a gated side road, which I volunteered to explore. I walked by myself, in the dark of night, rocks crunching beneath my aching feet, black forest around me. I rounded curve after curve; each turn presented me with more darkness, more nothingness. After a quarter mile, I came to a sign that read "Pacific Crest Trail." I had no idea how I could have re-crossed the PCT which we had left several miles behind up on the ridge. I shook my head; the Twilight Zone factor set in.

"Nothing down that road," I said to Muse. "Let's keep going."

A full moon rose, like a dead man hoisted up on the gallows. We descended the mountain in wide-arching switchbacks of ivory sand.

"It's no wonder Nate never made it up here," I remarked as we rounded another curve. "Look at this steep, sandy road. It's hard enough just to walk on."

Hours passed. We crossed over a stream in the foothills; the land flattened into the broad desert plains of Kelso Valley—dark hills miles away in every direction. My feet ached terribly; the bruised footpads sent a shock throughout my body with every step.

"How far do you think we've gone," someone said.

"Probably six or seven miles," responded the other. We took a break. Cows lingered out in the flats like a dark tide, rumbling here and there as we startled them into stampedes.

When we resumed hiking I noticed a large bird, silhouetted against the dead moon, and circling us as we made our way down the road. It seemed to fly with exaggerated slowness, not moving a wing—as if dangled against the moon like a plastic Halloween bat.

"See that bird," Muse said.

"Yeah, it's kind of creepy; a bad omen. It's been following us." Cows rumbled off in the distance. We sat down again.

"What time is it?"

"Midnight." I had the watch.

"Think we should camp soon?"

"It's gonna be hot here when the sun rises tomorrow." I was lying with my back against the edge of the road. The night was still and warm. "I think we should put away as many miles as possible tonight."

"Yeah."

The time was two a.m. when we saw a dim light ahead of us on the road. They turned into headlights; a car slowed.

"Hey, how's it goin'" I said, exhaustion in my voice. "Our friend was supposed to pick us up at the pass, but he didn't show; we're out of food. We started walking to get to the Fourteen Freeway."

"Where are you guys coming from?" asked the man.

"We walked down from the mountains; we're hiking the Pacific Crest Trail. Do you know how much father the Fourteen Freeway is from here?"

"Eh, it's probably another ten miles that way," he said, nonplussed with our adventure.

I asked the question. "Do you think you could give us a ride to the freeway?"

"Oh, I don't know," he said. My heart sank. "I just got off of a twenty-hour shift at Edison. I'm real tired." He thought for a second. "But I'm coming back this way tomorrow morning. If you guys camp out here, I'll drive you the rest of the way tomorrow."

As tired and pained as I was, camping out another night was not what I wanted to hear. I tried another question. "Do you have a cell phone? Maybe we could call our friend."

"Yeah, but you won't get any reception here in the valley." He shifted in his seat. "I'll tell you what though; we'll drive to the top of that hill; there should be reception there."

I collapsed into the back seat of his car. Once we were in, and driving back towards the Fourteen Freeway, he said he might as well drive us all the way. Thank God!

Miles of dirt hills, dry washes, and sheered cliffs passed by my window. I could not believe how much farther we would have had to walk. At Jawbone Canyon and the Fourteen is a Bureau of Land Management Office. We phoned Nate at 2:30 a.m. and waited for him on a picnic bench. The Mojave was blowing sharp, warm wind. I dug a hole and crapped in front of the BLM office. Nate finally arrived sometime after three am. He was as calm and reticent as always.

The night that Nate picked us up from Jawbone Canyon and the Fourteen Freeway, I had a terrible dream while sleeping in his guest room—a dream in which Meadow broke up with me. "You just need to get over it and move on," were her words to me in the dream. I woke up the next morning with the lingering emotions of having been dumped—a wholly terrible feeling. I sat down at Nate's computer and emailed Meadow at work; I had big plans for us the coming week I would be home. We had both been looking forward to this time together. She responded with an email reading as follows:

Dear Joel,
The time has come. Joel, I am so sorry but I can't do this. I have

a past that keeps coming back. There are things you don't know about me that I wanted to keep from you. I was hoping the more I ran the better I would get, but it hasn't. I just need to deal with myself and stop masking things with distractions. I have been going to a counselor and she advised I take some time for myself and to not get attached to anyone. This hurts but I know she is right. I really hate doing this via email but I didn't think it would be fair to keep you in the dark till you got back. It hurts to write this, I am sorry. I think you are a wonderful, sweet, thoughtful person and you deserve the best. And I cant give you that right now. Please understand what I have to do.

-m

I sat back on the couch and stared at the wall as it melted away, my veins ran dry; I was weak. I felt like I had been drugged; my head swirled. Then I got down on my knees and prayed earnestly for Meadow, and myself. I emailed her again, telling her of my dream. We arranged to meet face to face for due explanation the upcoming Monday; currently it was Friday—an eternity of time away.

This event brought to light my old insecurities of girls and their prior relationships, and how males take advantage of women so often, ruining their future relationships with a man who really cares for them. Granted, I did not know what her "skeletons" even were, but there was no doubt in my mind that some dude was the cause of her distress. The world is a very unfair place, and it shall continue to be so, for a long time.

My parents drove up to Lancaster the next day, Saturday, at noon. This was to be the week that Meadow and I were to spend every free moment together; the week we had both reminded each other about in glowing expectation. I would see her but one time, on Monday night. My parents drove me home.

Three nights prior to my dream about Meadow, I had a dream about my best friend, Drew. In my dream he had a terrible rash on his shoulder, running down the top portion of his back. Oddly, pieces of bacon were stuck to the raw, irritated skin. "You know," I said to him in the dream, "there's bacon stuck to your rash?" Nonchalantly, he replied, "Hey, it happens."

On Saturday night Drew and I converged on a coffee shop. "How's your shoulder?" I asked as we sat. Drew gave me a sideways stare.

"How do you know about my shoulder? Did you talk to Sarah or something?"

I told him about my dream and the bacon-covered rash on his shoulder.

"Yeah," he said. "All week my shoulder has been popping and scraping and giving me pain! I don't know *what* it could be from. I'm gonna go see the doctor about it."

I took my broken camera to the Nikon service center, inconveniently located in El Segundo. When it is fixed, they will mail it back to my parent's house. I also ordered a solar charger for my ipod, which Meadow had been borrowing until she dumped me. Her counselor advised against having any reminders of me in her house. I had brought a green-hued rock back from Panamint Valley for her; she had requested that I find her an interesting rock. The rock also had to be removed from the house and put in the garden. It is nice to feel so potent.

I told Muse he had better bring his MP3 player, which he had decided to leave behind to lessen weight; he would not be borrowing my ipod. His bad attitude is rubbing off on me to the point where I do not feel like extending him favors anymore.

Since we would be waiting a while for my camera to be fixed, Muse went out and bought a new camera to use while we were off the trail. He bought a Nikon Coolpix like mine, but a more expensive and superior model. He also made sure to purchase the protection plan. I awaited the camera safety speech, which came when we returned to the trail; do not drop the camera into a Ziploc bag; always have the safety strap around your wrist when taking pictures, and so on. I decided not to take pictures until my own camera was back in hand.

Last Friday I convinced myself to see a podiatrist, hoping to cull some helpful information regarding foot care to take back with me to the trail. Sitting barefooted in the medical room, I explained to Doctor White my unfortunate situation with blisters, bruised footpads, and the mysterious pain in my right foot.

"I wear a knee-high nylon underneath polypropylene socks," I said, trying to sound esoteric and conscientious. Muse had convinced me that a knee-high nylon and sock combination was blister-proof, and I had worn them from day one.

"Get rid of the nylons," said Doctor White. "Nylon traps moisture against the skin, and that's what gives you your blisters." I nodded, protruding my lip in thought. "How do you treat your hot spots when they come?"

"Well," I said. "I usually cut a segment of foot tape and put in on the hot spot."

"No. Don't put foot tape on your hotspots; especially don't put them on your blisters, because the adhesive is gonna tear the skin from the blister. You wanna try to *save* that top layer of skin. If you're gonna use foot tape, adhere it to the part of the shoe that is rubbing your foot." She went on. "Do you carry Vaseline with you?"

"Yes."

"When you get a hot spot, put a big glob of Vaseline on it—not foot tape. Vaseline will reduce the rubbing." It all made perfect sense. "Let me also recommend some insoles for you." She pulled a pair of green Super Feet insoles from a drawer.

"Oh! I use those!" I said successfully. "Well, I did use those until my blister problems; I've been switching out insoles like nobody's business."

"Put your Super Feet back in. The high arch in the Super Feet insole is going to preserve the natural arch of your foot, which will take pressure off of your bruised footpads. Furthermore, preserving your arch means that the front of your toes won't rub your shoes and cause more blisters.

This last weekend, Drew and I drove out to Pioneertown in the Mojave Desert. I had originally made reservations at the Pioneertown motel for Meadow and myself. That's life! While there, we visited the Integratron in the nearby town of Landers. Landers claims the largest freestanding boulder in the world. I have been there. It's big. The Integratron was built entirely of wood by George Van Tassel back in the 1950's. The blueprints for the domed building, according to Van Tassel, were given to him by aliens from the planet Venus. The aliens had visited him one night by the largest freestanding boulder in the world, and told him to build the structure, which was originally supposed to function as a time machine. Van Tassel died however before its completion.

These days the Integratron is operated by some stinky, unshaven, New-age women. The general public can visit the Integratron on specified weekends to participate in a "sound bath", wherein participants lay on mats with heads towards the center of the upstairs domed room while one of the unshaven new-age women plays quartz bowls with a soft-tipped drumstick, producing vibrant sound waves in the perfect acoustics of the domed room in the Integratron, in the High Desert. The purpose of the sound bath is cellular regeneration. George Van Tassel was trying to build a time machine, and I, as I lay there on the floor, my cells regenerating, was trying hard to go back in time. Perhaps I would have been successful had my concentration not been broken by several large individuals who had fallen asleep and were snoring next to me.

After the sound bath, Drew and I drove in to Pioneertown. Our room at the Pioneertown Hotel had not been thoroughly cleaned as evidenced by the jacket hanging on the bathroom door, hair all over the shower, and a cache of pornographic movies left on the television.

Aside from being dumped, last week was everything I so *sorely* needed. Everyone remarked on how skinny and tan I had become. I had sushi with John, lunch with Navin, dinner with Ninh, dinner with Maddie, repeated coffees with Drew. But after being stuck in traffic half a dozen times, and encountering an equal amount of road detours along my seasoned driving routes, I had had enough. I wanted back on the trail. The fresh air has awakened the psychic part of my mind, and I wanted to nurture this latent ability in an effort to become a real life X-man with psychic powers. My name could be "Psycho!" Oh wait. That would not be good.

Yesterday, Drew, Sarah and I got together for a barbeque at Sarah's house—a going-back-to-the-trail party in my honor. That evening Muse was coming to pick me up so we could drive back to Santa Clarita, drop off his car, and be driven back to the PCT. When Muse arrived to pick me up, he immediately cited how stressed and tired he was from the rehearsal dinner and the wedding. I think he was an usher. Muse had recommended to me that I spend my week staying in shape— running and walking and so on. I did not lift a finger all week, unless there was food at the end of it.

Tired as he was, I drove his car to Santa Clarita in just over an hour—record time for him and me. It is 3:35 here at Nate's in Lancaster. Tonight, after he gets off from work, Nate is going to drop us back off at Jawbone Canyon Road—as far as his car will make it up the sandy mountain switchbacks. He sure has been a valuable resource for the last three weeks. I cannot thank him enough.

Tuesday, June 20, 2006

6:07 pm

The Explanation

Muse is making dinner in the knife-edge shade of a Joshua Tree. We have hiked slothfully today—our first day back on the trail since our week break. I almost forgot to write about my "skeletons" meeting with Meadow two Mondays ago now. We met at a Starbucks—my choice; corporate coffee with plenty of uncrowded outdoor seating. I had a fresh pack of cigarettes with me at the table, and smoked them with purpose—first driven to smoking by Muse, and now by Meadow. A frazzled man bummed a cigarette from me, trying to pay me with some change. "I've been through hell this week," he said. I said I had too. "Don't ever get involved with a married woman!" he admonished. "It is not worth it!" I said I believed him. Women.

I was five minutes early. Meadow was five minutes late. She had fallen asleep after work, and rushed straight here after she woke. We hugged. I will spare the details of the whole conversation, over the heart of the matter. She explained having been in a seven-year relationship until less than a year ago. She had been engaged to a closet drug user who hid his addiction while telling her he was clean. He eventually crashed his car into a telephone pole while hopped up on something, landing himself in jail. Meadow returned to him the engagement ring and since that time she has felt ashamed for being involved with such a person, and has been unable to become seriously involved with anyone since.

"That's it?" I asked her. My cigarette was astonished. She nodded.

Wednesday, June 21, 2006
6:07 pm

Ipod

Anyhow, that is the story Meadow gave me. At her car, she handed over my ipod, which now accompanies me on the trail.

Nate drove us back up Jawbone Canyon Road, getting his Saturn stuck at the same steep, sandy curve that prevented him from picking us up two Thursdays past. Tragically, the spot was about two miles shy of where we sat and waited for him for five hours.

It was late in the day when he dropped us off. The sun had dipped behind the Piutes. Nate and I glanced at each other quizzically as Muse applied sunscreen on his face and hands.

Today is another day. We are walking in six thousand foot mountains of scrubby pines. Muse is walking incredibly slow and is being a little shit: quiet, with smart little answers to any of my questions. When I asked him what the matter was, he said he was tired, and sick of the desert sections. He usually takes out his bad moods on me.

We had a nice distant view of some snow-capped High Sierras today, which actually choked me up a little bit. A Coldplay song was playing in my ears as I saw them.

Last night we met up with Hoosier where we made dinner beneath the Joshua Trees. He was joined by an equally aged hiker named Caboose.

"Your trail name is Mojave?" asked Caboose.

"Yes, like the desert."

"Y'ever get out to Death Valley?"

"Sure, I was just out in Panamint Valley two weeks before I started the trail. We visited Darwin Falls, and drove on some dirt road up in the Hunter Mountains."

"Oh, there's an old cabin up in the Hunter Mountains!"

"Right! We went there too."

Caboose and I volleyed interesting corners of the Mojave for a while. He has been around. I was impressed.

Since I knew he was not feeling well, I had volunteered to walk the extra two miles down a dirt road and back to replenish Muse's and my water at a spring. I did it earlier in the day too, tramping down another dirt road to retrieve water for both of us as he lay in the shade of a pine tree. Luckily, I ran into Cuervo again and got a good look at him in the light of day. I asked Cuervo the name of his wolf dog. "Well, I'm just calling him Little Shit for now."

I just spilled hot chocolate all over the porch of the old McIvers cabin, where we are camping tonight. There is a spring just behind the porch and this is a perfectly pleasant camping spot for the evening.

I was surprised yesterday, talking with Cuervo by a dirt road. A truck with two Mexican men drove by, yelling something in Spanish at Cuervo. They exited the truck, shook Cuervo's massive hand and proceeded to have a lengthy conversation in Spanish. Cuervo sounded more Mexican than the Mexicans.

The spring here by the cabin is flowing out of a pipe at the speed of a slow faucet, free falling about two feet into the wet boggy grass. The only drawback of this spring is that the water smells of cow dung, and with the all the cows in the area, I am worried that there is cow crap in the water.

Kurt from Wisconsin is camped here with us tonight. He seems like a pretty nice guy—though he is disgusted with the cow water from the spring.

The front porch of McIvers cabin is perfect for settin' on as the sun goes down. Inside the cabin are some shelves of empty water bottles, note pads, empty cans, and other random things. Half of the room is carpeted, while the other half is wooden slats. I think I will sleep in the cabin tonight.

It dawned on me today how the first six hundred miles of this trip for me were typified by one pain or another—be they blisters, bruised pads, torn ligament, shin splints; there were problems, constant problems, and constant pain. Ibuprofen became my drug of choice, but after a while, even "vitamin I" could not suppress the pain. Now that I have had a week off however, my feet are feeling pretty solid. But a new pain has arisen—the pain of a broken heart. I think about Meadow all day. Mainly, I think about the good times we shared, and I long for more. I think about what I want to say to her when I contact her next. I am not supposed to talk to her until I finish my WHOLE trip, but I have been thinking of simply having any anonymous friend call her to read a scripted message: "You have a message waiting from Joel Clark; would you like to accept?" And if she answers in the affirmative, "Joel would like you to know that his love for you grows every day. He thinks that you're a wonderful and special girl, and he'd like you to know that he prays for you every day, and he'd like to encourage you also to lay all your cares down before God." Something like that.

Muse is clearing his throat off in the distance.

Having my ipod along has transformed this trip. I am in such a great mood while hiking and listening to music. Before commencement of this trip, I went against my common sense by adopting the purist attitude regarding music in the Great Outdoors, thinking that I would simply enjoy the beautiful sounds of nature. Bologna. All I heard for the first six hundred miles was the loud swish of nylon pants and the crunch of gravel beneath my feet, and Muse clearing his throat; some soundtrack. Now, my favorite music provides a wondrous soundtrack to the beauty around me. The mountains look more uplifting and majestic, the trees and flowers more spiritual. I cannot wait to get my solar charger as my ipod is about to die.

Tonight for dinner we made buckwheat pasta with miso soup mix. Though it tasted great, I am left feeling very hungry, and will go to bed feeling the same. It is 8:30, but still light outside, and I have nothing to do. I just saw a mouse run by the door of the cabin.

Saturday, June 24, 2006

6:44 pm

The Pistachio Argument

Several days have passed since I have written. Muse and I generally hike from sun-up to sundown, leaving me with no light to write.

Kurt and I talked until ten o'clock on the porch of McIvers cabin. He told me about the family business that he stood to inherit some day. His parents, who live in Appleton, Wisconsin, buy huge rolls of paper from paper mills. With specialized machines, they cut the rolls down into usable sizes, such as for receipt tape and so on, depending on who the client is.

Kurt's parents did not want him to leave home to hike the Pacific Crest Trail, even offering him money to stay. But it did not work. He was tired of operating the same factory machine day after day and so he had an idea—a vision. Perhaps, on another ordinary day as Kurt stood there pulling the same lever on the same machine in that humdrum stretch between lunch and evening, he envisioned that rocky trail, traversing miles of canyons, hills and mountains. Kurt saved his money wisely, bought pieces of equipment here and there, made the final arrangements, then found himself standing on a sage and chemise covered rise one day at the border. His is a familiar story—an old story, of young men and wanderlust. I told him the same.

That night at McIvers cabin was a sleepless one. I bedded down on the crispy wooden porch and heard vermin scurrying around in wooden crevices all night.

The next day Kurt, Muse, and I paused at a picnic bench midmorning and refilled from a water cache. Muse had been busy all day thinking of trail names to bequeath on Kurt. When Kurt complained that the water from the cache had a funny taste to it, Muse blurted out, "Oh! I know what your trail name should be! Water Nazi!" Kurt smartly passed on this sobriquet. I thought back to how angry Muse became when I joked that he change his trail name to "Weight Nazi."

A day or two later, we met John and Ivajoe, a married couple in their late twenties. They live with a community of Christians in the Church of the Sojourner in the Mission District of San Francisco. John and Ivajoe are two of the most pleasant people I have met.

Muse and I have made the distance to Kennedy Meadows, gateway to the High Sierras, and are lounging around the General Store. John and Ivajoe are here, as well as Bean and Rabid, Wild Thing, Redneck, Bear, Ladybird, and others. The general store of Kennedy Meadows is the cynosure of town, and everyone who is hiking, fishing, or camping in the area hangs out on the porch to drink beer and look dirty. Sometimes, the porch looks like the set of an old Western film, replete with hard characters wearing beards, boots, and beer. They watch you come, and they watch you go, in between conversations about fishing.

There was a town potluck here tonight, which I just partook of. I am still hungry though, even after having had a chiliburger upon arrival, and a pint of Ben and Jerry's Double Fudge Brownie ice cream; then the potluck.

Yesterday, we hiked half of the day in extremely hot temperatures before reaching a lonesome campground where we stopped to make mashed potatoes. A tall, dark-haired man with possibly a German accent wandered down from an unseen campsite to ask us if we were hiking the Pacific Crest Trail. He wore a straw hat like mine, with dark ringlets of hair retreating from the sides. He was a geologist, most of the time researching fault lines in interior Mexico.

He was on his way home to Tucson and offered us his extra food, which we gladly confiscated. The food included two apples, three tomatoes, three carrots, half a loaf of bread, a bag of pistachios, teriyaki jerky, and a container of figs. I left that campground feeling whole, though Muse and I had an argument at the picnic table wherein I accused him of acting very immature and I cited recent examples of him bursting into anger over trivial matters—most recently at this picnic table. The incident happened as follows: I was pouring half of the pistachios into the Ziploc bag that had previously contained our mashed potato flakes. "No!" Muse yelled when he saw me doing this. "I hate mixing foods together! Just leave it alone!" His unwarranted aggression pissed me off enough, and the argument was underway. I showed him the Ziploc bag, which was completely free of any residual potato flakes. "Look!" I said forcefully. "There are no potato flakes in this bag!" I could not believe what he was yelling at me about. "Man, you need to learn how to talk to people in a civilized way!" I said to him. Muse sat down, silently staring at the picnic table. I laid into him about his poor attitude. He shot back saying that I am never willing to hear about *his* annoyances with me. So, I asked him to give me some examples of how I had crossed him. He became flustered, responding that he did not remember anything specific as he prefers to forget about my offences against him and move on. What a noble man!

The temperature was in the nineties the next day. But the trail wound along the upper Kern River where we stopped to swim several times, walking ourselves dry. When we arrived at Kennedy Meadows, Muse was on the phone immediately to find out the status of Grandma Eleanor. Whomever he was on the phone with gave him the bad news. She had just died. The funeral was scheduled for the coming Tuesday. I was on my way home again.

Wednesday, June 28, 2006

7:08 pm

Home Again

At long last, this is looking a lot like the Sierras. Muse and I started hiking today at noon after his father dropped us back off at the trailhead by Kennedy Meadows. We were happy to run into Dude just heading into Kennedy Meadows. Muse's dad drove Dude to the general store after we got ample pictures together.

Packing up my gear on Tuesday, I tried to imagine what I should prepare for in the High Sierras. Rain pants? Hmm. They just seem like they would be extra weight. After all, when we left Kennedy Meadows on Sunday, the temperature was in the nineties. But I find myself sitting in the tent right now; heavy drops beat down on the tarp. Pit, pat, pit pat. We walked through Monache Meadow today, which is the largest Meadow in the Sierras. Then we walked east over a hill and down into another meadow where flowed the south fork of the Kern River in a sandy brown bed, twisting through mammoth fields of wild grass. We ate dinner on a footbridge over the river and watched as distant dark clouds crept closer, threatening with lightning and thunder. Lightning and rain came earlier in the day as well, wherein I stupidly sat under a tree, waiting for Muse to catch up.

On that fateful Sunday at Kennedy Meadows, Nate was kind enough once again to pick us up from the trail and drive us back to Lancaster. From there, I called on several friends, none of whom I was able to reach immediately. But good old John Tran, who was trying to take a nap, answered his phone and ended up driving the two and a half hours to Lancaster to pick us up.

I arrived home at 5:15, put on some proper clothes, and went to the six o'clock church service. Brad Waymann, a kid who I knew from church surprised me with his presence and with some blonde eye candy hanging on his arm. Standing there in the evening sanctuary, he asked, and I told him what I was up to: walking from Mexico to Canada. Then I asked and he said, dejectedly, that he was working at a mortgage office.

I would have to say that Muse's Grandmother died at a perfect time—if such a thing were possible. When I walked into my room on Sunday, there sat Solio, the solar powered ipod charger. And the next day, Monday, my busted camera came back to me in the mail, fixed, and working square again.

John and I went to Gen Kai for sushi on Monday night. I let myself in to his house before he was home from work and downloaded a wealth of new music from his computer to my ipod.

While we ate sushi, John suddenly had a random quirk in his neck muscle, keeping him from swallowing. He thought the spasm may have been caused by a high note he hit while at band practice. Either that or the piece of steak he had choked on the night before at Morton's Steak House. I don't think John has ever cooked a meal for himself in his life. Whatever the reason of his neck problem, he sat there at the sushi bar with a morose and crestfallen expression on his face. I finished off the sushi and we left. On the way back to his house, I saw Meadow walking her pit bull, Knuckles, along Pacific Coast Highway. My heart leapt in my chest. I moaned to John and we philosophized about the inscrutability of women.

Speaking of women, a girl named Andrea, who I slightly knew in college, found me on myspace.com, and suggested we hang out. I told her to meet me for coffee at 8:30. She suggested "drinks." A clove burned in her fingers as I hugged her and sat down at the table. She gave me the abridged version of her life since college; she had married a worship pastor named Moses, bore a son with him, got divorced, had her house flooded by a pipe leak, and is currently trying to move back to Redding. She smiled. Andrea had a great attitude about life, and we had a great time talking—finding much common ground.

On Tuesday, she called me wanting to hang out again, claiming a friend had bailed on her. I explained that I had to drive to Santa Clarita, and continue hiking the following day. Such is life on the trail; no time to nurture relationships with the opposite sex.

Tuesday night I drove Muse's car up to his late Grandmother's condo in Santa Clarita, arriving at 9:30. Everyone was in bed: Muse, his father, and his cousin. Muse breached the door of the bedroom when I entered the house. "Did you lock my car doors?" I said yes. The door closed.

I found myself sleeping on the bathroom floor with my ground pad, a pillow, and one sheet. That night I had a dream that a truck carrying a "wide load" had tipped over on the 55 Freeway, shutting down all but one lane. On the way to Kennedy Meadows the next morning, we saw one of those "wide load" houses crumbled on the side of the freeway.

Friday, June 30, 2006

7:54 pm

The Olancha Incident

We have been hiking for two days now in the semi-High Sierras. Our maximum elevation so far has been eleven thousand feet, and we have stayed consistently above nine thousand. Mount Whitney is close, and we have had views of her shrouded peak for most of our hike today, which was a gorgeous hike through Gomez Meadow, Big Dry Meadow, Brown Meadow and other meadows presided over by Olancha Peak in the Golden Trout Wilderness. Carefully monitoring upcoming water sources is no longer a worry as water flows in small creeks everywhere. We forded Rock Creek a short time ago—our first serious creek ford. Rock Creek is about ten feet wide and flowing swiftly with snow melt. On the opposing creek bank stood Detour, a bearded hiker of much girth. He stomped effortlessly across the creek in his shoes and joined me where I stood.

"How come you're coming back across?" I asked him.

"Well, I'm gonna go to Trail Pass" he said in his slow, shaky voice, "and hitch forward to Lone Pine to meet up with my friends."

"Oh. Did you do Whitney?"

"Yeah, I got about ninety percent of the way to the top, then I slipped and fell down a snowfield about a hundred feet and hurt myself, so I came back down."

Hence the name, Detour.

Muse charged through Rock Creek first—bare footed, and in his briefs. I am not sure it was necessary to go pantless, but he made it. I removed my shoes started across, facing the current, walking sideways like a crab, and steadying myself with trekking poles; one sure step at a time. The water stung ice cold; the stones under my feet were slippery—

sometimes round, sometimes jagged. I felt their cool texture and took care to avoid jagged edges.

Mosquitoes have become a nuisance, especially since they cluster heavily around water sources and gorgeous green meadows—seemingly everywhere we would prefer to stop to enjoy. Beauty always seems to come with a curse.

Yesterday, I came to a junction well ahead of Muse and thought I knew which way to go, but I was wrong. Among the oatmeal bark lodgepole pines, I followed the Olancha Pass Trail because I had heard Muse mention Olancha Pass several times. The proper direction was the left-trending trail to Gomez Meadows. I hiked a good mile in the wrong direction, eventually intercepting an overnight camper who informed me that I was not on the PCT, and that the trail I was currently on would take me to a parking lot. While we chatted, I was able to score three donuts, four packs of peanut butter crackers, some lemonade mix, and two cigarettes from the man. He resembled John Denver, but with thicker prescription glasses.

Needless to say, when I found my way back to the PCT and eventually found Muse where he sat on a bluff, he looked panicked and red in the face. I did not ask, but it looked like he may have been crying. I apologized profusely for my error, feeling bad about my cavalier drive, and forced myself to sit there and listen to all the new rules he wanted to implement as a result of this fiasco. He did not mind taking two packs of the peanut butter crackers I offered him though.

Today, as I hiked along in pristine wilderness, far from freeways and cars and hordes of people, I came across a balloon snagged in a bush. It was a shiny Mylar balloon—the type that people release on sunny days to watch drift up into heaven where God catches it, smiles, and winks a blessing upon their charmed lives. Wrong. I consider it littering even when your trash happens to float along for miles before touching the ground. Probably the most frequent piece of trash I have seen littered in the mountains has been Mylar balloons. The balloon I saw today said "Congratulations!" as I walked by. Thank you, whomever you are; and congratulations to you for littering the Inyo National Forest.

I am lying on my pad on the ground at the moment. My no-see-um head netting keeps the mosquitoes from landing all over my face. Mosquitoes are incredibly slow but audacious. Should a hiker become terribly frustrated, vengefully killing a couple hundred mosquitoes could be done quite quickly. But mosquitoes are amazing creatures in their fearlessness. Their one objective is to land on me and suck my blood. And they will not stop until they either succeed or get slapped dead. The red bumps on my feet, legs, hands, neck, shoulders, and forehead are a testament to their periodic successes. Mosquitoes instinctively target the back of my shoulder, where my capilene hiking shirt lies flat against skin. I cannot see them back there, and their proboscis easily penetrates my shirt. They also enjoy biting me through my polypropylene thermal underwear, which I subsequently removed to zip on the legs of my nylon pants. They have not evolved enough to penetrate nylon, yet.

Sunday, July 2, 2006

1:12 pm

Atop Whitney

We have paused by a creek to make lunch. Our food supply this week is incredibly insufficient, especially considering that the High Sierras will be the most physically exhausting section of the whole trip. Tomorrow we are supposed to reach the spot where Muse has hidden a bear can full of food. He stashed it by Bullfrog Lake the week we were off the trail. By leaving a re-supply box in the backcountry, we will not be forced to hike miles out of the Sierras to re-supply in Independence.

This week though, besides our hot dinner food, I have found myself with a bag of mixed dry fruit, beef jerky, GORP, bland crackers, and bean dip. Now, throw in the fact that we summited Mount Whitney yesterday, after hiking ten miles in the morning just to get to the base of Whitney. We did not summit Whitney until 5:30 p.m., by which time every hiker had left, leaving us all alone on the highest mountain in the contiguous United States. On the way up, at around thirteen thousand feet, my ipod stopped playing songs, and the unit itself began making a strange grinding noise. I have tried repeatedly since then, at different elevations and temperatures to turn it back on, but it remains silent and unmoved. Not having music and not having much food has left me depressed and lethargic today. Yes, I conquered Whitney, but the mountain took my energy and my music in exchange.

All complaints aside, I did much enjoy the sunset from atop Whitney. It took a bit of cajoling to convince Muse to camp on Whitney, as he was rightfully fearful of sudden thunderstorms. But we had perfectly clear skies all night, and the next morning we rose at dawn to watch the sun rise out of Death Valley—that molten sink out beyond Owens Valley, beyond the Inyo Mountains, beyond the Panamints, where the sun was rising from the hot, briny bottom of Bad Water. Meanwhile, I was shivering in the wind atop Whitney where my watch registered the temperature at twenty-nine degrees.

I felt it necessary to overnight Whitney in an attempt comprehend the sheer immensity of my surroundings. In every direction I looked from my celestial perch, mountains retreated in an eternal reign to the twilight edge of the earth—to the edge of my vision—to the edge of my imagination; endless, and forever. I looked north upon the wind and crumbling peaks of the Sierra crest—my small brain grappling the grandeur, fathoming the height of their lonesome summits, the expanse of their valleys—wondering where and how my trail will traverse those sovereign ridges with epaulets of crystal snows—jeweled lakes and turquoise buckles cinched around their granite waists.

In the late afternoon mountaintop luminescence, I laid flat on my back in a sandy area between the scattered golden granite slabs of Whitney and watched the strange death and birth of clouds in the sky. A solitary white lamb of cloud would make a benevolent appearance overhead. Seconds later the fluff unfurled and doubled on itself, tripled on itself while the center turned a pale gray—a brewing storm cloud. Then, like the blowing out of a match flame, like a puppet disappearing behind a felt screen, like a magician vanishing a coin into emptiness, the cloud would disappear...until a short while later, another solitary white lamb of cloud would make a benevolent appearance overhead.

Hiking back down Whitney is a snap compared to ascending. There were about three snowfields at different spots along the switchbacks. Their placement on the trail made for dangerous situations if one were to slip, but they were easily navigable, having been beaten down by many feet before mine.

Crabtree Meadows could be the most edenic area on the trail so far. The deep stream flowing through the meadow is of diamond clarity; the water flows like slow molten glass shimmering in the sun, boiling and swirling in the gentle curves and elbows of the meadow—the grasses of which terminate exactly at the water's edge, leaving no eroded banks and stony messes. Deer step with sacred care through the glade.

Tuesday, July 4, 2006

3:42 pm

Stomach Problems

Happy Fourth-of-July to me; there is rain and hail as we head up towards Mather Pass. We walked in the slight rain for a while, simultaneously fording a stony creek. The day before yesterday, after descending Mount Whitney, we strained further above timberline to conquer Forester Pass. Standing at 13,180 feet, Forester Pass is the highest point on the entire Pacific Crest Trail. The final steep switchbacks leading up to the pass were covered here and there in winter snow like a scattering of collapsed circus tents, forcing us to scramble around them and up the exposed ridge, grabbing and pushing boulders behind us until the dizzy saddle in the sky was attained. A metal sign at the summit informed us we had just left Sequoia National Park and were entering Kings Canyon National Park. The northward descent from the pass was a snow trail cutting diagonally and down an expansive snowfield for a good half mile, leading to broken snow patches at a lower elevation; then the muddy, shoe-soaking tundra across which ran the hundreds of run-off creeks, seeps and trickles into ponds, lakes, or larger Bubbs Creek.

Late in the afternoon yesterday we summitted Pinchot Pass, then found our way down to the stunning Rae Lakes where we stopped to camp under the ruddy pinnacle of the Painted Lady. Pinchot Pass had a good amount of snow to negotiate on the downhill side, and there were some scary moments stumping through the snow along a steep, exposed ridge. By the end of the day I was dead tired. My quads were fatigued and shaking from having carried me up and over two major passes: Glenn Pass near twelve thousand feet and Pinchot Pass at twelve thousand feet, both of which had precarious snow fields hiding the trail, forcing us to take difficult alternate routes.

For several days now, I have been plagued with stomach problems that have left me feeling weak and gassy, and my bowel movements resemble the consistency of a Slurpee as they exit. Muse and

I had talked about having a rest day in the backcountry so that we would not be hiking eleven days straight through the High Sierras. Today is supposed to be our rest day, and I desperately wanted to hike about five or ten miles then camp, for my stomach problems have left me feeling a weak.

The trail descended to eight thousand feet today where we crossed a cabled foot-bridge that swayed back and forth as one traversed its planks over the south fork of the Kings River. A rattlesnake was contentedly curled up on one of the steps on the far side of the bridge, and presumably sat there all day as hikers stepped down, just feet away. At the far side of the bridge were good camp spots beneath the shade of pines and I suggested to Muse we relax there for the rest of the day. The temperature in the valley was warm, and there were no mosquitoes. Muse was not content however. He wanted to get back to the high country to be out of mosquito territory, even though I pointed out that there were no mosquitoes anywhere around. As usual, I acquiesced to his wishes, and we hiked further, gaining elevation—which is when a cloud of rain and hail floated over forcing us to put up the tent in a mosquito-ridden grove of lodge pole pines from which I currently write.

Friday, July 7, 2006

7:06 pm

Muir Pass

It is hard to believe, but this is our last night out before we reach Vermillion Valley Resort. It has been a long, tiresome, but majestic ten days in the High Sierras. Yesterday, we conquered Muir Pass, which was covered in seven miles of snow. The ascent was not particularly steep, but very tiresome as the pass seemed always just beyond the summit of the next ridge, ascending higher and higher as we slogged through the snow, struggling to find breath in the thin air. At one point, the trail of footprints crossed a snow bridge over a rapid creek. I reluctantly crossed, fearing I would be that one hiker for whom the snow bridge collapsed, dumping me into the ice-cold rapids of the creek, and sweeping my body beneath the dark cave of snow into which it disappeared.

At twelve thousand feet on Muir Summit is a round shelter built entirely of rock—it's purpose: to provide shelter to hikers who find themselves in angry weather atop the pass. A hiker named By the Book stepped casually from the entrance like it was his house, and he was just checking the mail—sipping from a mug as we approached. The guidebook informed us that hikers are not supposed to sleep overnight in the Muir Hut save for emergency situations, which sounded like a ridiculous rule to me, and I attempted to convince Muse that we should camp here for the night, leaving the descent for tomorrow. "Ehh," cringed the ever-punctilious Muse. "I don't feel comfortable breaking the rules." So I gave in and we said goodbye to By the Book to begin our descent.

Muse and I attempted to reach Sapphire Lake at the bottom of the pass, but by seven p.m., as sunlight faded, we were still dragging wet shoes through miles of slushy snow; the temperature was dropping fast. We fretted for a bit, trying to locate somewhere to camp in a veritable snowfield, and darkness was coming on. Finally, we chanced upon a rock outcrop breaching the snow, with a flat enough area to secure our tarp tent. The dusk light behind the cold blue peaks created a terrific holy alpine glow, intermixing hues of burning orange, crystal blue and the scintillating white snow. Sometimes, I find myself camping in such rarified landscapes, in such moments of terrible beauty, that I am frightened. This little rock life raft, surrounded by an ocean of rippling snow, and electrified peaks, felt sacrilegious to be sleeping on. I felt as if we had pitched our tent in the Notre Dame cathedral, tying the guy lines to church pews. It felt like I was about to sleep at the foot of the Cross, on Crucifixion Day. The silence was tremendous, like the trembling calm after a bloody war. You expect it to come back—the anger, the clashing of weapons; the wind, the blinding storms. But the miles of razor peaks of the Goddard Divide are silent and trembling in suspended animation, in Christmas beauty, while we humans—ephemeral creatures—slowly explore the mountain valleys and ascend their peaks declaring ourselves triumphant, for a moment...

I was cold that night, surrounded by snow on the slope of Muir Pass; much like sleeping in that frosted-over freezer that sits half-neglected on the back porch. All night outside of the tent I heard what sounded exactly like someone eating potato chips. The noise started an hour after dark and continued on as often as I awoke during the night. Perhaps it was the slow grind of the giant moving glacier, or the snow refreezing during midnight hours. Though I cannot imagine how either one of those processes could produce such a sound.

One reason for my waking during the night was a wet dream. In my dream I found myself in a room and surrounded by women trying on a new line of see-thru lingerie.

But today I felt great as my stomach issues seemed to have passed. We hiked about twenty miles today, fording the infamous Evolution Creek around noon, on whose banks we met up with Stomper and the foul-mouthed Whiptail. Despite all the acrimony about it, Evolution Creek was not scary, but beautiful—a wide green creek with a sandy bottom, moving at a relaxed pace through Evolution Meadow. The water came up to my waist as I waded across the creek on a perfectly warm day.

Friday, July 14 2006

10:01 a.m.

Vermillion Valley Resort

The Vermilion Valley Resort does injustice to the word "resort." The refinement associated with the word has been lost at the bottom of Lake Edison; the lake upon whose shores lingers VVR: a strip of rooms for paying customers, general store and restaurant, and off to the side three tent rooms reserved for thru-hikers. It was perfect.

Muse and I had eighteen miles to accomplish yesterday before we would reach the far end of Lake Edison to catch the twice-daily ferry to the resort. The night before, Muse advised me to set my watch alarm for four a.m. to ensure that we would not miss the last ferry pick-up at 4:45 p.m. Come morning, my watch alarm either failed to respond, or we simply slept through it; thus, we woke at the disrespectable hour of five a.m. and began hiking by six.

We summitted 10,900 foot Selden Pass by eight a.m. On the descent, I slipped on a snow bank, and snapped one of my trekking poles in half. Soon after Selden Pass, we forded the notorious Bear Creek—a creek that every hiker had been warning us was treacherous and time-consuming. Muse had pre-calculated an hour for us to ford Bear Creek. It took us about ten minutes.

Before descending to Lake Edison, we ascended Bear Ridge where we traversed a spooky lodgepole forest—wholly unlike the lush riparian forests we have encountered in the Sierras so far. The thin pines sheltered a forest floor of dead wood—not a plant grew anywhere—not a stream flowed, and all was silent. It seemed an inhospitable environment. No birds flitted from branch to branch—jays did not fuss at me from treetops, chipmunks did not raise their alarm squeals.

The trail dropped down from Bear Ridge into a monotonous fifty-three switchbacks down to Mono Creek, which flows into Lake Edison. We reached the ferry dock at Lake Edison around 1:30—three hours early—and sat around eating and talking to the other hikers and fisherman in the area.

The ferry arrived at 4:40 and left as soon as the last person boarded, which was me. I bummed a cigarette from the ferry captain—a bearded, smoky man, slouched nearly in half behind the helm of the boat.

The grounds of Vermilion Valley Resort are littered by the trailers that house the derelict onsite staff of the resort. The maintenance man has a crop of marijuana growing somewhere out in the woods. When he wanders off the premises to smoke weed, he declares quite euphemistically, "I'm goin' to church." At first, I thought I had this icicle-bearded, dirt man all wrong; that was before he explained to me what "Goin' to church" actually meant.

Jim is the Brains behind VVR. He greeted Muse and me at the counter of the general store and restaurant, and give us the run-down. "Okay folks," he said to the city people. "Lemme help my hikers first!" That was us. "What's your name?" he asked me.

"Mojave."

"Mojave..." he scrawled it in a register. "You look like a Mojave!"

I liked Jim right away.

"I'm putting' you guys up in tent three; first night's free, and first beer is on the house. It's two dollars a minute to use the satellite phone, five dollars for a shower, and five dollars for the laundry."

There were not too many hikers here yesterday, and even less today on Sunday. Yesterday's dinner was my first square meal in ten days, and it was by far the most heavenly barbeque I have sat down to in all my years. I ordered the "Special," which was comprised of pork ribs, tri-tip, quarter chicken, pork loin, barbeque beans, and potato salad. I ate it all. For dessert, I had a slice of boysenberry pie a la mode.

I did not sleep well in the tent cabin last night as there were five people sharing the room, and the constant rustle of nylon sleeping bags on plastic covered mattresses, and Muse snoring next to me, chased off any chance of sleep.

My friends Dave and Dianne live somewhere nearby in the town of Big Creek where Dave works at Edison's hydro-electrical power plant. I was hoping Dave and Dianne were going to drive up from Big Creek to house us on our zero day. I had called them from Kennedy Meadows with my arrival date. But after spending a small fortune on two-dollar phone calls from VVR, I had only succeeded in leaving them several voice messages, and currently await a return call.

Having given up on them at the moment, I broke down this morning by purchasing a five dollar shower, and felt of hot water for the first time in two weeks. In front of the bathroom mirror I removed my shirt and shorts; I gasped at my stick figure in the mirror. My skin was pulled tight against ligament and bone; my genitals hung there sadly like two deflated party balloons. I reminded myself of E.T. when Elliot's brother discovers the emaciated alien surrounded by raccoons and dying on the banks of a creek. I had easily lost another five to ten pounds over the last ten days of technical hiking in the Sierras. There is not much left of me.

Today is our zero day. I have been relaxing, watching the World Cup soccer match, and smoking Marlboros at the outdoor wrap-around bar with the tree stump stools. Muse and I sorted our re-supply food first thing this morning, presumably leaving us free of all worries for the remainder of the day; at least that is how I see it. But Muse has been racing around the premises, unable to relax or act in a normal fashion. He buzzes around me like a mosquito, coming at me from all directions with new worries, concerns, and delegations. He has repeatedly confronted me about the status of Dave and Dianne, while I sat watching the soccer game. Zzzzzzt "Any word from them yet?" Zzzzzz.... Zzzzzzt. "Have you heard from Dave?" Zzzzz.... Zzzzt "Anything yet? Did you call them again?" As if I would not inform him if I knew Dave and Dianne were on their way. Dave and Dianne are notorious latecomers to every event, and I would not be surprised were they to simply arrive unannounced. And I would not be surprised if they did not show at all.

The cook here has a fake eye, or a dead eye; or perhaps an evil eye that sees into your dark side. He is quick witted and feeds on the unsuspecting and vulnerable mind, like Muse's.

"Still serving lunch?" asked Muse, seating himself on a stump stool.

"Nope," the cook responded quickly. "Kitchen's all closed." The evil eye waited for Muse's sorrow to appear.

"Oh, darn," responded Muse.

Then the cook handed Muse a menu. "Kitchen's open now though! Ha ha ha!"

The hilarity.

The bearded maintenance man, who resembles the quintessential bum holding a cardboard sign at freeway off-ramps, and the cook whose appearance is equally sour, generally sit around all day, smoke, and make fun of each other, and everyone else. They are a synergistic pair who work themselves up into professional volleys of insults when they are together. I often sit with them to augment my own stores of insults and also to have a good laugh. Their recreational insult-fests remind me of Drew and me, and I imagine Drew and I will be just like them when we reach such a grizzled age.

Muse has engaged By the Book in card games at the moment; he thrives on competition. His hands and mind must always be engaged in some activity. I on the other hand take my rest day in their most literal definition: I sit around and rest.

Muse stresses me out; his presence means he is searching for some kind of competition to engage in or has dreamt up some new task that must be accomplished immediately in order for our hike to continue. I wish he would start smoking or drinking, or taking depressant drugs—anything to put him under for a while.

The Lake Edison ferry brought over more hikers today: Ridgewalker, Oatmeal Stout, and Gnome Sherpa. Ridgewalker works at an REI in Seattle, and is a wealth of knowledge on absolutely every subject that I ever heard raised in his presence. Oatmeal Stout hikes with specialized trekking poles fixed with a hollow shaft and a screw top, into which she pours hard liquor for nips on the trail. Gnome Sherpa earned his trail name for carrying around a gnome on his backpack—not a real one. This gnome accompanied him on the Appalachian Trail in a past year wherein he earned his trail name. The gnome, by the time I was introduced to it, was in an advanced state of deterioration—cracked, chipped and missing appendages.

A thundershower poured down on Lake Edison this afternoon. The Sierra Mountains create their own weather systems, and the clouds usually come suddenly late in the day, pour a bit of rain, then move on just as fast as they appeared. I sat, unmoved from my stump stool at the outdoor wrap-around bar, protected by the overhang, watching the rain. Today has been a good day.

Friday, July 14 2006

10:01 a.m.

Mammoth Steve

I just finished breakfast at Nicely's, a restaurant in the town of Lee Vining situated along Highway 395. Lee Vining claims itself the gateway to the Sierras; gateway to Bodie Ghost Town, and perhaps Death Valley would not be too far either.

On our last night at Vermilion Valley, I relaxed by outdoor fire pit along with By the Book, Oatmeal Stout, Gnome Sherpa, the derelict maintenance man and the evil-eyed cook. Muse had just retired to bed when a burgundy Isuzu Trooper stopped in front of the general store. From its open door strode Dave, Budweiser in hand, and a broad grin in my direction. He said he was camping with his family somewhere nearby, and had not been home to check his messages. Dianne, his wife, had made up a care package for me, but since Dave drove off from where they were camped without explanation, the care package was never delivered unto me, and Dave was the recipient of a firm scolding from his wife after the fact.

Muse and I hiked twenty miles yesterday, up and over Donahue Pass, and down into Tuolumne Meadows where flows the Tuolumne River, like a winter fresh squeeze of blue toothpaste. We had been hiking the day with T-Bird and Bama, and at a wide bend in the river, where the water slowed and deepened, Bama and I stripped to our shorts and dove in headfirst, thoroughly stunned by the horrendous cold of such beautiful and inviting water. I climbed out and stood on the bank in the grass, dripping and warmed by the sun. My eyes were transfixed by the sapphire blue and emerald green of the rippling water. What an irony that something so inviting should be so cold as to disallow a prolonged touch.

Day hikers began to appear as we drew nearer the highway at Tioga pass. Typical of Yosemite National Park, all the campgrounds in the area were full, so I thumbed a ride for us out front of the general store along Tioga Pass. A commercial airplane mechanic and his wife picked us up and drove us eleven miles down the mountain into Lee Vining, a town perched above the anomalous Mono Lake with its smoke-stack spires of tufa.

We are zeroing in Lee Vining due to Muse's recurring foot pain, which he contracted by long jumping across swollen creeks. He also seems very tired. We rented a room in a cabin-style motel where, upon entering, Muse drew the blinds and went straight to bed. The time was near six p.m. I left the room saying over my shoulder that I was going to get something to eat. He groaned into the pillow. It would be nice to eat at Bodie Mike's Barbeque restaurant up the sidewalk alone with my thoughts, and not have to worry about Muse delegating new tasks to me. Ten minutes after I was seated at a nice corner table on the patio, I see Muse power walking down the sidewalk—the apocalypse close behind him; he spots me on the patio and sits down.

We had been hiking the last couple days with Gnome Sherpa and Oatmeal Stout from Iowa and Ohio respectively. By The Book has also been leap-frogging with us since Mammoth. He is solo hiking the PCT, having left his wife and kids at home. People frequently ask him if his wife cares that he is away for nearly half a year. "Care?" he says, humored. "She *encouraged* me to do this. In fact, she bet me five thousand dollars that I wouldn't finish! But if I *do* make it all the way, she owes *me* five grand!" He did not make it the whole way.

Muse, By The Book, and I overnighted in Mammoth on the living room floor of a red-faced man named Steve who was taking advantage of the fact that his wife and kids were visiting San Diego. Steve builds low-income housing in the Mammoth area. This is how we met Steve: we had all hiked into Red's Meadow, an equestrian resort a short walk off of the PCT. Steve had ditched work for the day and drove up into the mountains to have couple beers at the Red's Meadow diner and see what kind of trouble he could find. He found the three of us wanting a ride into Mammoth and immediately offered a ride; and his living room floor, laundry, and Internet. We jumped.

We wound down the mountain together in Steve's truck on a sunny afternoon. Steve is a round-faced, slaphappy man in his late forties; a proud beer gut challenges his t-shirt, and a baseball cap squeezed the top of his fat head like a cherry atop a scoop of ice cream. Steve mumbles quick sentences when he talks, sounding perennially drunk, which makes him difficult to understand sometimes.

It became obvious to me that Steve was in search of some drinking buddies, which is how we wound up at a cantina in Mammoth Village straight away. By The Book is not much of a drinker, and Muse, forever fearful of dehydration, had lemonade, leaving me delighted to be Steve's designated drinking buddy. He gave our young Australian waitress elevator-eyes as she kept the three-dollar margaritas fresh. By The Book attempted to engage Steve in professional questions, but Steve was content to tell us, as he ran his hand over his head and replaced the baseball cap, all the *things* he could do with our blond waitress.

Later that evening, Steve drove off to play softball with his buddies, leaving the three of us alone in his house. We walked through Mammoth Village over to a restaurant called Bergers; Steve had recommended it. Muse ordered a big salad, which did not fill him up. I knew it wouldn't. He is always ordering these stupid salads everywhere we go, repeating his mantra of eating healthy in town to increase performance on the trail. What he needs is meat and carbohydrates, which is what I ordered: buffalo steak and fries. Mmm, good.

Around ten p.m. Steve was ferried back to us by his friend Dave, as he had gotten too drunk after the softball game to drive himself. If I thought Steve was difficult to understand sober, he was near impossible to understand when drunk. His buddy Dave, who I suspected was drunk too, was a hyper-active loud-mouth who talked at the top of his voice indoors, cutting everyone off constantly. Dave stood in the doorway yelling at us for near an hour about a near-death-experience he'd had. Steve would occasionally mumble something unintelligible from where he was slumped red-faced and smiling on the couch, "Frada-bada-gaga!" The story went like this: Dave's signage company had provided the signs and banners for some kind of big-city dinner at a convention center, to which he had been invited as a vendor. While sitting in the grand ballroom eating dinner, Dave had a heart attack. At the hospital he was declared clinically dead. But there he stood in the doorway, yelling at us at the top of his voice, clearly not dead—or else the loudest zombie ever to haunt the earth. Dave's story could have been told in its entirety in ten minutes, but I guess he felt we were quite enamored by his near-death-experience and repeated the story forwards and backwards, middle to end, end to beginning, until he was sure we understood him—this Lazarus.

The following morning we took the shuttle bus back up the mountain, past Devil's Postpile to Red's Meadow, and began hiking again around one o'clock. Muse's new nightly worry, besides bears and rain, is mosquitoes. He has backpacked in the Sierras at least once a year for upwards of fifteen years, yet his disproportionate irritation with this insect is renewed and more pathological with every passing day.

Hiking out from Red's Meadow we engaged in conversation a nice lady who turned out to be the accountant for Gossamer Gear—the company whose backpacks Muse and I both wear. It was a beautiful warm day—no mosquitoes anywhere. As we all talked, Muse suddenly exclaimed he was "being eaten alive by mosquitoes" and hiked off. Every conversation we have with a stranger out in the backcountry is centered on Muse's delusion of a mosquito pandemic. For myself, I have pretty much gotten used to having them around and will swat them when they get too friendly. When mosquitoes are particularly bad I apply Deet to the exposed parts of my skin, which does away with the issue immediately. Muse walks around a fair amount of the time with his rain jacket on and hood cinched over his head. Like I have probably written already, Muse is covered every day from head to toe in fabrics to protect himself. I have asked him why; he cites his Grandfather who had skin cancer later on in life.

After hiking with us several days, Gnome Sherpa and Oatmeal Stout suggested the trail name of "Blind Shepherd" for Muse because of the bandana he has over his head, and safety pinned under his chin; combined with the sunglasses that have an elastic strap securing them around his head, and in his hand the stalk of a nolina plant he uses as a trekking pole. All of these items give him the appearance of a blind shepherd. But Muse is Muse; someone who is a deep thinker and musical, and I do not imagine he will tolerate being renamed.

I seem to have lost my sunglasses some time between yesterday and today. The last two pair of sunglasses I have worn on this trip have been sunglasses I have found along the trail. I also left my food cup and my titanium spork somewhere around Rae Lakes. Is it considered littering to accidentally leave something somewhere? Other than those three items, I have hung on to all else I am responsible for.

There are many Europeans staying here in Lee Vining. I see them at dinner and around our hotel, looking thin and fashionable, but not thinner than myself. In contrast, my white hiking shirt is stained all about, particularly with a dark dirt stripe down each shoulder from my shoulder straps. My facial hair is at that dirty stage between an acceptable shadow and a tangible beard. I wear a bandana around my head everywhere I go to control my head hair, which has not tasted scissors in three months. I wear hiking shorts and beat up Brooks running shoes with no socks. I am a mountain man and look the part. My nature is free and my needs basic. I eat up day hikers with my lithe legs when I pass them on the trail, and chuckle to myself at their rolls of fat bunching over and under their hip strap.

Most of the Sierra's high country and high passes are behind us now. I am happy about that. I am sick of the Sierras. They suck. There are miles of ankle twisting snow to navigate across, hoping I can find the trail again on the other end. And the snow is never flat. It resembles the surface of a choppy ocean were it flash frozen—peaks and troughs called sun pockets for miles. Overnight the snow freezes and is hard and slippery to walk on during the morning hours. As the day progresses, and the snow softens, my feet sink into it as I walk and my shoes remain wet all day. And the trail, when it is not covered with snow, is covered with water from snow run-off from high above. Half of the time the trail is quite literally a creek, forcing us to walk amongst the boulders off the side of the trail or through a muddy field. And when the trail is not covered with snow or water it is usually a hardscrabble walk over uneven stones and exposed roots making it still difficult to hike with any alacrity. That is the Sierras, folks—a hard country, challenging mind and body. I have conquered the worst of it, with Muse clearing his throat the whole way—constantly worrying of rain and bears, complaining endlessly of mosquitoes, and delegating tasks to me just as I have gotten comfortable in my sleeping bag. I am alive and feeling stupendous. My feet and legs are strong, bearing no compromising pains, and on our zero days I sit around and smoke like a Jap, then return to the trail and tear up the mountains like nothing. Praise God!

Sunday, July 16, 2006

8:57 p.m.

Hiking Blind

I journal by the light of a campfire I made. She is popping and dancing against the dusk sky. "Are the mosquitoes gone yet?" Muse just asked me from where he lay in his sleeping bag, the hood of his rain jacket cinched tight over his head. He hiked most of the day with his black mosquito netting over his head, and sunglasses on underneath. He looks like a veiled, mourning woman, walking an eternal mosquito-ridden trail of sorrow. I think it dangerous for Muse to walk around with sunglasses *and* black mosquito netting over his head. In fact, earlier today, he said to me from beneath his veil, "You lead. I can't see anything." I have offered him the Deet but he is reluctant to use it for some reason. Maybe his other Grandfather had Deet poisoning later in life. I guess it is more fun to hike blind and in a rain jacket on a hot day than to apply some insect repellent.

Campfires rebuff the onslaught of mosquitoes to some degree, and I enjoy lying by the fire at day's end to relax and be hypnotized by the flames. I built a fire last night as well, as there have been frequent fire rings along the trail. Muse never sleeps by the fire for fear of popping embers. He systematically chooses his sleeping location each night by laying his pad down on a potential flat area, laying on it for a few moments, then gets up and repeats the process somewhere else. He rarely settles on the first lay-down. Sometimes, the process can go on for five minutes or longer.

Last night I settled down in my sleeping bag beside my fire for the night, joined soon after by Muse. No sooner had he sat down to enjoy the warmth when a log popped, sending embers all over his clothes. He jumped up, brushing them off and repeated his safety mantra of never sleeping next to a campfire. Later in the evening, from where he lay in the distance, he suddenly yelled out, "Mojave! It looks like your sleeping bag is on fire!" which it was not.

When we camped a few nights prior, at Thousand Island Lake, we had just stopped to camp beneath some pines and had both chosen our spots when he called over, "Could kind of organize your stuff to make room for me to come over there, in case it starts raining and we have to put the tent up?" There was not a cloud in the sky.

"Do what?" I asked incredulous. "It's not going to rain!"

"Wanna bet?" he said smiling, thereby transforming his worry into an attempt at humor. I gave up.

We passed several lakes today, two of which lay so close to the trail that I stripped to my shorts and dove in as I walked by, experiencing the wonderful shock of sudden immersion in snow melt—water so cold that my breath is stolen away, and I regain the surface with a horrified gasp. There is nothing to do in freezing water but madly swim back out and stand on the shore feeling as if you have just had a religious experience—an invasive cleansing; the split-second antithesis between being hot and sweaty, and sudden immersion in ice water.

Six days until we reach our next re-supply point. I have been eating too much food lately, and fear I will run out before our time in the backcountry is up. I still have my dry salami with me that I purchased in Mammoth. Salami tastes good in everything. Tonight I added it to miso soup, and last night I simply cooked it on a stick over the campfire.

I hiked well today, always having to take longer breaks to wait for Muse to catch up. Our rest day in Lee Vining was not enough to cure the pain in his foot, and I know it is slowing him. I hope and pray it will pass so that we can start making some good mileage. It is ironic that I should finally reach hiking utopia only to be slowed by Muse's first foot pain on the trail. But I do not complain about it, as he was patient with me.

Wednesday, July 19, 2006

5:23 pm

Sonora Pass

Two days ago we breached the boundary of the Toiyabe National Forest, passing the ice-crusted Dorothy Lake at Dorothy Pass. A Sierra storm threatened us from the east, sending winds through the pass, and raising a dark storm-head up higher and higher like a cobra about to strike. But the storm in the waning sunlight created such a terribly beautiful fire over the artistry of mountain crests. With the broken clouds, the sun spanned a double-rainbow touching down gently the atop distant granite crags.

Descending the canyon towards the West Fork of West Walker River, the mosquitoes horded in heretofore-unseen density. We had entered what is called "mosquito alley" where clouds of fearless mosquitoes followed us for miles, even in the rain. Yes, rain *and* mosquitoes at the same time; hike the PCT everybody! The mosquitoes were a thin cloud, ever-present in front of my face, and humming in my ears. Though I was lacquered with Deet, sporadic mosquitoes would hold their breath and dive bomb out of the cloud on suicide missions. We walked around masochistically slapping our arms and faces all day. Jackalope and Eagle Eye—an engaged couple from Oregon, leap-frogged with us today. I enjoy their company very much.

The composition of the mountains changed drastically yesterday as we entered the Emigrant Wilderness, nearing Sonora Pass. The trail gained elevation out of mosquito alley as the forests grew thinner, giving way to a barren volcanic ridge walk at ten thousand feet. Muse and I stopped to enjoy the silent air, finally free from the burden of marauding mosquitoes. We hiked along crumblesome volcanic ridges, over-laid with patchwork snows.

We leap-frogged with Chewy, who has been hiking solo after Magnet left the trail due to migraines. Highway 108 at Sonora Pass was in sight when we came to the last stretch of trail. The trail was covered in snow, of course, rendering the descent a difficult one. At first, I stepped slowly out onto a precipitous slant of snow, kicking holes into the snow with each step, and sinking my trekking poles deep. My heart raced and every muscle felt. It was a foolhardy attempt, fraught with the real danger that I could slip and fall quickly against the rocks below. I turned slowly back and sought another option. Muse took a crumbling dirt slope and I followed, inching down on my butt on a slant of loose dirt and gravel to where the snow was not so steep. From there we shoe skied to the bottom and found the trail to the road.

Girl Scout was hitching at the pass as we approached. He informed us that By The Book had slipped on the snow we just descended and slid down a hundred feet or so, breaking a couple ribs on the jagged rocks. I felt lucky and protected. Though there were several ways to descend Sonora Pass—none were safe or easy.

Muse had reached the highway ahead of me, and when I caught up, he was in conversation with a tall, thin, white man standing with his Asian wife. They ended up driving us eleven miles down the pass to Kennedy Meadows resort—yes, a second Kennedy Meadows.

Muse initially wanted to hitch down the pass to get lunch at the resort, but we were soon overtaken with enough laziness that we rented a cabin for the evening. Perhaps our lethargy was divinely inspired, for several hours after our decision to stay overnight, storm clouds materialized in once-blue skies, and dumped more rain with lightning than we have encountered on trail so far. I enjoyed the show from the wooden porch of our cabin. Jackalope and Eagle Eye stepped out of a car just as the rain started, and the four of us congregated for dinner, having a thoroughly enjoyable conversation. Jackalope, who was in her early thirties, had just earned her PhD in biology, and was celebrating by hiking the PCT. Eagle Eye said that he wanted to start a high-end audio/video store in Las Vegas. The two of them are on schedule to hike to their wedding in Oregon, marry, and presumably continue on from there.

Later that night we met up at the saloon for drinks where there was a group of about six cowboy types who, upon learning of our trek, appeared roundly impressed and proceeded to ask us many logistical questions on the matter. One cowboy left the saloon to retrieve all of his leftover backpacking dinners to contribute to our hike. The grand congratulations continued as another bought us a round of drinks. Jackalope and Eagle Eye are quite the drinkers and seem to have a beer at every meal—then they find the nearest bar to top it all off. I am not sure what Muse initially ordered at the bar, but whatever it was, he did not finish it before he left the bar for bed. I overheard Muse explaining to the bartender in a serious tone, how alcohol dangerously leads to dehydration on the trail, which was why Muse was not taking advantage of the cowboy's generosity. In all, I drank two Long Island Ice Teas and a rum and Coke, then staggered warmly off to bed, feeling wonderfully dehydrated.

Sunday, July 23, 2006

1:12 pm

Cookie Monster

We are in South Lake Tahoe now, the largest city we have seen since Lancaster. We walked the seventy miles from Sonora Pass in three days: two 27 miles days, and the remaining miles on the last day.

Hitch-hiking back up the deserted Highway 108 to Sonora Pass from Kennedy Meadows was our most difficult hitch to date. Muse and I took turns standing beside the quiet forest road. Five or ten minutes would pass before a single car whooshed by, but none would stop for us. The morning was sunny and warm—the fresh air smelled of mountain pine, and I was happy. I stood hitching for my designated twenty minutes, then called over to Muse who sat on a rock reading. "It's your turn."

"Your twenty minutes is up already?" he would say, forever fearful that I was cheating. Muse sighed in exasperation. If hitching ever took more than ten minutes, he became extremely frustrated.

He stood on the shoulder, glancing up and down the highway. "This is ridiculous!" he said, spiraling quickly into depression. "This makes me never want to hitch-hike again!"

"Don't worry about it," I said in my most consoling voice. "We'll get picked up; it's just going to take longer than usual because this highway is so empty. Don't let it affect your attitude. Turn that frown, upside down!" Muse cracked a smile and simmered down. I was tired of battling his mood swings though. Finally, a car full of teenagers picked us up.

At dinner in Kennedy Meadows, Eagle Eye and Jackalope had given us a bag of brownies and a bag of chocolate chip cookies from their re-supply box. Muse took hold of them, and I never saw them again. Meanwhile, the last two days Muse had been complaining of running out of food, repeatedly asking me if I had anything I was not going to eat. We were making lunch at Carson Pass when I thought to ask him, as I stirred a boiling pot of quinoa, what had happened to all those brownies and cookies.

"Oh, those were like totally gone on the first day!"

"Really!" I said, nodding my head. "Wow, that must have been nice."

"Well, you didn't really eat any of them during dinner. I didn't think you liked them!" His speech was defensive; he was lying.

"Yeah," I said. "How were you supposed to know that I would want any chocolate chip cookies or brownies?"

"Well, you didn't ask for any! Besides, I was carrying all that weight around, so I ate them all. You have to say something, or they're gone!"

Muse raced off to use the phone at the ranger station. I had not even seen him eat the brownies and cookies while we hiked, which meant that he only snacked on them while I was out of sight. His defensiveness told me he knew he had acted selfish. What really irked me though was that he should ask me for food after having devoured all of his in two days, including a wealth of cookies and brownies. The whole situation made me angry and I took out my anger on the trail, hiking fast and taking very few breaks—only stopping long enough for Muse to catch up wherein I got up and hiked off out of sight again. Our twenty-eight miles the day before had been difficult for Muse, by his admission, leaving him tired and hungry; I felt great after the twenty-eight, and hiked even harder this day without the aid of cookies and brownies.

We hiked through a beautiful volcanic portion of the North Sierras. The brown crags around Leavitt Peak and Tower Peak reminded me of the pinnacles, spires, and hoodoos of the Southwest. We had a spectacular sunset, and an impressive array of wildflowers on our last day.

Bears are notorious for robbing food from unsuspecting campers. The more time I spend in the wild, and the hungrier I become, the more I associate with the mentality of a scavenging bear. As we neared Carson Pass there were a good amount of day hikers out to enjoy the wildflowers. As I breached the ridge from the backcountry—a starving animal—I did not see fellow humans anymore; I immediately saw their backpacks, their fanny packs, the florescent colors of their clothing; food was there, and my mind starting entertaining ways to secure it for myself. I was startled at the primal instinct developing within—to see city people merely as sources of food.

When at last we came down to busy Highway 50, we were able to hitch a ride within minutes from a gruff guy in an SUV. The sky had rained on us for the last couple hours of our hike and we clambered into his car like musty wet dogs. He dropped us off in South Lake Tahoe where a string of hotels lined the street. I started talking to some off road Jeepers in front of one hotel who turned out to be from the city of Orange, which neighbors my home town. They had just spent the last couple days driving a renowned ORV (off-road-vehicle) trail in the Tahoe wilderness. I explained our hike to them, which once again garnered respect and admiration to no end; they were men after all, and rewarded us with a box of peanut butter crackers, pop tarts, apple crisp bars, granola bars, dry salami, pastries, and other sundries that we eventually had to start thankfully denying.

Monday, July 24, 2006

11:46 a.m.

Lake Tahoe

Muse and I were sitting at the bus stop this morning in South Lake Tahoe when we were offered a ride back up to Echo Lake from a hiker named Rig, who I had briefly met back in Idyllwild, and his friend who lives in the area. Muse and I are still waiting on our re-supply box, which did not come to the Echo Lake post office on Saturday as we expected. Rig and his buddy furnished me with a beer, which I drank in the car on the way up to Echo Lake.

The last couple days in South Lake Tahoe have been enjoyable. Friday night, the night we first hitched down Highway 50, we spent in a seedy hotel, the patrons of which seemed to live permanently in their rooms. Cheap hotels bear certain earmarks regardless of their location in this continent. Cheap hotels will always have someone working under the hood of a broken down Trans Am in the parking lot. Cheap hotel rooms are usually devoid of telephones, television remotes, and air conditioning. And cheap hotels always have a fat woman in a mumu who walks around smoking cigarettes and cracking jokes through blackened teeth. The pool, if there is one, will have been filled with dirt and turned into a lawn, which is where the fat woman sits and smokes all day.

Based on the informed recommendation of the front desk staff at the hotel—a greasy tank-topped man with a thin mustache—Muse and I walked down the street to a Chinese food restaurant for our highly anticipated off-trail pig-out dinner.

"How about this one," I said, looking at the menu. "The two-to-three person meal, which comes with soup, salad, fried rice and all the appetizers."

"Eh, I think I'm gonna be hungrier than that."

"Really?" I said. "Then what do you want to get?"

Based on Muse's hunger calculations, we ordered soup, appetizers, about four entrees, fried rice, and a side of steamed rice for Muse. Twenty minutes into our meal, with plates still full of food, Muse sat back with a bloated look on his face. "It's so much food!"

"Yes, it is."

"I feel sick to my stomach," he said.

"Oh?"

He moved to leave our table. "It's your turn to pay right? I'm gonna go back to the room." Muse was never one to stick around for after dinner small talk.

"No, actually it's your turn to pay," I responded. Muse sat back again, looking even sicker. He had mistakenly thought it was my turn to buy dinner, which is probably why he ordered an exorbitant amount of food. He was more than happy to leave me with the tab of sixty dollars. "But you know what," I finally said, allowing the dramatic pause to set in. "Since this is an unusually large bill, I think it best that we just split this one down the middle. I know you'd do the same for me."

I returned to the room with bags of Chinese food and put it in the small refrigerator. It made a swell breakfast the next morning.

On Saturday, after we checked out of the derelict hotel, we took the bus down to the main strip where the casinos reside at State Line. We found another hotel without a pool or air conditioning, but felt better about our location near downtown. This one even had a ceiling fan.

The buffet at Harras Casino is on the eighteenth floor. People were lined up behind the register as if it were a rollercoaster at Disneyland. People glanced quizzically at me as the line advanced. I was thin, and wearing dirt-stained clothing—a bandana wrapped around my head. We ran into Chai Guy, Eagle Eye and Jackalope, and two other hikers at the buffet. It seems as though we had all calculated the cost/benefit of a buffet for the starving hiker. After dinner Muse and I walked to the movies to watch M. Night Shayamalan's new movie, Lady in the Water. Muse is a huge fan of Night's movies.

Yesterday, Sunday, seemed to fly by too quickly. The sky remained overcast, and I sat at the Laundromat journaling. We saw another movie; Pirates of the Caribbean, Part two, then walked to an Indian cuisine restaurant for dinner. Two hikers were already seated as we entered the restaurant. We had never seen or met them before, but they recognized us as dirty, starving hikers and waved us over. They were Samantha and Matthew from Boulder, Colorado. After dinner I walked by myself over to Coldstone Creamery and tried the Cherry Loves Cheesecake in a waffle bowl, "Like It" sized.

Muse pointed out to me the other day that the burn scar on my leg from the motorcycle has taken on the same triangular shape as the Pacific Crest Trail emblem. He is right! I have been keeping it out of the sun as much as possible as the scar is reddish and is taking quite a while to heal. At least the scab is now gone.

Muse claimed to have some friends in the bay area who wanted to hike with us out of Echo Lake. I did not know that he had any real friends besides Nate in Lancaster. But his friends, a married couple, showed up to Echo Lake ready to hike for a couple days. Our re-supply box had not shown up to the post office though, rendering Muse and me incapable to hike out with them. "It's fine," his friend Alex said. "I mean, we were going hiking anyways so, no big deal." Muse and his friends talked like people who did not really know one another. And though we were hiking from Mexico to Canada, they seemed uninterested in helping Muse out in the least. It seemed more coincidental that Muse and his friends had converged on Echo Lake at the same time. As a closing courtesy, Muse and his friends decided that we should all meet up for lunch on Sunday in Tahoe when they were done hiking. They took the ferry across Echo Lake and were gone. On Sunday Muse called and left them a voice message. They never called back.

I had been calling my mom for two days trying to contact her to see when our box was sent out. She is visiting my grandparents in Missouri. Finally on Sunday afternoon she answered, claiming that she had just barely missed the phone each time I called. Apparently, things are a mess in Saint Louis where record-breaking thunder and lightning storms have knocked out electricity to thousands of people. They all retreated into the basement because the house was so hot without air conditioning. All of the food in the refrigerator rotted and had to be thrown out.

I hung up the phone. We were about to leave our hotel room to get dinner when I informed Muse our box had been mailed out nine days ago. He flipped out about the box having been mailed a mere nine days prior; not enough time, by his estimation—especially in hindsight. I tried to get him to leave the room so we could eat dinner, but he sat there on the edge of the bed, his bowl haircut frayed, his nostrils flared, his blue eyes fixed on that distant point over my shoulder; a land where re-supply boxes never came late to post offices. "Just let me think about this for a minute," he snapped. When Muse is thinking he cannot walk to restaurants, or do anything else whatsoever. I tried to calm him by laying out our options in a pragmatic presentation. But he was waiting on some new shoes he thought were in the box, without which he was reluctant hike on. "I have five-hundred miles on these shoes." His shoes looked fine. "If I don't get my new pair, I'm afraid I will start to get blisters."

Finally we ate.

Tuesday, July 25, 2006

6:30 p.m.

Easily Lost

I promptly became lost yesterday as we rejoined the PCT out of Echo Lake. I guess I was not actually lost; but I kept walking on a trail bordering along Echo Lake and missed where the PCT forked off to begin ascending a ridge. When Muse did not catch up with me after I sat for a while, I decided that something must be wrong and started walking back; I walked all the way back to where we started at the Echo Lake Lodge without finding him. David, another PCT hiker, informed me that I must have missed where the PCT broke off the trail to climb the ridge, as there was no sign at the junction, making it an easy miss. Perhaps if I carried the maps every once in a while, I would not have missed the trail.

I started up the PCT finally as it entered the Desolation Wilderness, and asked everyone passing me in the opposite direction if they had seen a guy in pants, long sleeve shirt, gloves, and a purple bandana pinned beneath his chin. Most said they had. Several hours later I caught up to Muse where he sat on a rock overlooking Aloha Lake. He was silent as I sat down. Relieved to find him, I explained to him how I had missed the junction, realized something was wrong, and walked back to the last place where I had seen him, which is our protocol if we become lost from each other.

"Well, did you learn anything?" he asked in a smug, fatherly voice.

"Umm, not really," I said. Muse chuckled, shaking his head as if I was the densest oaf that ever walked the earth. "What was I supposed to learn?" I asked. He had no answer. "I simply missed the junction," I said again, "because there were no signs. So I went back to the last place we had seen each other, which is what *you* decided we should do if we were lost, and you were not there."

"You're right, I didn't follow procedure," he said. "I heard you were back down at the store, and I thought to myself, 'Do I really want to go all the way back down to the store? Or risk our friendship if I don't?' I wonder if anyone else gets lost like you do? I wonder if anyone else has to deal with this?"

It was a terribly self-centered thing for him to say. I quickly reminded him of Amyloid, the hiker we had met just two days ago at Echo Lake Resort. Amyloid had become lost from his friends for weeks, and had been calling the home of his friends to find out where they have checked in from. Yes, some were worse off than we were.

He talked calmly in an affectation of maturity, claiming he had pushed aside his anger, which I knew was not true. I could have strangled him at that moment, for all the useless stupid rules and plans he promulgates—rules which he never follows through on—plans that never come to fruition. He could never just be happy to see me; he could never act relieved that I had found my way back, especially since I never have the maps. I would never hear, "There you are! What happened? Really, you missed the trail? Well, thank God you found your way back." My becoming lost was a personal insult to him; another excuse to be angry, another excuse to point a finger in my face. Not only did I have to deal with my own emotions of being lost without maps, but I had to deal with Muse's attitude whenever I found him again. Now I would get the silent treatment for a while—maybe days.

Today as I write, is the next day—Muse has been silent and withdrawn, giving me short, tart answers to anything I ask. I asked him today if he was still having fun on this trip. Staring straight ahead he said he was "enjoying his time." Sigh.

When we began hiking this morning, I let Muse lead off to alleviate his fear of my becoming lost again. But not a mile into our hike, I spied Muse step over a log and hike down an embankment in the wrong direction. The log had clearly been placed on the trail to guide hikers to the left where we were to ford a creek. I hiked quickly and caught up to Muse who was standing at the bottom of a hill.

"You're going the wrong way," I said.

"Are you sure?"

"Yeah, that log you stepped over—it was guiding us to the left, to the creek. The trail continues on the other side of the creek." We backtracked and found the trail, and nothing more was said of it.

I am not sure if it dawned on the deep-thinking Muse how easy it really is to walk in the wrong direction. I had walked down the wrong path yesterday and continued down the wrong path because Muse was so far behind me as to be out of sight. When Muse leads though, I hike close enough behind that I can see him from a distance which gives me the opportunity to stop him when he goes the wrong direction, which has happened several times. If I did not hike with him in my sight, I dare say he would have become lost more often than the two times I have become lost from him.

We camped early tonight because Muse has new shoes and new soles and is complaining of hot spots. We are sitting by our campfire along the shores of Richardson Lake in the El Dorado National Forest. We found an old beat-up grill in the dirt and have employed it to steady our cook pot over the campfire, thereby saving fuel. Muse is reading "The Heart of Darkness."

Richardson Lake is accessible and welcoming, surrounded by grasses, firs and pines. We both took a swim in the lake whose waters were a perfect temperature to cool the body, without being so cold as to require immediate abandonment with every orifice clinched. I swam to the center of the lake, lying on my back in the drowsy afternoon sun, imagining a slimy lake creature suddenly pulling me under.

Camping by Aloha Lake last night was typified by a consistent attack from mosquitoes. In the morning I woke up to find heavy dew had soaked all my gear, requiring me to hike today with various items tied to the outside of my pack to dry in the sun. Aloha Lake is a gorgeous lake though, with rocks, dead lodgepole pines, and small islands breaking the surface everywhere, even into the center of the lake; and the lake all around is surrounded by stark gray granite cliffs and the mountains of the Crystal Range. Aloha Lake took on the fantastical appearance of a haunted body of water—beautiful in its stark appearance.

In civilian life, Muse was most recently an actuary, pricing homeowner's insurance back in San Antonio, Texas. In college he was a math major, with a minor in music. Yesterday evening while we hiked, Muse choked on a mosquito that flew into his mouth. For the next hour at least, he was hacking and coughing as we walked along. I have never seen such drama. I would have laughed had it not been so annoying.

Muse is generally quiet all day. I rarely find him in a jovial mood anymore. He is either silent or brooding, or both. Most of his irritation comes from the pockets of mosquitoes we still encounter from time to time. In fact, the other day he stopped and said to me, "With these mosquitoes and the pain in my foot, I could seriously quit the trail." To be honest, I had to withhold some excitement at the prospect. I am probably another major source of his irritation, as he complains frequently of my not sharing equally in the logistical work of our hike. But I wake up in a good mood each day, complain not, and am happy to be hiking. I am doing my best.

I am laying by the fire in shorts, shirt, and bare feet—not having seen a mosquito in at least ten minutes now. Muse sits on the far side of the campfire, hidden in his rain jacket with the hood cinched over his head, long pants, socks, and his mosquito head net over his feet.

8:06 p.m.

On the trail I have two different levels of concentration. At the height of the day, I stare at the ground as I hike, watching my steps as the trees and rocks fly past. There is generally not a lot going through my head during this time. I am usually thinking about Meadow, or fantasizing about pulling Muse's elastic sunglasses to let them snap back against his face. But come early evening, my energy mysteriously peaks, and I become intently aware of my surroundings: every tree, every rock, every button-small wildflower catches my attention, and I find it all beautiful. This is the time when I douse my music and become acutely aware of every sound, reverting to some kind of hunting instinct at the time of day when animals start to haunt the forests. But the most enjoyable time of day is the moment when I climb into my sleeping bag next to the campfire, and stare up into the stars through the silhouettes of the swaying pines. The forests are quiet, save for a solitary owl, and the lapping of my campfires that I build every night now. Yes, this is my favorite time of day, especially if I happen to have a cigarette with me. To lie on my back and smoke a cigarette beside a small Indian campfire while staring up at the stars—with Muse off under the tarp tent for fear of rain and mosquitoes—THAT is my favorite moment of each day.

Friday, July 28, 2006
5:05 p.m.

Back To Work

I am in Citrus Heights, a suburb of Sacramento. My married friends, Dani and Sam picked us up from the trail on Thursday where we waited in the ski resort at Donner Pass. Our hike between Echo Lake and Donner Pass took us over the Tahoe Rim Trail where we had glimpses of Lake Tahoe throughout the day on Wednesday and Thursday. Dani and Sam have two rambunctious boys, both under two years old, whom Dani tirelessly restrained and regrouped at the dinner table in El Torito on our first night in town.

Dani is having a phone interview at the moment, interviewing for a teaching position. I went with Sam to work today where the masonry company he works for is revamping the brick-work on a house. We drove through the Arden Arcade portion of East Sacramento—right by the last branch office I had opened near El Camino and Howe before leaving my job. I told Sam I would like to drop by the office. I have recently been collecting feathers on the trail, which I have been duct taping to the long hair directly behind my ears; the feathers, minus thirty pounds—I look much different. I walked into the office where sat Susan Delacey, the lady I had hired about four months ago to run the operations of the office.

"May I help you?" she asked, not recognizing me.

I laughed, feeling a bit giddy. "I hired you!" I finally said, standing there in shorts, tank top, bandana, and feathers in my wild hair. What a glorious moment. Susan sent an email off to the corporate office that I had stopped in.

At the jobsite I helped Sam mix cement, then scoop it into a pastry squeeze bag and so on. Muse came along to the job site as well, applying sunscreen on his face as we left. While Sam and I worked with the bricks, Muse walked down to a store, returning with an Oreo ice cream cake, salad and salad dressing, which we all enjoyed. Thank you, Muse.

I stepped on the bathroom scale today, which totaled my skin and bones up to 140 pounds. If the scale is accurate, I have lost a bit over thirty pounds since I started hiking.

Monday, July 31, 2006

8:33 p.m.

Peter Grub Hut

Tomorrow is the Mew concert; my favorite band that almost never plays in the U.S. I am a little bitter about it. My friend John will be going without me. Muse is off clearing his throat in the background. He has been in a much more agreeable mood after we left Dani and Sam's. They are a wonderfully loving couple who radiate a lot of positive energy.

Dani dropped us back off at the trailhead at six p.m. three days ago. In testament to Dani's greatness, the following events happened on the day she found time to drop us off. Early that morning she helped a friend give a water birth. Then her cousin dropped by to visit and left a copy of a book she had just written and published. Then three sixteen-year-old neighbor girls stormed into their house having just returned from auditioning for a commercial. Then her parents and brother with Down's syndrome came over to drop off some items. Her husband Sam had gone fishing that day. I began to feel insignificant as I sat on the front porch drinking a beer. Muse was inside on the couch listening to the neighbor girl talk to Dani's cousin about bras. Time to start hiking again.

Our first night out from Donner Pass and Highway 80 we breached Castle Pass as the sun went down, then fumbled around in the dark, looking for the side trail to the Peter Grub hut. The Peter Grub hut is actually a log and stone cabin with working lights on the inside, and a picnic bench. A precipitous ladder takes one up to an attic of wooden rafters and floorboards, where several mattresses lay.

On a counter downstairs sat a Captain Morgan bottle with a candle in the spout. I lit the candle and proceeded up the ladder to bed down on one of the mattresses. "Do you think there's black widows?" asked Muse. I told him that I did not see any. I may have slept well that night if it were not for the mouse that repeatedly visited my bedside, chewing on something crinkly. In the morning, I saw that I had dropped my bag of chocolate just below my mattress.

Thursday, August 3, 2006
8:18 p.m.

Robert and Beans

Journaling is becoming more difficult as we hike longer into the evening, racking up between twenty-seven and thirty miles per day. We pushed hard to reach Sierra City, accomplishing a thirty-six mile day by nine p.m. Late in the day the trail descended upon Yuba Pass and highway 49. Our guidebook informed us that Sierra City was about a mile walk down the highway. In waning light we headed down the road, passing a dead deer on the shoulder as we reach the town limits. The occasional headlights illuminated my gaunt figure haunting down highway 49 lined with fragrant incense-cedars, tall sugar pines, and Douglas fir. The evening was warm and I walked shirtless down the highway, dizzy with hunger and excitement for a restaurant meal.

Quiet and tucked away in the crags of the Sierra Buttes, Sierra City was first established in 1850 as a gold mining town. The historic buildings of Sierra City glowed with nostalgic warmth, and wrapped around me on both sides as highway 49 blended into the main street. I felt like Ishi, the last member of the Yahi Indians, who mysteriously walked out of Lassen forest into a town one day in 1911, the last of his tribe, bridging the gap between the ancient life in the forest and the white man's new world of cities.

At the Mountain Creek Restaurant and Buckhorn Tavern, Muse and I found Groomsman sitting by himself in the loneliness of the empty wooden restaurant. I did not recognize him at first. We sat. "Groomsman!" I said. "Wow! I haven't seen you since you hiked off with Ray down by Silverwood Lake."

The manager of the restaurant assisted us by calling all the lodges in town to secure a room for the evening. Our arrival had coincided with a bicycle marathon, rendering most of the hotels without vacancy. However, there had been a no-show at a hotel half-mile down Highway 49. I spoke with the manager on the phone who explained that the available suite was normally $140 per night, but he would charge us $80 if that would help. Muse, Groomsman, and I split the room three ways and enjoyed a commodious rustic suite with a porch, kitchen, reclining chair, couch, and adjoining bedroom.

For lunch the next day, we went back to the Mountain Creek Restaurant. The outdoor seating in the garden had a natural stream that flowed down from the mountains right through the center of the patio. Along with the sweet smell of the surrounding cedars and black oak, the Mountain Creek Restaurant patio is absolutely the most beautiful setting in which I have dined. By this time, we were a table of nine hikers—GQ,

Switch, Cole, Ridge Walker, Ben, Elan, Heidi, Muse and me—enjoying malts, ice cream, pie, cheese steak sandwiches, and anything else laden with calories. The waitress brought out Muse's hot fudge Sunday and mistakenly handed it to Elan. "Alright!" Elan jokingly rejoiced. "A hot fudge Sunday!" Nonplussed, Muse found no humor in the situation and grabbed his ice cream from Elan with resolve. Elan can be a loud, bull-headed know-it-all, and I could see that Muse did not care for him.

Walking main street Sierra City, I was overcome with its old-world Western nostalgia. Across the street on a lamppost an official sign read *No Parking, Excect for Bob's Wife, city ordinance #...*. Nowhere was Sierra City spoiled by fast-food restaurants or miles of convection-oven parking lots, and even though all the hotels were booked, Sierra City was quiet and empty; no crowds, no lines to get into restaurants, no traffic. Stellar Blue Jays fussed at me from every branch. I gathered several blue feathers to stick into my hair: Ishi the Indian. I only wish we had more time to stay.

Joined by Paparazzi, Muse and I hitched a ride back up to the pass and the trail. Continuing north from Yuba Pass the trail immediately climbs two thousand feet, but having stocked up on calories in Sierra City, I breezed up the mountainside. I generally hike faster than Muse these days, and find myself taking long breaks until he catches up.

Two nights past, Muse and I pitched camp within view of a deserted highway. Not one car passed all night; only in the morning a couple logging trucks broke the silence. We had hiked twenty-nine miles that day, and my feet felt great as I walked around collecting branches for a campfire. I bedded down next to my campfire, relaxed by the hypnotic glow, and fell peacefully asleep. Around midnight, my sleep was interrupted by the sound of branches cracking out in the forest. I opened my eyes, staring out into the blackness. The cracking continued. I found my LED light next to me, which I directed, into the forest, but the animal was too far to be illuminated by a little squeeze light. Whatever was out there, it walked in a slow, full circle around our campsite, sizing us up; I followed the steps with my light as it walked just far enough away not to be seen; crunch, crack, snap. After circling us once, the crackling stopped, and I assume whatever it was, drifted back out into the darkness. Muse was still snoring as the forest fell silent once again, and I did not sleep well for the remainder of the night.

The next morning we rose early and came across Groomsman where he was camped just a mile beyond us. He told us he had seen a bear in the area tearing apart a stump to get at the termites; probably the object of my unseen visitor last night. But in the darkness of a midnight forest, hearing slow footsteps conjures up images of every legendary monster imaginable.

We continued on as Groomsman packed up. Not a mile past him as I walked along in the lead, a dark object climbed out of a tree ahead of me: a bear cub. Then a momma bear with two cubs in tow ran directly across the trail in front of me and down the slope on the other side. I called back to Muse, but by the time he caught up, they were well gone.

Groomsman and I hiked together for the rest of the day as we both hike quickly and generally enjoy each other's company. I suspect Groomsman had assumed I was some kind of liberal hippie when he first met me; resplendent with feathers in my hair. But after he told me he had been a medic in the army and had recently returned from Iraq, I broke into a soliloquy about the benefits of freeing Iraq, and the slanted reporting of the war by the media. He was all smiles after that.

We reached the Middle Fork of the Feather River around lunch and climbed down beneath the high footbridge where the water branched off around some smooth rock outcroppings forming slow pools with picturesque waterfalls and so on. I took advantage of a high rock to dive into the river where the water flowed into murky depths. GQ and Switch caught up with us a little later and joined the pool party.

That night Muse, Groomsman, and I camped on a sandy plateau off the trail with panoramic views of surrounding mountains. It was a beautiful evening as we all sat about a campfire laughing and farting and pondering the night sky.

Late in the day yesterday, the three of us were traveling the crest of a mountain top when we came across a truck affixed with a camper parked on a lonesome old logging road. We were in the ancient mountains of the Plumas National Forest. In every direction I looked were soft, rolling mountains, heavily forested and generally rising no more than seven thousand feet. No stark rock outcroppings or saw-toothed peaks broke the rolling ocean of forest. Robert Cooper and his dog Beans were enjoying the evening with some marijuana by his camper. He was high and happily called us over to outfit us with some fresh coffee he had brewed. Robert Cooper is a blowed-in-the-glass prospector, mining gold out of the rivers and streams of the Plumas and surrounding areas. He showed us his photo album; page after page of gold nugget photographs—nuggets he had prospected. He employs an interesting method of gold extraction wherein he digs a seven-foot hole right in the center of a streambed; then he attaches led weights to himself and free dives down into the hole to inspect the layers of bedrock underwater. He showed us an old cracked coin from the 1800's—it was worn, but I could make out the words San Francisco on it. Robert makes a living from prospecting. He furnished for us a glass vial of gold stones of significant size. Some of the small nuggets he fashions into earrings and such to sell down at the store by Bucks Lake.

Robert is pretty detached, and generally rambled on from subject to subject regardless of any questions we directed at him. Finally getting through to him, Muse asked him if he has seen Bigfoot to which he responded he has heard Bigfoot walk around his trailer at night.

"Old Beans here, she aint afraid a nothing'. She barks at bears and mountains lions—you name it, but I always know when there's a Bigfoot walking around outside at night cause she don't bark at Bigfoot. She stays real quiet." He went on. "You watch; you'll know when Bigfoot is in the area cause you'll see the tops of saplings broken right off. That's how they mark their territory; they break off the tops of small pine trees. Nothing else could do that! That's like twelve feet high!"

Tonight as we had dinner at the Caribou restaurant in the dank town of Belden, I saw gold earrings for sale beneath the glass of the counter. They were not Robert's wares, but the waitress knew of Robert well enough to roll her eyes and say, "Be careful around him. He's kind of crazy," She went on. "Robert was house-sitting for a family in town, and tried to run over a couple people with the family's tractor." Robert and Beans.

Friday, August 4, 2006

11:41 a.m.

The Braatens

The Braaten family host hikers in the near-bust town of Belden. On our last day out, Groomsman and I charged three thousand feet down the mountain into the valley where the lackluster town of Belden clings in decline along the Feather River. We walked across a pair of railroad tracks and found a skinny, bearded man living by the river in a grove of trees. He said he was about to drive into Belden and would give us a ride…on the hood of his truck; all the free space being occupied with the eccentricities of a man who lives in his truck by a river. Groomsman and I found a spot on the hood with reluctant stares at each other, and off we went down a winding road beneath a canopy of bay tree and live oak as the bearded man yelled questions to us from the window.

We found a couple chairs outside of the saloon and general store and sat. A half hour later Muse found his way into town and joined us while we waited for the Braatens to pick us up. Spying a ping-pong table in the saloon Muse was quick to challenge either one of us to a game; I accepted. Just as I had pictured in my head, Muse held the paddle in the downward position and served the ball like the professionals on the televised matches. I returned the ball and he attempted to slam it back but hit the net. This went on for some time—him trying to slam the ball, either hitting the net or missing the table altogether. It was not very fun. "Besides tennis, I consider ping pong my best sport," he said, slamming the ball into the net again. I suppose if he were properly warmed up and practiced he could be a formidable opponent, but Becka Braaten arrived just in time and we left the table, me having won most of the rallies.

Becka Braaten, the daughter in her late 20's, dropped us off at the Caribou restaurant situated next to a trailer park. GQ, Switch, Chai Guy, Groomsman, Muse and I dined together. Along with my beer, I had a salad, pork chops, mashed potatoes, and green beans. Still hungry, I ordered a basket of French fries and a Dr. Pepper, topping it all off with a Haagen Daz ice cream bar.

As I left the restaurant, I caught yet another Racer snake and brought it with me to the Braatens, a half mile down the highway. Becka's two-year-old daughter was overjoyed to see the snake, but it pooped on my arm so I released it into the bushes.

The Braatens have sectioned off a portion of their house just for PCT hikers: two bedrooms, bathroom, kitchen, common area, and a wooden deck, which is where I slept last night on an old chaise lounge.

Cucumber Boy is a flirtatious Russian girl who complimented me on the feathers in my hair. She offered to use colored thread to properly weave them into my hair instead of the duct tape I had employed. I sat on the floor eating peanut butter from a jar as Cucumber Boy sat behind me working the feathers into my hair, like an Indian Squaw preparing a warrior for battle—or so I would like to imagine.

Breakfast this morning was spectacular! Eight hikers sat at the Braatens dining table and were served by Mr. and Mrs. Braaten, and their hippie daughter Becka. They made scrambled eggs mixed with veggies, country potatoes, English muffin, and a huge bowl of fresh fruit. Amazingly, there was plenty of food for all eight hikers and the family. After breakfast I snacked on my jar of peanut butter for the rest of the morning, then walked to the Caribou restaurant at lunch and had the Diablo burger with onion rings and a chocolate malt. Finally, I am starting to feel full.

Later in the day, Ridge Walker, Cole, Ben, Heidi, and Elan hiked in to town. On the deck outside, Cole sprayed cheese whiz into Ben's mouth while Heidi unpacked her re-supply box. Most of her re-supply food was going to be contributed to the community hiker box as she had become tired of eating the same food over and over. There are hiker boxes at every major hiker stop along the PCT. The purpose of the hiker box is to discard food and supplies that you do not want or need, and hopefully find something that you do need. It is a community box, to give and take—but not to be abused.

Muse had been monitoring the status of Heidi's re-supply food from afar. "Are you going to put all of that in the hiker box?" he asked right when she finished. He was twitchy and excited.

"Yeah," she said. "You can have any of it." Muse grabbed the box and paraded excitedly from the porch into the house with a triumphant laugh as if he had earned a great reward, "Ah ha ha ha!" I found it selfish for Muse not to give anyone else an opportunity to look through her discards before he raided all the good snacks—not to mention his gloating laughter. But Elan stopped his parade through the house by taking hold of the box. "Is that Heidi's box? She didn't say you could have all of that."

"Yes she did!" Muse said assertively.

"No she didn't."

"Yes she did!!"

"No she didn't."

"Fine! Let me ask her then!" Muse stormed back out onto the porch. "Heidi! Didn't you just say I can have anything in here?!"

"Um, yeah."

"See!" Muse yelled at Elan, clutching the box like a pissed off kid guarding a handball on the playground. "You are really starting to get on my nerves!" he added.

I cannot be sure, but it looked like Elan laughed a little bit as he walked off to have dinner at the Caribou restaurant. Elan is the kind of person who likes to tease and get under people's skin. Muse is a perfect target; his emotions are always lurking just beneath the surface. I have never seen a twenty-seven-year-old behave quite like Muse.

Wednesday, August 9, 2006

8:52 a.m.

Drakesbad

I just woke up in a waterbed in a house in Redding. My buddy Bryce picked up Muse and me from Old Station yesterday.

Days ago at the Braatens, my friends Dani and Sam drove up to hike out of Belden with us. They brought their two-year-old Elias, and their one-year-old Everett in Kelty kid backpacks. At 6:30 p.m. they arrived to the Braatens in their van and off we drove to the PCT trailhead. The sunlight waned low as we started hiking and we accomplished three-fourths of a mile when we made camp due to the fading sunlight. We camped at a flat area by the footbridge spanning Indian creek, tumbling down from a canyon lined in fir, maple, oak and bay. Sam brought his fishing pole and threw a line in the water. He caught a fish that was about three inches long.

We began hiking the next morning at nine a.m. After a half mile, Dani and Sam were drenched with sweat and the kids were crying. Unfortunately, the trail was traversing an exposed burn area lined with poison oak on both sides. It was not a good situation, and they turned around to begin the journey home. They are a great couple.

The four hundred miles of Sierra Nevada Mountains are officially behind us now. Climbing out of Belden, we officially entered the southern tip of the Cascade Range, which will see us into Canada, still some 1600 trail miles ahead. We caught up with Chai Guy at the end of our first day out of Belden. He was reclined on the ground by a campfire and invited us to stay. The time was just before eight p.m. so we decided to hike further while we had some sunlight. But we only attained another quarter mile before coming to a grassy, tree-lined, mountaintop meadow where a fire ring invited me to stop for the evening. In no time I had settled myself beside a dancing fire with a bundle of wood piled next to me to keep the fire burning indefinitely. I stretched out and let my mind drift.

"Guy! What are you doing?!" Muse sat down across the fire and started freaking out.

"Huh?"

"There's grass growing over the fire!" A handful of green stalks leaned over the fire ring close to the flames. "What would you do if you started a forest fire!?" he asked me, hurriedly yanking the stalks from the ground.

"There's not going to be one," I said.

"No, seriously!" he continued. "What you do in a forest fire is to determine which way the wind is blowing; then run the opposite direction of the wind."

"There's no wind here."

"And there is supposed to be a five foot diameter of cleared area around a fire ring."

Another campfire spoiled. I tenderly picked a stalk of grass and held it over the flames. It would not catch fire. Muse watched.

"It doesn't burn does it?" he said.

"No. No, it doesn't."

The next day we hiked through more low forest, coming to a branch of the Feather River where the modern day Civilian Conservation Corps (CCC) was lacquering a footbridge. I washed off in the river and spoke with the supervisor for a while about the CCC, which I had assumed did not exist post World War II. They are a hardy group of kids from all over the U.S. who camp at night and work by day. As I walked over the footbridge, one kid stood up and yelled out "hiker!" Then the next stood and yelled "hiker!" until all the workers paused from their activity for a moment of salute as I passed. I felt honored.

Towards the latter part of the day, we emerged from a dusty forest of Jeffrey pines to highway 36, which led to the one-horse town of Chester. Muse asked me if I wanted to hitch in to Chester, to which I responded that I would rather skip it and hike on. Muse was dissatisfied with my answer, saying that he really wanted to shower and sleep in a hotel. As usual, I acquiesced to his wishes and stood on the shoulder of the quiet highway with my thumb in the air. We happened to converge on the highway at the same time as Floater, an older man who is hiking Southbound from Ashland. In civilian life, Floater is a pot-smoking, criminal defense attorney from Washington State.

After a half hour on the roadside, an SUV pulled over, driven by Haleh a half Iranian, half German girl. In the passenger seat was a hiker named Graham. We all had dinner together at a railroad-themed hamburger joint in Chester. The restaurant cooked the patty and provided me with a hamburger bun. Everything else, such as tomato, lettuce, pickles—I had to get from the condiment bar situated in the middle of the restaurant.

Haleh is working in Yosemite National Park this season on a team that studies squirrels in the Sierras. Evidently, there are many teams that perform different tasks in the Sierras each season. The members of her team are referred to as the "Squirrel Girls." Haleh met Graham as he was hiking through Yosemite on the PCT after which time they kept in contact. She had just driven up to Chester to meet up with Graham again, and after dinner, they disappeared into their hotel room with a bottle of wine.

The next morning we hitched back up the pass from a quiet woman who had been car camping in the area. We crossed into Lassen Volcanic National Park that day—thick with green forests and streams. Mount Lassen loomed snowcapped in the distance. Towards the end of the day we hiked a side trail down to Terminal Geyser, which was an eroded hillside of coral-like rocks between which emitted clouds of sulfurous, boiling steam and ebullient gray water.

Further along, the trail wound along the edge of Boiling Springs Lake, which is a shallow and steaming thermal pond of electric blue water lying on a white mineral lake bed. Bubbling mud pots and fumaroles line the edge of the lake giving it an otherworldly appearance.

Between Sierra City and Lassen Volcanic National Park we started to hear talk on the trail about Drakesbad. Our guidebook gave a brief description of Drakesbad as an exclusive resort nestled within Lassen National Park, which sometimes offers services to PCT hikers. The buzz on the trail was that Drakesbad is an awesome resort which welcomes PCT hikers, feeding us gourmet meals at a discounted hiker rate. Not far beyond Boiling Lake, the forest opened up to reveal an expansive mountain meadow in the middle of which sat the scattered cabins of Drakesbad, encircled by mountain flanks forested in white fir, sugar pine, incense-cedar and Jeffrey. In a green ocean rising into mountain peaks, Drakesbad is surrounded by edenic beauty—tenuously connected to the civilized world by a thin dirt road.

We walked up to the restaurant and office where a lady greeted us with a smile and a short speech, assuredly given to countless hikers before us. "You're PCT hikers? Feel free to use the showers down by the pool. After you shower off, you are free to use the pool [hot spring fed pool] until dinnertime. Come back to the restaurant at seven. We have a special meal for hikers." Muse and I looked at each other, overcome by the no-strings-attached generosity extended to us. The lady brought me a beer and frosted pilsner, telling me to pay for it later. The honor system was alive at Drakesbad. At the mineral pool sat a cooler full of sodas: take a soda and pay for it later. Drakesbad is unspoiled hospitality; no micro-management of guests; no fences or warning signs. Deer stepped through the meadow nearby. I walked around Drakesbad feeling like I owned shares in the business.

Muse, Chai Guy, and I lounged around the pool in the late afternoon sun. The day was warm and perfect and I glanced up and down the long meadow, as the pool was conveniently located in its center. People sat in chairs around the pool; children splashed in the water; they spoke French, and Spanish, and languages unrecognized.

At seven o'clock we converged with purpose at the shore of the restaurant patio, waiting to be seated; three starving hikers with backpacks at heel, watching the elegant patio gourmands sip wine from balloon glasses and slide fork tines across red lips. I felt again like some feral creature that had wandered out of the deeps woods to raid food from the resort dumpsters.

Just as we were seated, Graham and Haleh arrived, happily carrying a six-pack of beer to the table. "Hi guys!" exclaimed Haleh. "We have a six-pack to share with everyone!" The waiter de-capped our beers: Corona—one of my favorites. Muse, thwarted by Haleh's good looks and generosity even accepted a beer. I watched as he took his first drink, furrowing his brow as if he had just drunk sour milk. He left the rest.

For dinner we were first served perfect roasted tomato bisque, accompanied by bread and olive spread. The main course was vegetable lasagna, a chicken breast smothered in a lemon butter sauce, grilled asparagus, and wild rice. For drink I had a beer, Pepsi, and coffee. Despite my ravenous appetite, I could not quite finish all the food, eventually priced out at ten dollars per plate!

Drakesbad Ranch is over 110 years old, and generations of families have come back to the ranch for years to enjoy the solitude, beauty, and unparalleled hospitality. In a world of commercialized vacation spots, Drakesbad is truly a gem of California. I was almost a little leery at Drakesbad, watching my every step in paradise, making sure not to eat an apple from the tree of good and evil, making sure all tabs were paid so that I was not the one to ruin the feeling of all-access trust and exclusiveness.

Chai Guy, Muse, and I sat around an outdoor fire pit that night, in relaxed conversation. The fire was popping and dancing away, started by somebody, though no one but us hikers sat about. Later that night we hiked off up the ridge out of Drakesbad. Without a reservation, staying at a Drakesbad cabin was not a possibility for us, though hikers were welcome to sleep outdoors if they chose.

Sunday, August 13, 2006

1:03 p.m.

Shasta Mysteries

We have stopped by a creek to make lunch. When it is my turn to cook, I perform the task wholly without any assistance from Muse—drawing water from a stream, cooking the meal, and cleaning the pot—during which time Muse is free to sleep, wash in a creek, or do whatever. But today is Muse's turn to cook, and as always, he tries to delegate to me tasks that are his responsibility. "Do you think that if I get lunch started you can watch it and stir it every now and then so that I can go wash off?" I told him that *I* had planned to go wash off by the creek while he cooked. He looked disappointed.

We have had some stunning views today of Mount Shasta, standing a bit over fourteen thousand feet above sea level. The slightest bit of research on Shasta will reveal all kinds of strange beliefs about this lonesome volcanic mountain. There are those who claim the mountain is a major energy vortex on the earth's energy grid. Allegedly, there are many UFO sightings over the mountain; the UFO's are supposed to have a base in the center of the old volcano. People believe an ancient race of humans live in cities in the center of the mountain. Some believe them to be an ancient race of dwarfs; others believe them to be the giant, white-robe-wearing descendents of the lost continent of Lemuria, and still others believe them to be from the lost continent of Atlantis. And the Native Americans of the area believe the mountain to be inhabited by the spirit chief Skell. I was also told by some hikers that good old Bigfoot lives in caves at the base of Mount Shasta. It seems that nearly every crypto zoological and archaeological legend finds its home in Mount Shasta for some reason, probably placed there by the over-active and gullible minds of the many New Agers living in the area. If the aliens, Bigfoot, dwarfs, giants and a spirit chief all dwelt together in the confines of one mountain, I would imagine much pandemonium; Bigfoot constantly trampling the dwarfs and befouling the white robes of the Lemurians; aliens attempting anal probes on everybody, and the spirit chief Skell cursing them all for inhabiting his native mountain. It is amazing they have all dwelt together this long and yet maintain their secrecy.

Muse secretly got up early this morning and hiked off a half hour before I was ready to go. Knowing that I easily outpace him, he left first in an attempt to be the next person to see a bear. If he had simply asked me to let him lead for a while, I would happily have done so. But off he went, leaving me without any knowledge of upcoming water sources. Unfortunately for him, the large black bear I encountered this morning wandered into the area after Muse had already passed. I stood on the trail looking down a ridge into the forest where the bear swatted logs left and right, wandering its way towards the trail. I hiked off when it came close enough, frequently looking back over my shoulder.

When we hiked the final dusty miles into Old Station about four days ago, we sat at the local deli and snack shop by the Hat Creek Resort waiting for Bryce to drive up from Redding. A fourteen-year old boy sat down with us at the outside table along Highway 89. He was a bit chubby, with blond hair and glasses. The day was hot, yet he positioned his chair directly in the sun and explained to us how he had caught a couple rainbow trout in Hat Creek using a combination of power bait and salmon eggs. One by one, he commenced showing us all of his personal belongings. Then he repeatedly invaded the store, each time bringing out a different item, which he thought might be of some interest to us. He saw the burn scar on my leg, inquired about it, then left and came back with a burn and scrape ointment. I thanked him.

Bryce picked us up from the broken down deli and drove us down into Redding around five o'clock. Being an outdoor enthusiast, Bryce was intuitively hospitable—furnishing us with shower towels right away, and throwing our dirty clothes into the laundry. He dropped us off at the Hometown Buffet while he went for a run up in Whiskey Town. The Hometown Buffet in Redding is like the Hometown Buffets in every other city—full of white trash, grossly-overweight-marathon-buffet-eaters.

That night I slept in his waterbed.

Monday, August 14, 2006

3:30 p.m.

The Dunsmuir Checker

We just got a quick hitch to the post office in Castella with two guys. They were also nice enough to drive us into the old railroad town of Dunsmuir, which is up the road from Castella.

We have been hiking with Rig for the last couple of days, but lost him today as Muse hikes slow, and Rig generally keeps a good pace. The Calabama boys were sitting outside of a café when we walked down main street Dunsmuir.

In the local market I was buying food when I met Funnybone for the first time. We both laughed at all the junk food in our baskets. The checker at the counter was a tall blonde girl, smacking a piece of gum as I laid out my junk food on the counter. She glanced up at me.

"Are you, like, one of those people from Mexico?" she asked snootily.

"I'm *hiking* from Mexico, if that's what you mean."

She fell silent, processing the information while sliding my candy bars across the scanner. She looked up at me again. "So, do you, like, sleep on the ground every night?"

"Yeah, pretty much."

She turned her head, rolling her eyes slightly. It continues to be fascinating, the different reactions between men and women when faced with the prospect of camping and hiking for five months.

Groomsman has hiked the whole PCT so far without the aid of trekking poles, and as he has become a major influence in my life, I threw away my ski pole (which had replaced my broken trekking pole) in a trashcan as I walked down the street in Dunsmuir. My other trekking pole I collapsed in on itself and stuck in my pack. I quickly became so enamored with hands-free hiking that I did not use trekking poles for the remainder of the trip.

Muse and I seated ourselves in a pizza parlor and used the spacious tables to sort our re-supply box. Main Street Dunsmuir has the charming old buildings one likes to see in small American towns, but quite a few "for rent" signs hung in windows of empty storefronts. While waiting for our pizza I walked across the street to an old brownstone hotel to check on room rates. The ground level was sectioned off into shops, which stood silent and vacant now; an ornate fountain was dusty and dry in the center of the bazaar, and a solitary woman sat rotting on a couch in front of a large television set. A hand-written sign indicated the manager on the second floor. I walked up the wooden staircase to the office door, which was closed. I rang the buzzer twice—waited—but nobody came.

Barney and Sandy Mann are trail angels in San Diego—having given numerous rides from the airport to the trail head to hikers. This year they have been driving lengths of the PCT, keeping up with hikers along the way. As Muse and I stood on the main street of Dunsmuir, in want of lodging, Barney, topped off with a yarmulke, and Sandy pulled up to the curb to ask us if we knew the whereabouts of GQ and Switch, to which we responded that they must be but a day from Dunsmuir. They drove Muse and me down the road to a rustic hotel with individual cabins overlooking the Sacramento River where we stayed for the night. We made plans to meet for breakfast the next morning.

Though I had just eaten pizza, I was struck with hunger again, which moved me down the sidewalk to a small grocery store. I bought some potato salad, rotisserie chicken, a pint of Ben and Jerry's ice cream, and a forty-ounce Corona. After dinner I whiled away the evening with some old men watching a television set up on the spacious green lawn.

Wednesday, August 16, 2006

10:24 a.m.

Restless Leg Syndrome

We have had some good views of Shasta today, which has a skirt of low clouds at her base, but the peak is clear. After breakfast with Barney and Sandy in Dunsmuir yesterday we hiked up into Castle Crags National Monument. We were immediately hit with a five thousand foot climb, which consumed most of the hiking day. Having eaten a lot of good food in Dunsmuir, I felt strong and powered up the mountain without flagging. Muse is lying on his pad on the ground at the moment. He thinks he might have Giardia as he often feels like throwing up and claims to have the runs. This has been going on for about a week now.

I bought some New Balance 908's, size twelve, while in Redding. As we hiked out of Old Station on the dry Hat Creek Rim days ago now, they felt pretty good, and continue to feel good, though the backs of my feet bore small blisters from the stiffness of new shoes. Muse strongly suggested that I keep my old shoes with me and switch off until I break in the New Balances. It is not a bad idea, but I ended up throwing out the old shoes after carrying them just a few miles. Muse saw me dump them in a trashcan, but said nothing—biding his time until the moment when he could say, "I told you so." His moment has not really come, but he tried to slip it in anyhow when we reached Burney Falls. We had hiked twenty-eight miles with GQ and Switch, finally reaching the store at the Burney Falls campground. Muse had arrived there ahead of us; he saw the falls, bought food from the store, and announced not long after I had arrived that he was ready to hike further. "I could do another five to ten miles today," he said to me in one of his characteristic, yet unpredictable mood swings. "I think we should keep hiking!" Rig was at the campground and had invited us to stay with him and his family at their campsite for the night.

"I think we should stay here at Rig's campsite tonight," I said. "We've done twenty-eight miles today and my feet are a bit sore from the new shoes."

Without missing a beat, "Well, why don't you get out your old shoes then, if your feet are hurting!"

"You know I got rid of them," I said. "Besides, we stopped early for you and your new shoes at Richardson Lake."

"Yeah, well what about the first six hundred miles?" was his response. He chuckled successfully, glancing over at GQ and Switch for confirmation. They sat there quietly, not knowing what he was talking about.

We ended up camping with Rig at Burney Falls. Muse stayed up late, playing cards with Rig and Rig's relatives at the picnic bench, thoroughly enjoying himself.

Hiking with GQ and Switch into Burney Falls, I learned something interesting. "So, I hear you get lost all the time," GQ said to me as we walked along.

"Lost?" I said confused.

"Yeah, Muse was telling us at the Heitmann's how frustrated he is because you get lost all the time."

"Oh really," I said, realizing that Muse had been talking about me behind my back. "Well, I took a wrong trail in the Sierras, and I took a wrong trail out of Echo Lake. So, in over a thousand miles of hiking, I have been lost twice for a couple hours. Do you think that's bad?"

"Not really," said GQ. "We've been lost more than that."

11:56 a.m.

Muse is lying down again. His stomach must really be giving him trouble. The air is chilled today, and scattered clouds alternately hide the sun, and move away, floating like ghost whales over the slopes, ridges and alluvial fans of Mount Eddy, and White Ridge. I reckon we are not going to make good mileage today with all of Muse's breaks. At least I can catch up on journaling.

After a night with Bryce in Redding, he drove us back up to Old Station and dropped us off at the Heitman's hiker house for another night of rest. Georgi and Dennis Heitman have a beautiful rustic home at the end of a dirt road. A barn and a tree house adorn the yard, and a creek flows at the property's edge. Georgi scampered over to welcome Muse and me, thanking Bryce profusely for dropping us off. The Heitman's are an older couple enjoying their retired years up in Lassen forest. There were other hikers at the house such as Twisted Sister, Girl Scout, Groomsman, Chai Guy, GQ and Switch.

Assisted by Twisted Sister, Georgi cooked dinner for everyone. In all, I ate three sloppy joes, two ears of corn, two helpings of peas, salad, ice cream, and a brownie. When I told Georgi I had eaten three sloppy joes, she said excitedly "Good for you!" Georgi loved her hikers like they were her own grandchildren. In the morning she cooked biscuits and gravy; best I have ever had.

After breakfast Georgi saw me sitting at a table bouncing my leg nervously like I often do after meals. She sat down at the table and asked me if I had RLS.

"What's RLS?"

"Restless Leg Syndrome! It can turn into Parkinson's later in life if you don't treat it!"

I told her I did not think that I had RLS—just a nervous leg I inherited from my mother.

"I had RLS," she continued "and I have taken several different medications to treat it." She scrawled the names of three medications on a piece of paper for me—giving me the pharmacist's warning of side effects for each one. "This one worked well, but it can cause you to fall asleep at weird times; I woke up driving a car one time. It can also cause compulsive gambling."

To the best of my interpretation, these are the medications she recommended to me: Requys (glaxosmithkline), Carbidopa/Levo (mylan), and Miraplex, which can cause somnambulism and compulsive gambling.

As I sit and wait for Muse near Deadfall Lake, two of the Calabama boys have walked by, as well as three day-hikers—one of which asked me "Is there a lake this way?"

"Yeah, there's one up there," I said pointing, "and I think there might be another one over there." She laughed hysterically and walked off. I didn't see anything funny in what I had said.

Leaving the Heitman's we hiked along the Hat Creek Rim, an ancient lava flow stretching for miles. GQ and Switch were with us as we took a side trail to see the Subway Caves, which is a tunnel system of lava tubes large enough to walk through. Near one of the caves, a sign said that the Hat Creek Indians did not use or go near the caves because they believed an evil ape-man lived there.

Thursday, August 17, 2006

11:59 a.m.

Bigfoot

We hiked about twenty-five miles yesterday, which felt like eighteen miles due to all of our long breaks. We paused for lunch in the parking lot of the Shasta/Trinity trailhead at Scott Mountain Summit by Highway 3. I stirred the pasta as a brown van drove up and parked. The driver door creaked open spilling out an old man resplendent in camouflage shorts, no shirt, and a black round-rimmed hat beneath which straight, white hair retreated. He asked us if the trail heading south was steep terrain as he was looking for a nice place in the mountains to do his rituals, but could not walk far due to health concerns. I asked him about his wristband, which was made of several dozen teeth. He said they were Elk Teeth. The old man turned out to be part Pomo Indian. "The Pomo are a coastal tribe," he said. "The abalone is a sacred animal for the Pomo. The holes in the abalone shell align with the handle of the Big Dipper." I told him I used an abalone shell as a soap dish back home. "Well," he said, "the abalone is sacred to us, but I suppose it's okay since you're using it for cleansing."

I asked him what tribal land we were currently hiking through. "Kurok," he said. "And there are only ten full-blooded Kurok left. There is a Kurok elder who hosts a sweat lodge nearby, just down the road here, which anyone can attend."

"Do the Kurok believe in Bigfoot?" I asked. They did. The old man said that Bigfoot migrates down from Canada, crossing right through this area, and continues as far south as the mountains east of Oroville, which would be the Plumas National Forest. I told him that I was camped one night in the mountains east of Oroville wherein some creature I could not see walked in a circle around my campsite in the middle of the night.

"You could not see it because it was out of your paradigm," was his explanation. "People cannot see things because they do not believe in them." Makes sense. Before leaving, he gave me a small bundle of sage and what looked to be juniper—covered all about with lime green wolf lichen. The whole bundle was wrapped together by a thin vine like the stripe of a candy cane. I secured the bundle to my pack—a good luck charm. My luck came that very evening.

Muse and I hiked through the hemlocks and beautiful weeping spruce of the Klamath Mountains until late in the day; the sun dispersed behind the distant crags of the Trinity Alps leaving but ambient twilight. I was hiking a good five minutes ahead of Muse, hoping to find a place to camp, but the trail wound along a sloping ridge, in and out of breathless forests where the dark trees were silent, tall and brooding. Walking through one pocket of forest, I had the distinct feeling, which happened but twice on the trail, that I was being watched. I shrugged it off as my overactive imagination in a dark forest where my vision was drunken and hazy, like that of a dream.

At last the ridge gave way to a small meadow through which flowed the run-off of a trailside spring. Just inside the meadow's tree line were some flat cleared areas and an old fire ring. Perfect! The time was 8:40 p.m., nearly dark. Within minutes I resurrected a fire and laid out my bed next to its cocoon of warm flames and light. Muse arrived and laid out his sleeping area twenty feet away. I cooked a small meal, cinched up my sleeping bag and laid back. The night was moonless and frigid—Muse snored off in the distance.

Around eleven o'clock, a creature took up such a scream in the forest—a primal scream so wholly unfamiliar to my ears, that the hair was raised on the back of my neck. It emanated with the frequency of a dog's bark, but replace the barking sound with that of a banshee scream. The screams lasted several minutes, sounding a bit farther away with each broadcast, fading to the edge of imagination. I managed to fall asleep some time later, though unnerved.

Much deeper in the night frost, I awoke from the urge to urinate. From the cinched opening in my sleeping bag the night air froze my cheek, and I could see the funereal black of the forest. I did not want to leave the comfort of my sleeping bag, but if I did not relieve myself, I would not fall back asleep. I sat up, pushing my bag down to free my shoulders and arms. But when I did this, I startled some *thing* standing just at the tree line in the meadow about twenty feet away. The creature went stomping away across the meadow—two heavy, thudding, footsteps, sounding like an old lady beating the dust from a rug with a broomstick; thump, thump, thump. After about eight stomps the creature paused, as if looking back at me, then resumed stomping across the meadow until the night fell silent again. I was absolutely frozen in place, while my hand took up a failed search for my LED light. The darkness of the forest closed in around me like an unseen hand—exposing my vulnerability.

During the whole experience, I thought of only one thing: Bigfoot. It seems to me that the stomping I heard was exaggerated—perhaps deliberate, as if whatever I startled was trying to sound loud, trying to sound heavy; a defense mechanism maybe. I cannot now imagine what species of *known* animal in the Pacific Northwest could make such a sound. The only other possibility I could think is that the sound was a startled deer, bouncing across the meadow on all four feet. But the thudding steps—they sounded so solid, so distinctly like two feet—not four hooves bouncing across the meadow. Ah, mystery—what is life if we do not leave room to entertain the fantastic angles!

Saturday, August 19, 2006
11:45 a.m.

Blackberry Blonde

The night after what I call my Bigfoot experience, Muse and I slept directly on the trail for want of finding a proper flat area by sundown. We had joined three of the Calabama boys stranded on the same ridge: Nate, Raw Dawg, and That Guy. I sat listening to these guys who were in good spirits, teasing and poking fun at each other until they were all laughing—the way in which guys bond; the way in which Drew and I, and the rest of my friends constantly rip on each other in good humor. Then I thought of Muse, and how early on in our journey he said, "I don't like to be teased. I don't want you to make fun of me like you and Drew do with each other." I honored his request, and have not teased him—not even in good humor in the presence of others, or any time whatever. I just stopped, though he is never reluctant to take shots at me when he is in a playful mood amongst others.

The next day, yesterday, we hiked into the Russian Wilderness portion of the Klamath National Forest, coming to Highway 3 by noon. The town of Etna, our next re-supply point, was a good twenty-mile hitch down the pass. Glancing up and down the highway, not a car was in sight. Muse and I stood there as the minutes passed in the blinding sun.

Hours earlier I had stopped and spoken with an older couple who were out for a short hike on an intersecting trail. They promised to drive us into town if they saw us hitching at the pass. Twenty minutes later the same couple made good on their promise.

Muse and I coasted down the mountain road in the bed of their pickup truck accompanied by a black and white dog. The air was perfectly warm as the road leveled off into the grassy flatlands; farmhouses and decrepit old barns passed by in the fields. The road was lined with grand oaks, their crooked branches swatting at the sun as we passed. Once again the world was surreal—as if I had passed through a time-portal somewhere in the mountains, and emerged into the America of black and white photographs.

We waved bye to the dog and the amiable couple who rolled on down the road in no hurry beneath the oak shadows, leaving us standing in front of Alderbrook Bed and Breakfast. The two-story farmhouse, now a bed and breakfast, was beautifully restored with all the whitewashed gingerbread of a dollhouse, a wrap-around porch with outdoor ceiling fans. After ringing the doorbell to no avail I found Vickie in the backyard on a riding mower, grooming a minty summer lawn with a pond at its far end. She glanced up and saw me standing on the porch. Instantly, she threw the machine in park, calling to her husband that they had a couple of hikers!

Vickie's husband Dave told us that their house had been built in 1877, and the old barn on the property they had recently converted into the "Hiker Hut." Swinging the Dutch barn door wide Muse and I were surprised to find the barn carpeted, two bunk beds, a fold out couch, bathroom with shower, refrigerator, sink, microwave, and computer with Internet access. This was the most hospitable barn I had set foot in. The price, we were told, would be twenty dollars per night.

After showering, Muse and I grabbed two bikes leaning against the fence and rolled down tree-lined Highway 3 which melted into Main Street Etna, California. Main Street is lined with large historic homes floating on seas of green lawns; no fences, no gated communities—just trust separating neighbor from neighbor. Like Sierra City, Etna is an anachronism of a town—no fast food chains, no modern buildings—just a small town where changes have come slow since 1950.

At the far end of town is the Etna microbrewery. I entered and found Rig journaling at the bar with a pint before him. I sat and we both ordered the sampler, which included eight glasses of locally brewed beer. I was won over by the blackberry blonde: light, with a hint of blackberry—a perfect beer to end another week on the trail. After beer, I stopped at the ice cream parlor for a sundae. At the marble counter sat a Grandfather, a Father, and a young boy—all smiles and ice cream, moving in slow animation as if time itself has slowed in Etna. I shook my head, feeling like Marty Mcfly in *Back to the Future* when he walked into the diner in Hill Valley of 1955. A Norman Rockwell girl busied herself behind the counter. She explained to me that ranching was the business of Etna. I believed it. I stood outside of the Trailhead Restaurant around dinnertime and watched a cowboy on his Indian pony trot down Main Street. I shook my head again.

The one saloon in town was alive that night with local cowboys in Wranglers and Stetsons—hard men and fat women, and the overflow of a nearby wedding reception. Rig was in the bar along with all the Calabama Boys: Nate and Teflon from Alabama; Gouda, Raw Dawg and That Guy from California. I ordered a Heineken and played a couple games of pool with Muse to feed his competitive thirst. He is fun to watch—using his stick to measure angles, sizing up the table at eye level. I drank my beer and did my best not to draw attention to myself—aware that feathers still dangled from my hair. Muse disappeared to the store between games, returning to the bar eating an ice cream drumstick, and pouring handfuls of Nerds candy into his mouth. He offered some Nerds to That Guy who yelled out in his drunken state, "You're a nerd!" Muse left soon after.

I took up a game of pool with a local cowboy who was delighted to hear of my hiking adventure across California, but he still wiped the table clean. I abandoned the bar around midnight, a heated competition of darts still in play between some Calabamas and some locals, and walked down the silent main street of Etna. Away from the bar, not a soul was downtown. The world felt like it all belonged to me—all the storefronts shut tight and dark. A possum lay freshly dead in the middle of the road. Crickets buzzed, electrifying the air.

Back at the hiker hut Teflon, Gouda, Old Dirty and Stomper were watching South Park. Muse was in bed attempting to sleep, as popcorn popped in the microwave next to his head.

This morning I rose early, exiting the Dutch door of the barn into the quiet, cold air—the dewy green grass. I commandeered a bike and allowed the slight downhill grade to glide me through old town Etna—passing the old soda fountain, the old garage, the Trailhead restaurant, the Mason Lodge; my skin bristled against the cold.

Old Dirty sat by himself at the breakfast bar in Bob's restaurant, reading the morning newspaper. The patrons of Bob's watched me closely as I entered, and took up a stool next to Old Dirty. He provided me with a portion of the morning newspaper. A local woman had written an article describing the grandeur of the county fair, which I supposed was coming soon. Her favorite attraction was the smorgasbord of local foods to sample. Already wheelchair ridden from being overweight—she went on to contrast her pleasure with the fair with her displeasure at getting her wheelchair irredeemably wedged in a turn-style on the way in.

I am presently and pleasantly journaling from the bar in the microbrewery, indulging in a deli sandwich and another blackberry blonde. Today is another molasses day in Etna. The sky is tinted with a haze of tan from the smoke of the Marble Mountains forest fire—the next leg of our hike. For a while, the trail through the Marbles had been closed, but we have recently learned of its reopening, which is good news.

The guy we had Indian food with in Lake Tahoe has just arrived. We originally knew him by his slave name of Matthew, but somewhere along the way, he has been dubbed Goodness. His girlfriend he had been hiking with has abandoned the trail due to a broken ankle.

Monday, August 21, 2006

10:30 a.m.

My Name is Joel

Yesterday, Dave from Alderbrook Bed and Breakfast drove Muse, Goodness, and me back up the pass to the trailhead, with a wish of good luck. Muse and I hiked faster than Goodness and have not seen him since.

Last night in Etna, Gouda, Goodness, Old Dirty, and I went to the microbrewery for beer samplers and dinner. Muse joined up with us after a while, ordering a sprite or something. During and after dinner, Gouda, Muse, Old Dirty, and Funny Bone, who was laid out with Giardia, engaged in a deep discussion on politics, religion, and the forces that drive Human Nature. The deep-thinking Muse was now in his element—proffering his opinion and introducing new group questions to direct the discussion. Meanwhile, I borrowed Old Dirty's cell phone to touch base with those back home. I overheard Muse in the background, speaking excitedly; "So, what do you guys think about time travel?"

As I sat in the barn, making a peanut butter and jelly bagel, John returned my call on Old Dirty's phone. "Is Joel there?" he asked.

"Joel?" said Old Dirty. He looked at all of us. "Is there a 'Joel' here?"

I raised my hand.

"Your name is Joel!" everyone said at once. I blushed. "You don't look like a Joel!" The room erupted in laughter. I told John I would call him back as I could not hear a word.

We all retired to bed around midnight, taking turns farting and laughing ourselves sick.

The next morning, I exited the Hiker Hut into the chilled air and found the dirt road beside the barn lined with wild blackberry bushes. I filled a cup full—my fingertips stained deep purple, and covered a heaping bowl of cereal with wild blackberries. My heart sang. Life was vibrant! And the Oregon border was just one-hundred trail miles further.

We hiked into the Marble Mountains yesterday at eleven a.m. amidst a hazy brown sky. I am impressed with the character of the trees in the Marble Mountains. The red firs, hemlocks, and white pine seem larger, more exaggerated in their dripping and lacy appearances—almost dreamy like a fairy-tale forest. That night we paused by the creek at Shelly Meadows and camped out in the grass by Wilson Cabin. The deer in Shelly Meadows seemed to take exception to our intrusion. From where I lay in the grass near dark, a deer boldly approached to inspect my doings. When I aimed my flashlight towards the deer, it snorted and pranced around agitated, appearing as though it wanted to charge me.

Muse is collapsed on his pad at the moment, taking a prolonged 10:40 a.m. break. I am not sure why. Yesterday we hiked for two hour segments before taking any breaks, and he led the way all day. My shin splint is diminishing, yet is still a pain, causing me to walk slower and more carefully.

Muse's pack, with food and water, weighs no more than twelve pounds at the moment. He decided in Etna that he did not want to cook food for the couple days we have into Seiad Valley. I did want to cook; thus, I am carrying the pot, stove, and fuel—and several dinners. Muse is much lighter than me, but we wind up camping at the same spot each night, and I do not see him hiking any faster than me even when I do slow down. At the end of the day, I make couscous and spinach noodles with miso soup flavoring, while he eats whatever dry food he has brought. To each his own.

Thursday, August 24, 2006
12:47 p.m.

Guidebook of My Own

We are very near Ashland, Oregon having crossed the Oregon border yesterday where, perched on a hillside was a PCT register box. Inside the metal box is a register pad, a small bottle of vodka, some cognac, a marijuana pipe with some dusted weed in it, and a lighter; best register yet.

Muse and I are sitting in Callahan's restaurant, which is a short walk off of the PCT, down some dirt roads, over a set of railroad track, and under the eternal Five Freeway. It struck me how quickly things can change out here on the PCT; one minute I am hiking a dirty, dusty trail in the forest, the next I am sitting in a nice restaurant with a Heineken; not to mention the mysterious fact that one week later, the restaurant in which I now sit, burned to the ground.

The day before we reached Seiad Valley, we had hiked about twenty-seven miles into the Klamath River environs. The PCT at this point joins up with a dirt road lined with blackberry bushes, winding by backcountry homes and shacks in the Douglas pines sheltering angry dogs, barking as we passed. We camped on a ledge of pine trees beside the road just a couple miles out from Seiad Valley. Early the next morning we traversed the bridge over the Klamath River entering Seiad Valley by eight a.m. The Calabama Boys, Rig, and Crib were all crashed out at a campsite at the Mid River RV Park. John and Ivajoe were at the phone outside of the post office/general store/restaurant when we arrived.

Muse and I had breakfast with Rig and Stomper, during which time Muse exploded in frustration at me while trying to divvy up some maps between us. I had been confused with what he was doing and asked him why I needed this map and that map when he practically yelled at me at the table. Rig raised his eyebrows in surprise, glancing over at me. But it was not the proper venue for me to engage in an argument. I hope Muse never becomes a schoolteacher. He is a very impatient and explosive person.

After breakfast we sat against the wall of the store and sorted our re-supply box, then hit the road again by ten o'clock. The trail continues north from highway 96 via the Devil's Peak Lookout Trail, introducing us immediately to a four thousand foot climb out of the valley. About half way up the ridge was Lookout Spring. Back in Chester, Floater had told us that Lookout Spring is guarded by a rattlesnake. I had forgotten about his warning, but was soon reminded when drawing water from the spring; a Mojave rattler recoiled beneath a nearby fern. We all marveled at it for a while—Muse, Crib, Goodness and I. I grabbed the snake's rattle in an attempt to remove it as a souvenir. I determined the snake to be rather docile from repeated visits from humans to the spring, and I had heard that the rattles are removable. I failed in removing the rattle, but succeeded in causing Muse no end of stress and vociferous reminders of my foolhardiness.

We have a duplicate guidebook for this section between Seiad Valley and Ashland, which means I actually get to carry my very own guidebook the first time in all of California. This duplicate guidebook was part of my confusion at breakfast in Seiad Valley where the deep-thinking Muse lost his patience with me; truly a moment you had to see to enjoy. I had begun to think, as I walked the length of California, that the burden of carrying the guidebook was fully under-appreciated by me. Muse often carries the guidebook in the small mesh pocket of his pack, and each time he is wont to find the next water, or if I prevail upon him with an inconvenient question, he must stop, take his pack off, and open the guidebook for study.

I rolled up my cherished guidebook and stuffed it deep in my pocket, and when a question of water or terrain came about, I opened the guidebook and read while I walked along. The guidebook has lucid maps of the area, and explicit text of the surrounding terrain—pointing out nearby landmarks, identifying the various species of trees and plants, and so on. No longer do I hike in "the dark," and the burden of my questioning Muse has found relieved.

Our first night out from Seiad Valley, I can write with certainty that we camped on the saddle near Lowden Cabin's site, by Beardog Spring. The next morning of the next day, we met a southbound hiker called Notorious B.O.B. I did not ask her ethnicity, but she looked to be an African American woman—solo-hiking south from Canada, no less. I hiked ahead of Muse all day, as is usual, following my map to water sources, and at day's end, pushed us through the darkness to reach Long John Saddle, thereby totaling our day's hike at a solid thirty miles.

Today, we have crossed Interstate Five, where my section of guidebook ended, plunging me back into hiking ignorance.

Saturday, August 26, 2006

9:09 a.m.

Mayor of Ashland

It is a beautiful morning in Ashland, Oregon. I feel my head hurt a bit after drinking five beers yesterday, and am presently treating my headache with some Guatemalan coffee at Evo's Coffee Lounge, just down the street from my buddy Jeremy's apartment.

Jeremy had seen my Pacific Crest Trail schedule posted on myspace.com and told me to call him when I came near Ashland. I knew him in college, but have not seen him in years.

Muse and I hiked the final twenty-two miles of Douglas and White Fir forest between Callahan's and Hyatt Lake Resort where Jeremy was supposed to pick us up at noon. Ten miles into our hike out of Callahan's we came to Fenced-in-Spring where there is a pump faucet surrounded by a fence to protect it from cows. While at the spring, three other hikers caught up with us: On-On, Dave, and Amyloid. I did not think I had met On-On yet, but he tried to convince me that we had met the morning I came down from Whitney, which is possible since I was so battered and mentally retracted that morning. Dave was surprised to see Muse and me still together as he had mysteriously been present on both occasions when I had become separated from Muse; first at Olancha Pass, and second coming out of Aloha Lake. Amyloid, the round, curly-haired guy, we had last seen sitting at the Echo Lake resort, despondent from having lost his hiking partners.

We reached Hyatt Lake two hours early and called Jeremy. He stepped out of a Land Rover, still thin and stylish. We hugged and slapped each other on the back.

As we drifted back down the highway to Ashland, I noticed a hand gun between the seat and center console of Jeremy's car. "So, where do you work that requires you to work in the evenings?" I asked him. He explained to me that he was vice president of a private, nonprofit poker club in Ashland where he deals cards from 6:30 to midnight, or after. He keeps the Glock in his car for protection, as he often carries large sums of money around. His friends call him the Mayor of Ashland. When he walks down the street, there are usually a dozen people greeting him along the way. Jeremy is my age, and bears a slight resemblance to actor Edward Norton.

Entering Ashland, we stopped at a drug store to buy some supplies. As thanks for picking us up, I bought a twelve pack of Jeremy's favorite beer—Pabst Blue Ribbon. We ran into Goodness at a drug store and we all drove to the post office together to pick up our re-supply boxes. Jeremy had a lot of questions about our trip, as he is seriously considering the PCT some day soon.

At 6:30 last night we went with Jeremy to his underground poker club, entering the building from a back alley in downtown Ashland. Muse and I played a couple games of pool, and Jeremy put a beer on his tab for me. Muse did not have a drink from the bar, but had brought along some cheese, super juice, and more Nerds candy from Rite Aide.

Patrons trickled in to the club. Everyone knew everyone, and the men talked personal life and business with each other while sitting around on couches with their laptops before the card games started. Muse and I were introduced to each person as Jeremy's friends who are hiking the PCT. As I have said before, this will always spark the fascination of men. "Ah man, I wish I could do something like that!" they all say.

We ran into Stomper on the street who said the Calabamas and Rig were down at the brewery, which is indeed where Muse and I found them, hanging about a side street laughing and drinking liquor from brown bags like a gang of winos.

Rig abandoned the Calabamas and went with us to the poker club for some beers. We sat around on the couches and talked for a while. I liked Rig. I never knew him to complain about anything, nor was he ever in a bad mood. Rig is a man's man. I invited him to crash in Jeremy's apartment for the night, which he thankfully accepted.

Monday, August 28, 2006

6:36 pm

Push-up Marathon

We have hiked into the Sky Lakes Wilderness. The trail today has been composed of a fine dirt powder, which blackens legs and socks; it combines with the sweat in my shoes and makes little berms of mud. The weather is hot.

Muse just got out of the lake where we paused to wash off the day's grime. It is a beautiful lake—somewhat shallow, but ringed with pines; shoals of water grasses blow and bend in the afternoon wind. Too bad the scenery is somewhat ruined by Muse walking around in his briefs, which he pulls nearly up to his chest. Whenever we are in a hotel room Muse strips to nothing but his briefs—walking quickly about the room, clearing his throat, and doing power squats as he mechanically sorts and moves his equipment around. Muse has strong quadriceps and calves, but his upper body is featureless. And though he too has lost some weight—ten pounds, if I am not mistaken—his stomach remains mushy like a pot of mashed potatoes.

I was shocked earlier today when we paused by a creek to make lunch. Muse laid out his sleeping pad and proceeded to do push-ups. If I counted correctly, he was successful in completing five. Later on down the trail today, I walked up on him as he was doing pull-ups on a log that had fallen horizontally. He smiled at me as I passed, knowing that this would be a strange sight for me to behold. I gave him a quizzical look and continued on. My prediction is that this whole workout routine will fizzle out in a couple days when we encounter some mosquitoes or some kind of inconvenience that puts him in a foul mood. But if he does happen to stick with it, I am sure that I will hear more competitive comments like, "I can beat you up," or "I'm stronger than you now."

Tuesday, August 29, 2006

8:00 p.m.

Pyro

Wow, I am actually journaling two days in a row; just like the old days. We have about 850 miles left to Canada. How about that! Our last day in Ashland, Jeremy and I walked to his favorite bar in downtown where we waited for Rig, who Jeremy volunteered to ferry back to the trail that afternoon. The bar was his favorite because of the Pabst Blue Ribbon on tap, and a jukebox full of Tom Waits songs. Rig pulled up to the bar, joined us for a pint, and wrote some postcards.

Our first night back out on the trail from Ashland, Jeremy intercepted us by driving ahead to Dead Indian Road and walking south to meet us. I came upon Jeremy around five o'clock where we sat down to smoke and wait for Muse, whom I had last seen napping beside the trail miles back. It was another beautiful day. The trail stayed level and continued through a forest of Douglas and noble firs carpeted in green ferns; Spanish moss hung from everything like melted Christmas ornaments. Muse caught up about fifteen minutes later and sat down on a rock to eat. As soon as he arrived though, yellow jackets from a gray hive in a nearby tree began swarming our rest area forcing us to move on.

We continued north past Dead Indian Road to the Brown Shelter, which is a small log cabin with plastic strips hanging in the doorway to prevent insects from flying in. Inside the cabin is a wood burning stove, and a picnic bench. Outside of the cabin is another picnic bench, as well as a metal fire pit, and a nearby hand pump coaxing up cold, clean water from the earth.

Two bow hunters were in the cabin when we arrived, along with an old Tombstone looking guy who went by the name, Smoke. The bow hunters left before dark, but Smoke whiled away the night with us, talking about his travels here and there while puffing on a corncob pipe through his tall mustache. I built a huge campfire for the four of us—a campfire to be proud of. Smoke suggested that I call myself Pyro; not a bad name!

Muse and I are currently hiking through the Sky Lakes Wilderness portion of Oregon. In this section the PCT winds through beautiful forests dotted with lakes and ponds—refilled with water from the winter snowmelt. Every five to ten minutes on the trail, the forest opens up to a secret lake or a secret pond of the clearest emerald waters, shimmering in the afternoon sun. Fallen logs lay cross-hatched in the lakebeds below.

In the Sky Lakes Wilderness some alternate trails are available that would take us by many more lakes than if we stuck to the PCT. On the map the alternate route looked much more picturesque to me, and I suggested to Muse that we take it.

"I don't know if I want to do that!" Muse exclaimed, hidden beneath his rain jacket—hood cinched over his head, and long pants. "I got ten mosquito bites today! More water means more mosquitoes!"

I had hiked all day in shorts and no shirt. It became clear to me, especially as I have grown more intuitively acute with nature's consciousness, that Muse lives against his environment, which is why mosquitoes attack him, yellow jackets swarm in his presence, and campfires spit embers all over his clothes.

Another example of my heightened intuition happened this very evening just before we camped for the night. The forests and undergrowth here in the Sky Lakes can be thick in places. Around six o'clock this afternoon, I suddenly had the distinct sensation that I was being watched, and I felt quite firmly that something was watching me from the thickness of the forest to the east. As the sunlight grew lower, I stopped and waited for Muse to catch up so we could decide on somewhere to camp for the night. When Muse arrived, and before I had said a word to him, he exclaimed, "I had the weirdest feeling that I was being watched back there."

Thursday, August 31, 2006

10:33 a.m.

Crater Lake

The day Muse and I walked out of Callahan's Restaurant in Southern Oregon, a very strange thing happened. Twice while I hiked that afternoon, I had the distinct sensation that I was shrinking. I saw the earth come closer to me as I walked, and remember thinking to myself in an unexplained a state of mental euphoria, "Huh, so this is what it's like to be short."

The next morning, Muse approached and said to me, "I had something very strange happen to me yesterday. After we left Callahan's I felt like I was drugged—like I was losing my mind. Twice while hiking I felt like I was floating in the air.

We told our stories to Chai Guy as we all stood around outside of Jeremy's poker club in Ashland, and Chai Guy had a story of his own. "Hmm, that's weird because just *before* Callahan's I kept hearing voices ahead of me on the trail, but no matter how hard I tried to run and catch up, there was never anyone there. Later, I was looking down from a ridge saw a bunch of people marching on a dirt road, but I don't think they were really there—like, who would be marching out in the middle of nowhere?"

It bears noting that the Oregon Vortex, a tourist site of geomagnetic anomalies where tall people appear to shrink, and short people appear to grow, is fifty or sixty miles west of where my experience took place. I had visited the Oregon Vortex while on a road trip to Portland some years back. Our tour guide warned us that it is not unusual to experience euphoria in certain places. Ashland itself has always been a focal point of spiritualism and New Age, crystal-wearing hippie types who believe the area is a huge vortex of some kind.

7:31 p.m.

The feeling of "endness" is upon me. We still have around eight hundred miles left to Canada, but an excitement grows in me—an excitement of finality.

Muse and I camped early tonight because he was tired. He has been taking naps all day and continues to walk well under my pace—requiring me to take longer breaks to let him catch up. Left alone, I could be days ahead of him. Yes, Muse waited for me and my foot problems for the first six hundred miles, but I feel that I have out-paced him now for the last thousand miles, making us more than even—but still I say nothing, and I do not complain to him.

We walked into the forest of Crater Lake National Park two days ago, and camped three miles out from the Mazama campground in a whispering forest of mountain hemlock, then walked in early yesterday morning for the all-you-can-eat breakfast buffet. We were the only hikers there at 7:30 a.m., but the joint was filled with firefighters on their way out to regulate the controlled burns west of the Crater Lake rim. Our waitress, a speed-thin, crazy blonde with carnival eyes was downright excited to have two more hikers in her restaurant, and asked us all about our journey. She told us that Odessa, another hiker, had arrived at Crater Lake three weeks ago and passed-out due to sheer exhaustion. Apparently, Odessa never takes zero days and pulls huge mileage. "She's got bigger balls than you guys!" said our waitress with a smoky laugh. I asked her if she knew what the cat-like, ferret-like creature is that I had recently seen in the Crater Lake wilderness. She said they were Pine Martens. Of course, Martens. Anyhow, kudos to the nice waitress at the Mazama buffet for charging us five bucks a head for the breakfast buffet.

Instead of following the highway back to the trail, Muse schemed a quicker route using some defunct dirt roads and a trail that was listed in our guidebook. After a mile of hiking however, we came to an unexpected trail not on the map, rendering us unsure of our exact position any longer.

"I don't know…I just don't know where we are." Muse looked up and down the trail, then back at the map. "Which way do you think we should go?" he asked me.

"That direction." I pointed up the trail

"Really? That is the one direction *I* would think we should *not* go."

"Oh really?" I shrugged. "Well, whatever."

We ended up walking in the direction I suggested, and in less than a mile we intercepted the PCT once again.

The official route of the Pacific Crest Trail was closed in the section immediately west of Crater Lake, due to the controlled burns. As an alternative, we walked along Crater Lake's rim trail, which is an alternate trail that most PCT hikers take anyhow for its scenic overlooks of Crater Lake. I must admit, with the fear of sounding soft, that I did shed a tear when I attained the rim and first gazed across Crater Lake's awesome expanse of blue water, held in place by the crusty caldera walls that were once Mount Mazama, before it blew its top off thousands of years ago, creating the massive caldera. The once burning boil on the earth's surface is now covered with a blue liquid salve—a healing ointment of calm waters. The lake is 1, 943 feet deep—the deepest lake in America, and seventh in the world. As we walked the rim trail, I gazed over the placid waters looking for the "Old Man" of Crater Lake—a mountain hemlock log that has been floating upright in the water for over a hundred years, blown here and there by the winds over the waters.

On our way around the west rim, we took a side trail up to the highest peak over Crater Lake. The views were magnificent, but I still could not find the Old Man floating around the lake. A married couple asked Muse if he could take their picture with the lake behind them. The couple lined up for the photo. "Okay," said Muse, raising the camera to his face, "Do you want a portrait or landscape?"

"Whatever looks good," they said.

Muse was down on one knee now, lining up the photo to award-winning perfection. "Okay, do you want all of your body in the picture, or cut off at the waist?"

"Um, whatever," they said.

"Do you want to be centered or off to the side?"

"Just—whatever looks good."

Muse pressed the button; the picture was taken. Muse handed the camera safely back to the lady. When she turned, the camera was torn from her hand by the safety strap still around Muse's wrist; the camera fell onto the rocks and bounced a couple times before coming to a rest. "That's okay," she said politely.

Friday, September 2, 2006

Thirty-Eight Miler

We hiked into Shelter Cove Resort yesterday—a long day, just shy of forty miles. As I previously mentioned, two days ago Muse was hiking incredibly slow, laying down on his ground pad every half hour; finally we stopped to camp early due to his fatigue. When we woke up yesterday however, Muse performed his morning calculations, then declared, "We have about forty miles left to Shelter Cove; I think we should do it."

"A forty-mile day?" I said incredulous. We had not yet hiked forty miles in a day. "It's already 7:30. I don't think we can make forty miles."

"I think we can do it, if we hike fast all day, take no breaks and no lunch—we can do it."

"What is this?" I said, shaking my head. "Yesterday you're sleeping all day, and today you want to hike forty miles? There's no balance with you."

"Yup. Don't you love it," was his response. I did not love it. Muse's mood swings are a terrible thing to have to deal with.

"Well, if you can do it, I can do it." I acquiesced because arguing would make me sound like a spoilsport. But I knew that hiking all day without taking a break was another fantasy, like night-hiking into the Saufley's, like taking a picture of every place we camp, taking a picture of every road we cross, taking a picture of every mountain range we hike, and so on.

We set off—Muse in the lead, hiking at a terribly fast pace, which I knew he could not maintain all day, even *with* breaks. We passed up That Guy; we overcame Rig, who kept up with us for a while then abandoned the chase. I felt bad hiking off from Rig, shrugging my shoulders as if to say, "What can I do?" I wanted to hike with Rig for a while. But Muse pushed on, a dynamo of swishing nylon and stabbing trekking poles; no breaks, no lunch—straight to Shelter Cove…After three hours he stopped to take a break.

Towards the end of the day, I felt like I was going insane. We finally reached Shelter Cove at 6:30 p.m. having spent most of the day on the Whitefish Trail—an alternate trail that lessened our mileage slightly. The Whitefish trail is mostly an equestrian trail, and the horse hooves have pounded the trail into a fine dust that blackens shoes and legs. When I hike the PCT again someday, I will be sure to avoid the barren, hot and gritty Whitefish Trail. Muse led the charge all day; we did not stop for lunch, and took very few breaks.

It is Labor Day weekend and Shelter Cove Resort is busy with vacationers of all ages. Luckily for us, someone cancelled his or her reservation for a cabin, so Muse and I rented it for the night. Rig, That Guy, Raw Dawg, and Red Velvet arrived at Shelter Cove an hour after us. Rig ended up sleeping on the top bunk in our cabin, with Muse on the bottom bunk, and myself on a double.

There are no restaurants at the Shelter Cove resort, but I purchased some canned beans, mashed potatoes, and ground beef from the small store and filled our cabin with the happy aroma of dinner. Muse hung over the ground beef sizzling in the pan. "Do you want me to spice the beef for you?" he asked. I thought back to the inedible gruel he had made at Nate's apartment in Lancaster. "Naw, it doesn't really need any spices," I said. I made enough food to stuff myself as well as Rig and Muse, then laid down on my bed, polished off a bottle of celebratory Merlot, and went to sleep.

Monday, September 4, 2006

12:44 p.m.

A Lazy Zero

We had intended to take a full zero day at Shelter Cove, but our cabin had been booked the second night of our intended stay. As a result we hitched up the highway to a restaurant, then had another hotel come pick us up for the night. We got to the cabin around three p.m. and did not do anything but watch television until eleven at night. We watched *Back to the Future*, part of the *Jackass* movie, and some MXC. It was possibly the laziest I have ever felt on this trip. Yesterday, it took us two hitches to get back to Shelter Cove. When I called home to instruct my mother to add some items to our next re-supply box she told me that my great aunt Viola had just passed away that Sunday—age 93. She died of pneumonia.

Today we walked into the Three Sisters wilderness. Like the Sky Lakes Wilderness there are scores of lakes and ponds scattered amongst the moss-ridden forest of fir, pine, and the genteel hemlock. When we climbed into the Sisters wilderness from Highway 58, the aquamarine Rosary lakes—Lower, Middle, and North, were our jeweled entrance into this beautiful land. As usual, I have come to disagree with the prevailing opinion of hikers that Oregon is the least impressive part of the PCT. It seems that many hikers appreciate the Pacific Crest Trail most for its ridge and mountain crest traverse, which afford arresting views. Hikers seem nonplussed hiking through miles of old-growth forest however. Hiking beneath the under-story of these forests is just as arresting for me, as they are cool, dizzyingly tall, and spiritually quiet. And come night I lie on my back just before I sleep and watch the night sky sway through a canopy of black branches. Sometimes the wind makes that lonesome ghost-river sound in the treetops; sometimes the forest is total silence, save for a twitch in a bush here and there.

We have currently paused at a small lake where it is Muse's turn to cook lunch. I walked the shallow rock outcrop to where the lakebed drops suddenly into the blue-green, sun-shafted deep and dove in. The ripened summer sun is perfectly warm and lazy here in the Sisters, and I now journal on a rock beneath the shade of a fir tree.

Thursday, September 7, 2006

7:51 p.m.

Franken-route

The deep-thinking Muse has chosen a lava flow for our campsite tonight. The last couple days have been white-knuckle days for him as the fire in the Mount Washington wilderness has caused a sixty-mile closure of the PCT. The buzz on the trail is that most hikers are electing to hitchhike around the closure area, due to a lack of alternate trails.

The northern portion of the Sisters wilderness is a story of a volcanic past written in the bumbling lava flows, pumice flats, obsidian fields, and the secretive snow-mottled barren flanks of the North, South and Middle Sister's volcanic peaks. From the area around and north of the Wickiup Plane, I found myself most entertained by the ever-changing landscapes. The trail wound next to the fifty-foot-drop off of Obsidian Falls—a waterfall of mystic beauty. When we ascended to the top of the falls, the trail crossed Obsidian Creek and followed alongside where in less than a quarter mile I discovered the headwater of the creek to be the crumbling detritus and talus slope leading up the flank of the North Sister. I stood there amazed, watching the perfectly full and intact creek emerge from beneath a mess of talus rocks and flow on through a bit of grassland, then fall fifty feet over the obsidian ledge and continue on its merry way to who-knows-where. I got down on a knee, leaned over the creek's edge and drank deep of the cold water where it bubbled up directly from beneath a large boulder.

The final stretch of trail to highway 242 at McKenzie Pass snakes through the dormant flows and waves of the Yapoah Crater lava flow. My sympathy goes out to whomever forged this stretch of PCT, as the trail itself is composed of crunching, scraping lava rocks that wrenched my shoes and jabbed into the arches of my feet during my traverse. Yesterday at noon we reached highway 242, hitched east into Sisters to gather our thoughts and information from the ranger station regarding the forest fire. Muse did most of the gathering. The ranger suggested that we hitch around the closed area, but Muse would not take "hitch" for an answer. He asked for a map of the closure area, which the ranger made a copy of for him. Then he needed another map showing more land east and west of the fires; then another map, and another. Muse bought about three different maps and took a couple complimentary ones as well.

When we found ourselves standing on Main Street Sisters, we were at a loss as to where to go for a motel—which were cheapest, which catered to hikers. The downtown stem was lined with restaurants, markets, and bauble-shops. Across the street we spied two ragged hikers with packs. Muse yelled over to them, "Fellow hikers!" I looked around, embarrassed. The fellow hikers turned out to be Johnny Walker Red, who we had last seen at Warner Springs three months ago. He was hiking with a different girl now than when we first met him. She went by the name Librarian, if I remember correctly. We all had dinner together and learned that Librarian was Johnny's new girlfriend who had taken the place of his previous girlfriend, Lawn Ornament. Librarian and Lawn Ornament knew each other though. In fact, they had been girlfriend and girlfriend before they met Johnny Walker Red.

While I did laundry and swam in the hotel pool, Muse walked in to town and bought even more maps—topographical maps. He must have spent close to thirty dollars on maps, which I would be expected to help him pay for since this was a joint venture. Then, beneath the hanging table lamp of our room, Muse spread out the flock of maps and painstakingly plotted our route. The final product, as he showed it to me, was a patchwork of trails, dirt roads, yellow blazing (highway walking), cross-country hiking, and a river crossing. "But I'm not sure about this river," he said to me, pointing at the map. "There's no bridge, and I don't know what the river looks like, so…"

"So, what if we just walked along the highway the whole way. Wouldn't that be quicker and easier?"

"Eh, I really don't like walking along highways."

Today we hitched a ride back up McKenzie Pass and set off on our Frankenstein alternate route. A young man drove us up the pass after he had ridden by me on his mountain bike where I stood with my thumb in the air. He said that he had hitched all over Alaska when he was employed on a Halibut boat. He commandeered his mom's car, cracked a couple beers for us, and drove up the hill. At the top of the pass we talked to Stomper a bit, then set off on the first leg of our alternate route: a five-mile road walk west down Highway 262. The mileage markers slowly came and went; I timed our road-walking mile, which came to seventeen minutes. After five miles we turned off the road on to the Hand Lake Trail, which wound past a lava flow, Robinson Lake, then into a deep and tall forest—silent but for the sound of my feet. The trail seemed somewhat out of use; fallen trees lay across the trail—thousands of spider webs spanned across the trail collected against my legs.

An interesting, yucca-like bush in the area was presently flowering—sending a tall stalk up into the air from its spidery base. For some reason, Muse did not like the stalks of this plant and would walk off the trail when possible to avoid touching it. Then, as I walked not far behind him, I watched as he began hacking the stalks down with his trekking poles as he passed. I did not appreciate this, and neither did the two wasps that flew up and stung him on the arm. Muse jerked around, flailing his arms, and began running down the trail, yelling "There's something seriously wrong!" A black wasp landed on my leg, but I brushed it off and caught up to Muse where he stood examining the rising welts on his arm and shoulder. "Is there anything on me?" he asked, raising his shirt.

"No."

"See these red marks? I just got bit twice by some kind of bee. Maybe I stirred them up when I was swatting at those plants."

"Bad karma."

With my pen, Muse drew a circle around the red area then had me take a picture of the two "bites." He said he had been "bitten" by a bee as a child and taken to the hospital—as a precautionary measure, was my conclusion, since he had never gone into anaphylactic shock. Nonetheless, Muse believes himself allergic to bee stings.

The Hand Lake Trail terminated at the Robinson Lake Trailhead where the plan was to walk a dirt road. We did so for about two hours, finally coming to highway 126. We walked down this highway until about 7:30 wherein the Oregon sky turned towards twilight hues. There was a small dirt road I suggested we walk down and camp on.

"I don't know," said Muse. "What if it's a run-away truck ramp?"

The trucks would be driving up hill on this particular stretch of highway negating any need for a run-away ramp, but I did not feel like pointing that out. "Okay" I said. "Let's walk up to the next turnout."

We did, and this led us to a construction area of gravel roads between lava flows. Camping was looking stark. Muse called me over saying that he had found a place to camp—on top of a lava flow. There is a cushion of moss growing atop the lava in places making it softer to lie on. As is often the case he had found a soft, flat area just big enough for himself, but there was nothing else. I walked a bit further over the lava flows and found a better spot.

Muse has asked me to evaluate his wasp stings about five times now. They are swelling up and remain red. We will see if he is still alive come morning.

September 8, 2006

4:00 p.m.

The Celebrity Wasp Bite

Wonder of wonders—I am back in the town of Sisters. I slept okay on my lava bed last night. In the morning, Muse, who was still alive, remarked, "There's a high probability that I'll want to hitch to a hospital today."

We set off down Highway 124 again and picked up a trail that led to the Clear Lake Resort. We passed a reservoir on the way where a lady and her elderly father were fishing. "Do you know anything about wasp bites?!" Muse yelled to them. The lady walked up and Muse showed her his swollen, cabbage-patch-kid of an arm. Then the father wandered up and they all talked about the infamous wasp "bite" for a while. The lady said that he would probably be fine since the sting happened yesterday, and anaphylactic shock happens almost immediately after a sting, *if* one is allergic to bees and wasps.

We continued on to the Clear Lake Resort where Muse confronted a lady walking through the resort parking lot. "Do you know anything about wasp bites?" They talked for a while. She did not think that the sting would be a problem if he had not felt anything by this time.

In the resort diner we sat for breakfast. The waiter was a rough dude with camouflage pants, and a shirt that read, "Fish Tremble at the Mention of My Name." Muse showed the wasp "bites" to our waiter who reckoned that the sting was harmless by now. Soon after, the father and daughter from the reservoir arrived for breakfast and Muse continued the wasp "bite" conversation with them. She still maintained their harmlessness. At this point Muse was conflicted whether or not he should hitch back to a town and find a clinic, or hike on. I sipped my coffee and flipped through a scenic book of Oregon. The morning was sunny and warm—another perfect day to hike.

I walked along the Clear Lake docks just outside of the diner. The clarity of the water is remarkable. I could see Cut Throat trout gliding along the lake bottom through the crystal blue water; water like Indian moonstone. On the diner menu I read about the ancient explosion of Little Nash Crater on Sand Mountain, and the subsequent lava flows that ran into the McKenzie River valley forming Clear Lake. Stumps of trees, preserved and still standing on the cold lakebed, can be seen at a depth of one hundred feet.

After breakfast, we hiked down a dirt road, across a dry lakebed, then up another dirt road to a historical ranger lodge where a reunion of retired Clackamas Forest rangers was in progress. The present generation of forest rangers were serving the retirees on the lodge grounds. A guy sauntered up to Muse and me to find out who we were. Muse showed him the wasp "bites."

"Don't know nothin' about it," said the man. "Let me see if I have any EMT's here. He came back with a medical ranger who was himself allergic to bees. He told Muse that he should get it checked out, just to be safe. A female forest ranger became involved at this point. She examined Muse's welts. "Oh, that's how they all look. You'll be fine," she said. "But if he recommends that you get it checked out, then you oughta get it checked out."

The group of rangers said that they would offer us a ride into Sisters, except that they were legally prohibited from transporting non-employees in ranger vehicles. Muse and I thanked them and continued on up the dirt road, until a cute blonde girl came running after us. "Y'all need a ride somewhere, right? I can take you."

Muse searched my face, and asked me if I thought he should go back into Sisters to see a doctor. I wanted to tell him he was over-reacting regarding the wasp stings, but I did not want to sound selfish. "Either way is fine," I said. "Only you know how you feel."

So, after the father and daughter telling Muse he would be okay, the lady in the parking lot telling him he would be fine, the waiter saying the same, and a forest ranger saying that all stings look like that, Muse accepted her offer for a ride back into Sisters.

I weaseled my way into the front seat next to Jessica. Jessica turned out to be the twenty-three-year-old daughter of the lady forest ranger. On our way down to Sisters she asked us questions about the trail; Jessica was a hiker. I tried to impress her with stories of pain and danger on the Pacific Crest Trail. I made her laugh and inquired about her life. She seemed incredibly sweet and well adjusted. She loved to travel and read many travel books. Muse and I offered to treat her to dinner as thanks, but she declined. She would not even accept a refill for her gas tank. Her mother and she were attending a concert in Eugene at seven that evening, and she needed to be on her way back.

I told her that I would be taking a bus home after my trip, and planned on visiting a friend in Portland. She said that Portland was an hour and a half from Eugene, where she lived. I was hoping she would ask me to visit, or call, but she did not take the bait. Oh well. She sure was lovely.

Anyhow, now Muse has a headache, and tiredness, and still the swollen, cabbage-patch-kid arm. He thinks he is dying. I called some hotels while he was in the clinic and found space at the Best Western on the edge of town. Jessica dropped us off and hugged us goodbye. When we entered the hotel room, Muse closed the shades, stripped to his briefs, and retreated silently to bed with the pillow over his face. I hope the little guy pulls through this one.

I am journaling poolside now. A father and son are spraying themselves with water from floating foam tubes. There is not a pretty face for miles of here. A folk festival has taken over Sisters, rendering the cheaper hotels booked. Tomorrow we will have to hitch out of Sisters once again. Déjà vu!

Muse's general consensus is that he is tired of hiking now. He misses "the comforts of having a house." Sometimes I am concerned that we will not finish the trip before snow hits the North Cascades due to Muse's lethargy. He is slow on the trail, and likes to stop at every town or resort possible, so he can take a shower and indulge on expensive dinners. He admitted the other day that he and I have done a complete flip-flop: I was the slow one at first while he waited for me, and now the opposite is true, and has been true for quite a while now. I would not call it a complete flip-flop though. I have enjoyed hiking from day one up to this point—through deserts, mountains, and plains—despite my initial injuries. Muse hiked Southern California in a foul mood, loved the Sierras, and is now tired of hiking every day.

There are three lonely men at the pool now, all of us wishing that the other two men were two women. It is sad. Spotting gorgeous women in pools is about as rare as encountering Bigfoot on the trail; you hear stories of people who have seen them, but you never encounter one yourself.

Sunday, September 10, 2006

9:45 a.m.

Marion Forks

My hand is quite frozen now as I scrawl thoughts into my journal pad. The morning is frigid and still, and we have been walking up highway 22, past the nothing town of Marion Forks—still walking our Franken-route around Mount Washington forest fire. Soon though, we will take the Woodpecker Trail from the highway, which will meet up with the Pacific Crest Trail once again.

Yesterday, we hitched an easy ride out of Sisters back up to the Fish Lake historical area, and continued north on dirt road after dirt road. Everywhere we looked were orange-capped hunters hanging around their campers, waiting for evening to bring the animals out to haunt the surrounding forests. Muse and I started to get worried after a while, thinking that we probably should be wearing orange hats as well, lest we be mistaken for game. Walking the dirt roads was simply Muse's alternative to hiking down highway 22, which he disfavored doing.

By evening time the dirt road intercepted highway 22 once again where, off in the trees, a family was camped out. Muse and I went over to talk with them. Several matriarchal women in headscarves sat about and spoke in possibly an Eastern European language to the men, who were bearded, overweight, and had their faces smeared with black soot from the campfire. The soot-faced men wholly approved of our journey through the mountains and furnished me with a beer straight away. The scarved women seemed appalled with our journey though, frequently cradling their faces in a plump hand while we told stories, thinking us foolish and stupid. Several miles later, we walked down a small embankment from the highway and camped in a clearing by the Santiam River.

This morning, as we continued up highway 22 in the frozen air, we walked past a restaurant, which unfortunately was closed. The time was 8:15 and Muse wanted to sit and wait for it to open at ten. I practically forced him to continue on, not wanting to sit around for two hours. But around 9:40 as we continued up the highway, Muse stuck his thumb out, and a young man immediately pulled over and drove us back down to the restaurant. So, here I sit, waiting for the Marion Forks restaurant to open. I will be surprised if Muse does not find a reason to hitch back to Sisters for another night in a hotel. One waitress walked in already so we at least know that it will open some time soon. Meanwhile, I must say that I have never written so slowly in my life, due to this frozen hand.

Muse hikes with one trekking pole now so that he can keep his wasp "bitten" elbow elevated. We must be the last hikers on the trail by now as I am positive that most hitchhiked forward around the fire closures.

Tuesday, August 12, 2006

Federal Warning Water

Two days ago, after breakfast at the Marion Forks restaurant, we took the Woodpecker Trail from Highway 22 up to where it met the Pacific Crest Trail. We had circumnavigated the fire in the Mount Washington wilderness and rejoined the PCT, like an old friend, as it continued on into the Mount Jefferson wilderness.

Just before reaching Russell Creek, I intercepted a Sobo (southbound hiker) who went by the name of Crash Test Dummy. He had the largest beard I had seen on the trail yet. I talked with him for a while until Muse caught up and pummeled Crash Test Dummy with questions regarding Ollalie Lake, our next re-supply point, which was rumored to be denying hiker re-supply boxes.

Russell Creek was fairly shallow but flowing swiftly as I forded its dirty glacial waters. On the opposite bank I removed my shoes to clear all the sand and rocks that had invaded during the ford. At the top of the next ridge, I came to a trail junction. In pen, someone had drawn an arrow on the wooden sign and written "Canada" as an indicator to PCT hikers which way to go. But still, I sat and waited for Muse, who came stomping up the trail not long after. He thought not to stop and speak with me, but blasted past without a word, down the wrong trail. I thought about letting him go, as punishment for his rudeness.

"Muse!" I finally called in his retreat.

"What!" he responded, as if irritated.

"I think you're going the wrong way!"

He stopped. "You *think*, or you *know?*" he responded smartly.

"Well, there's an arrow here pointing to Canada," I responded with patience. Muse regarded the guidebook for several seconds.

"Yeah…you're right. I guess it's that way," he said calmly now. "Go ahead."

I hiked off.

The next day, Muse rose in the morning with a mission. "If they don't have our package at Ollalie Lake, I'm really gonna be angry. I'm gonna give them a piece of my mind," he said seriously. If Ollalie Lake was no longer accepting packages, I was sure there was a logical explanation. But he was already angry as we hiked off, Muse in the lead this time.

That morning we traded the Mount Washington Wilderness for the Mount Hood Wilderness. I hiked swiftly through the forests of hemlock, but Muse had disappeared from sight; Ollalie Lake must be reached as quickly as possible! The mystery of the re-supply box must be tackled at once! Miles later I intercepted him where he sat on a log, writing me a note. "I was just leaving you a note that this is the junction down to Ollalie Lake."

Ollalie is a sizable lake, with docks and motorboats, over which looms the white-capped backdrop of Mount Jefferson, when gazing from the lake's north shore. I entered the general store behind Muse, eager to hear the culmination of his volcanic anger that had been slowly building over the last week. He walked directly to the counter. "Hi, I'm here to pick up a package for *Nipper*," he said, adding a flair of authority to his last name.

"You're a PCT hiker?" asked the middle-aged man behind the counter. "I'm sorry we don't receive PCT packages anymore."

"Why is that?" asked Muse, drumming his fingers on the counter.

"See, when you mail a package to Ollalie Lake, the post office actually delivers them to the ranger station twenty miles down the road. The rangers are the ones who would deliver our mail to us, but due to rising gas prices, the Forest Service has stopped doing this. So, it's not our fault; we love our hikers who come through here! Sorry."

And that was the logical explanation I was expecting. Muse stared silently over the man's shoulder; his was fuel gone—his fire put out; the magma slowly sunk back down beneath the surface. The explanation made perfect sense. There was nobody here to blame—nobody to yell at.

The hiker box in the Ollalie Lake store was full of goodies, discarded by hikers before us. We cooked some Lipton pasta sides on the porch and talked with the teenage kid who worked at the store in the summer time. He brought us some fresh tomatoes from somewhere and told us he wanted to hike the PCT someday as well.

"What's with the federal warning about the water here?" I asked him.

"Oh it's nothing. We filter our own water, which is the water that comes out of the spigot over there. It does not meet federal standards, so by law we have to put that stupid sign up. We drink the water all the time. It's fine."

"That's what I figured," I said.

Before we left, I went into the store to buy a frappucino with the last two dollars in my pocket. Muse asked me if I had any extra cash, which I told him I did not. Muse does not carry cash, because it is unnecessary weight. He turned from me without a word and left the store, quickly. Irritation was written in his body language and I knew something was wrong yet again.

Stepping from the store I yelled after him to wait for me. We hiked back up the junction where I asked him if anything was wrong.

"No, I'm fine," he said.

"Are you sure?" I probed.

"Yeah, let's go."

We continued on the PCT; I was hiking in the lead. In no time Muse had fallen behind an undetermined distance, so I sat to take a break. When he caught up, I asked him a question, which he did not stop to answer.

"Hey!" I yelled with some starch in my voice. He stopped. "You can't stop and talk to me or what?"

"I'm in a hurry," he said testily, as if stopping to talk would be a major inconvenience. "I wanna get to Canada." He hiked off around the corner.

I sat there in dismay, thinking about his answer. He could not stop and talk with me, because he wanted to get to Canada.

Later down the trail, I confronted him again, and asked him what his problem was. He took a contrappasto stance, gazing over my shoulder for a moment. "I was just irritated," he finally said, "that I couldn't buy water at Ollalie Lake because you wanted to buy a frappucino!"

"Buy water?" I said in consternation. "You could get all the water you want at the spigot!"

"I didn't want to drink *that* water because of the federal warning on it!"

"Yeah, but you heard that kid say they filter it. The sign is just legal red-tape."

"Well, I didn't feel safe drinking it, and I didn't have cash to buy any water."

"I didn't know that. Why didn't you explain the situation to me?"

The deep-thinking Muse had no explanation. His emotions had gotten the best of him, and instead of reasoning, he became angry, avoiding conversation with me. And it was my job yet again to pin him down, to drag the issue from his lips for resolution, for a proper explanation—lest we continue on with a growing wall of silence between us.

Wednesday, September 20, 2006

10:53 p.m.

Forty-Miler

I am at the Village Inn at White Pass, Washington. It has been eight days since my last entry. Much has happened as we have finished Oregon, and entered Washington.

On the day we were to walk in to Timberline Lodge I had made up my mind to buy lunch for Muse in appreciation of his putting together the alternate route around the fire. But before we even got to the lodge he said, "Maybe you could buy me lunch for putting together the alternate route." I was irritated that he should volunteer kindness out of me, and I let him know how I felt.

Later on down the trail he stopped as I walked up behind him. "You know, I'm not angry or anything," he said, clearly angry, "but you are incredibly selfish and a mooch. I just had to get that off my chest." He walked off with me hiking behind. I really felt like quitting the trail then and there. But he started talking again, saying he did not mean to insult me, but I have just gotten him extremely frustrated. I was happy that this conversation was happening, because I knew that something had been eating him for a while as he has had a rotten attitude towards me every day. So I stayed calm and let him vent all of his frustrations, most of which boiled down to his viewpoint that he does all the planning while I do nothing. To this I explained that since he prefers to hold the maps, he is inherently responsible for any planning having to do with mileage, ambiguous junctions, and water sources. In my defense, I pointed out to him that we no longer take turns doing laundry, as I have consciously taken over that activity when in towns. I cook more often than he does as well.

I often think to myself, as I hike along, when and if I have ever acted maliciously towards Muse. And in fear of sounding self-biased, I have yet to think of anything. Nevertheless, Muse wanted me to admit, as we hiked along through a peaceful forest towards the raw flanks of Mount Hood, that I was equally to blame for the acidity between us. So, I asked him, as I have done on several occasions, to cite an example of when I have maligned him. Again he had no examples, but became angry. He stopped and turned to face me. "Do you really think," he said, red-faced and shaking, "that you have absolutely no blame whatsoever!?" I said I was sure I had done something, though I could not recall anything. My secret belief is that most of Muse's frustration with me is due to misinterpreted situations; a most recent example would be the water incident at Ollalie Lake, where I clearly had no ill intentions. I am not even sure what to do anymore to alleviate his growing frustration and anger towards me. Nevertheless, I gave him a nebulous, all-encompassing apology, in hope to restore peace between us. And having done so, hiking has been better between us. I feel that a weight has been lifted off of my shoulders.

Subsequent to our on-trail dispute, we ascended some sand hills at the base of Mount Hood—the tallest mountain in Oregon, standing a bit over eleven thousand—then invaded the luxurious Timberline Resort where we acquired our re-supply box and had lunch with Stomper,

Moose, and Popsicle. While I was waiting for my food at Timberline Lodge restaurant, I called ahead to a hotel in Cascade Locks to make a reservation for the following evening. We had planned on hiking thirty-five miles that day, and thirty-five miles the next into Cascade Locks, in the Columbia River Gorge.

We left Timberline Lodge around four o'clock and hiked on. Muse walked in the lead, and I followed close enough behind to keep him within my sight. Around dusk, the trail curved sharply to the left and down, but Muse continued in a straight line where a fainter trail continued down a sandy overgrown hillside. "Hey!" I called out to him when I caught up. He stopped, still pushing his way through a mess of bushes and looked back up at me. "You're going the wrong way."

"Are you sure?" he yelled back, knowing I was right. He came back up and followed my lead as the trail wound down a heavily forested ridge towards the Zigzag River.

I often wonder what would have happened if I had not seen him walk down the wrong trail. I would have continued hiking in the correct direction, thinking he was still ahead of me. After not catching up with him after a while, I would have hiked faster, and longer into the night using my headlamp to guide my way. Frustrated, I would eventually stop and camp by myself, thoroughly worried, confused, and angry. Meanwhile, Muse's LED light had fallen out of his pocket some time after we left Timberline Lodge, and it is nearly impossible that he could have negotiated his way through the thick, dark forest that the trail wound down into. Perhaps the next morning he would rise early at the break of dawn and hike quickly, knowing that I was ahead of him somewhere. And perhaps after four or five miles he would find me encamped beside the trail somewhere. Would I be angry? He would tell me that he had hiked down the wrong trail for a while, which is how I got ahead of him. His explanation would sound perfectly logical and there would be no hard feelings—no reason to be angry. These things can happen in 2700 miles. We would simply thank God, and walk on.

As I mentioned, Muse soon discovered near dark that his LED light was missing, and he could only figure that it had fallen out of his pocket when he sat down to take a break. I had a powerful headlamp on however, and I hiked slowly through the dark forest with Muse tripping on rocks and roots close at my heels. We had not reached the thirty-five-mile junction yet, and figured it to be still four or five miles ahead. Our night hiking was slow and labored due to Muse's blindness. And if his blindness was not enough to slow us down, we soon heard some creature baying and crying off in the dark forest. We stopped and listened as it went tripping and crashing around through foliage, coming CLOSER, then farther—then crying again as if lost and mad. We thought it might be a bull Elk in heat, but could not be sure.

"Do you think I should yell?" Muse asked me.

"I don't know. I don't think it's a human, whatever it is." My first instinct would not be to yell in the forest, thereby identifying myself, but Muse seemed to think it would be a good idea.

"HELLO!!!" He yelled. "IS ANYBODY OUT THERE!!"

The forest ate his voice and fell silent as we waited for an answer. I felt like dark eyes from hemlock boughs, from swampy underbrush, and moist caves were watching me now.

The trail descended in elevation, curving in broad switchbacks through the forest. We continued hiking slowly in the blackness—my headlamp sweeping the forest, illuminating mossy trunks, and overhanging spidery branches. Eventually, we heard the tormented creature above us, still crashing madly about in the forest as if insane. We put another couple miles between us and IT before we camped for the night. We were disturbed no longer.

The next morning, Muse figured we had a square forty miles left to Cascade Locks. When we took our first break in the morning, he told me he was going to do the forty-mile day, regardless of whether I was to join him or not. Since I had made a hotel reservation for that evening, I was determined to accomplish the forty miles, or lose the first night. I rose from where we had taken a break, and hiked swiftly into oblivion. I did not see Muse again until day's end.

The day passed before my eyes in a blur. I strode along the trail with a long gait, just below a run, past Sentinal Peak, past Preachers Peak/Devils Pulpit, through forests of swishing hemlock and petticoat firs. Fifteen miles later, I took my first break—a fifteen-minute break, at Indian Springs. I continued to Wahtum Lake, where several trails forked from the PCT leaving me unsure of which one to follow. I scaled down a brushy hillside to where three guys were camped on the lake. They had maps and pointed me in the right direction. Soon enough, a wood sign nailed to a tree read "Columbia River," and I knew I was going the right direction. After several miles, I intercepted a young couple coming towards me on the trail, whom I could see were just weekend backpackers. I asked them if they knew how much farther ahead Cascade Locks was.

"Cascade Locks? Oh gee, that's like twenty miles ahead of you yet."

"Oh, is that all?" I responded excitedly.

"I don't think you can make it in one day!"

"I've already done twenty miles today. What's another twenty?"

The couple looked at each other like I was crazy; maybe I was. I hiked off, calculating the miles in my head. If I hike four miles per hour for the next five hours—that puts me in Cascade Locks by eight o'clock. Easy.

The remainder of my trail food I kept in my shorts pockets, and without the encumbrance of trekking poles, I snacked all day as I walked along to keep my energy up. Dark clouds gathered in the northern sky as I counted down the miles. Finally, as I crested a saddle past Teakettle Spring, I was rewarded with my first view of the Columbia River far below. I could see the rectangular shape of barges moving up and down river—city lights edged the river. My brain raced along in excitement, yet the trail meandered in broad switchbacks, painfully taking its time descending into the gorge. The forests of hemlock gave way to Douglas fir and striking stands of maple, creating an emerald forest in which deer scattered frequently at my approach. The trail bottomed out then undulated up and down hills and ledges in the forest, heading in a west/southwest direction along the river for what seemed an eternity. Half insane by this time, I started yelling at the trail, scolding it for taking such a seemingly circuitous route into Cascade Locks. I was trail-running the down hills and still hiking quickly uphill—knowing that Cascade Locks might be around the next turn in the trail.

The forty mile day was tough, but not as tough as I expected—not even as tough as the thirty-eight mile day into Shelter Cove, wherein I could barely stand at day's end. I accomplished Cascade Locks by 7:15 p.m. having started at 6:20 a.m.—an eleven-hour hiking day, wherein I took about three short breaks between my running and speed walking. After checking into the hotel, I immediately walked to the pub down the street for some beer and dinner. The streets were quiet and darkened. At the bar, I sat by myself with my chicken dinner, flipping through the PCT register. The Calabama boys had been there the day before, along with Rig and some others. The waitress, a half-breed Klamath Indian gal, remembered well the Calabama boys who she said ate an inordinate amount of pizza and drank a sailor's cache of beer in one night.

When I returned to the hotel room, Muse sat on the bed in nothing but briefs, picking at his feet. "Hello," he said with a smirk.

"Happy forty," I said.

Sunday, September 24, 2006

3:36 p.m.

Cold Rain Washington

On our zero day in the quaint, riverside town of Cascade Locks, I exited our hotel room and gazed across the street in the morning sunshine. Broken storm clouds filled the sky, providing a gray and white backdrop for the Bridge of the Gods, connecting Oregon and Washington across the Columbia River. Amazingly, my current elevation was around 180 feet—one of the lowest points on the entire Pacific Crest Trail. There had been rain off and on in the morning and throughout the day. Across the street, I saw a hiker walking along the sidewalk. I waved him over. In shorts, beat up Montrail shoes, a wet raincoat with the hood over his head, Groomsman smiled and shook my hand. I had last seen him in Belden, California from where he had left the trail to attend a wedding, and was now hiking south from Canada to complete his journey. That evening a group of us had dinner together at Charburger; Groomsman, GQ, Switch, Moose, Popsicle, Muse, myself, and some other local hiker who latched onto our group.

After dinner I invited Groomsman to the pub and bought a round of beers. We told trail stories; I told him about my midnight Bigfoot experience in Northern California—a section he had yet to traverse as he continued south. The local hiker from dinner found us, and sat at the end of the bar, listening to our conversation. He had a cache of his own Bigfoot anecdotes, which soon dominated the evening.

"Do you want to hear a really strange story?" he asked Groomsman and me. We said yes and he told the following story: "Well, this happened years ago, when I was a little kid living out in eastern Washington; and I still have no logical explanation for it." He took a draught of beer. "You know on some older houses how they have an oil drum connected to the outside of the house, raised from the ground on wooden legs?" I did not know what he meant, but nodded my head. "Well, I was walking home through my neighborhood one night, and one of those oil drums started talking to me; it called me over, and started walking around on its wooden legs." Groomsman and I glanced at each other. "Then, it pulled its hose out from the wall of the house and sprayed me all over with oil! My mother opened the front door when I got home, and found me standing there, soaked with black oil."

The following morning I sat on the edge of my bed, gazing out the window where the gray rag sky dumped endless rain. GQ and Switch snapped a photo of Muse and me in front of the hotel, resplendent in our rain gear, hoods over our heads and reluctance on our face. We walked out of Cascade Locks in the rain; our schedule demanded we leave, regardless of bad weather conditions.

The only way across the Columbia River is to walk the steel-grated Bridge of the Gods. Below my feet, the brackish water roiled and boiled—cars drove slowly past the two poor boys walking in the rain. But the raindrops disguised the tears that filled my eyes as I entered Washington, our final state—our last five hundred miles to Canada. It was a momentous traverse across the bridge, and the entirety of everything I had been through, from that chemise and sage-covered rise in Campo to here, hit me all at once. By the end of the week however, I was crying due to frustration. The stretch between Cascade Locks and our first re-supply point at White Pass was six days of rain, sleet and snow. No section on the trail had been more miserable than this; no section had tried my will and perseverance as much as this. After our first several hours in Washington, my shoes and socks were soaked cold, and stayed wet until White Pass, six days later.

After crossing the bridge, the trail re-entered the deep forest, smelling of rotting, damp wood and wet vegetation. Brown newts twisted across the trail here and there, enjoying their moistened world.

On our first day out from Cascade Locks, Muse and I became lost from each other one more time. We had stopped to take a break wherein I said we should make lunch when we came to our next water source. Muse agreed. I hiked off once again with Muse behind. Before long, he was no longer within sight of me, which is his preference. I hiked for two hours without crossing any water, besides the water that fell on me from above. As is my protocol, I stopped at the two-hour mark and waited for Muse to catch up with me. The clouds had broken over the ridge where I sat on a dirt embankment, eating a candy bar. The air was cold, and a steady wind pushed over the saddle. I covered myself with another jacket. Forty minutes later, Muse had not caught up with me. This was frustrating. What should I do? Walk back? Continue to wait and freeze on this windy saddle? I got up and walked on; the trail dipped below the saddle into a shelter of firs, alders and maples. Before long, I happened upon Red Velvet, who was slack packing back into Cascade Locks. He confirmed that Muse definitely was not in front of me, so I continued on, hiking until about five o'clock. The clouds had converged again, raining steadily on me as the unseen sun went down, and my world grew dark. The dense, downward sloping branches of fir trees allow no rain to reach the ground beneath. This is where I sat and waited for Muse, who currently carried the tarp-tent. I reasoned that if I was lost from him for the night, I would stay dry beneath the fir canopies. A half hour later though, Muse came charging to a halt in front of me. *"There* you are!" he said in exasperation. "Where have you been!?"

"Where have I been?" I said surprised. "Where have you been? I hiked for two hours then sat and waited for forty minutes!"

"You said we were gonna eat soon! I was expecting you to stop!"

"Yeah, I said I wanted to eat when we came to our next water source. After two hours of hiking, I hadn't come across water, so I sat and waited for you."

"Well, I sat and waited for *you*, thinking you got behind me somehow."

"Until Red Velvet told you I was still ahead," I added.

"Well, what were you gonna do without the tent?"

"Just sit right here where its dry," I said, "and wait for you to show up—however long it took."

The situation was resolved without vitriol, and we continued on, hiking within sight of each other, until near dark. In a deep, damp forest, we tied up our tarp tent in a flat bottom by a stream. Felled trees lay crosshatched and crumbling on the forest floor; ferns grew daintily from mossy hillsides, and the windless forest dripped from every branch and leaf.

I sat on a wet log and heated water for some mashed potatoes. The night air was cold and every piece of clothing was wrapped about my body. That night was the first night I failed to make a campfire. I had peeled bark from trees, snapped dead branches from the under-story of pines, but everything was damp—like the air was humid yet cold. I ignited blank pages from my journal; they curled, turned brown and went dark again. I had failed. I retired to my sleeping bag.

Our third day out brought us into the Indian Heaven wilderness, where the continuing rain and clouds blocked out our views of Mount Adams, Mount Rainer, and Hood to the south. Luckily, the trailside huckleberries provided some mental relief from the wet weather. I will never forget that night spent at Sheep Lake. Nearing sundown, we walked a side trail to Sheep Lake where the guidebook informed of flat camping areas. The wind around the open meadow of Sheep Lake was intense and cold; laced with the wet sting of fog, it roared in the night like a cold-hearted beast, snapping the tent walls. I wore two wet socks on each foot, long-sleeve shirt, Primaloft jacket, down vest, nylon rain jacket, bandana, hood, and my torn-up silk bag liner wrapped around my neck. In the howling dark, I sat on a rock and made dinner as Muse altered the tarp-tent I had just pitched. He shortened the guy lines, lowering the tent walls almost to the ground to reduce wind invasion, which also reduced our space beneath the tarp. The longer I sat on the rock, the colder my body became. Quickly I scooped hot spoonfuls of mashed potatoes into my mouth; my hands had gone numb.

It was a cold night. They were all cold nights. I wore all my jackets while in my sleeping bag, a thermal shirt pulled up around my legs, and my rain pants pulled up over the end of my sleeping bag to prevent the wet ground from soaking in; still I was cold. Muse positioned the tarp tent so incredibly low to the ground, one had to be a contortionist to put anything on or take anything off without kicking the entire tent over.

The following day continued with sporadic rains as we climbed higher into the Mount Adams wilderness. We had been leap-frogging with Ryan and Tamara, two thru-hikers who I had never heard of or met before this section. They were a nice, but solitary couple—seemingly uninterested in the group aspects of the PCT; they had no trail names, nor did they sign a single PCT register along the way. Towards the end of the day, the four of us converged upon a curious sight while hiking through this volcanic area of the Mount Adams wilderness. Rounding a curve in the trail, we came upon a burnt and smoldering portion of ground, perhaps thirty feet in length and width. The grasses and shrubs were smoldering black sticks, and a tree stump smoked and bore red coals in its center, looking as if it had been burning for some time. None of us had seen a single flash of lightning from this storm, but we could not imagine what other kind of force could flash fry a broad swath of wet forest duff and tree stumps. Muse and I entertained the thought of camping here for the sake of warmth, but ultimately continued on, up and over some lava ridges, and down into a flat portion of black sand where we pitched camp. In the remaining light of day, I perambulated the surrounding forest, collecting the driest bark from the deadest trees; brushes of brown pine needle clumps, which burn better than anything; and the crooked dead branches from pine canopies. And with this, I ignited a small fire, feeding first on sizzling pine needles, which in turn ignited dry branches, then larger branches then sizable branches. After a day of much precipitation, I had made fire once again. Muse was thoroughly impressed.

In the cold, but still air, I sat on the black sand, laying my wet socks like strips of rotten bacon across the heated rocks of the fire ring. Throughout this wet week, the offensive odor of my socks reached new levels—dangerously high levels. Above, the sky was strangely silent, most assuredly collecting its next cache of rain. I stuck my bare feet close to the heat; slowly, feeling returned to my toes, which I feared had been nearing the beginning stage of frostbite. In fact, for months afterwards, the middle toe of my left foot remained somewhat numbed.

My fire licked and hissed on the damp branches for several hours; a couple raindrops fell from the sky. I ditched all my gear beneath the tarp tent and waited…the rain continued, and grew heavier. From beneath the tarp tent, I watched my beautiful fire murdered in the cold night.

I periodically woke throughout the night, when the rain tapped heavier on the nylon walls. Sometimes when I woke, the rain would tap with a sharp scrape: sleet. And other times the rain sounded a gentler hush and slide: snow. Come the light of morning, peaceful white flakes swirled down from the sky—dusting hemlock boughs and lava crevasses. As usual, I was the first one up, packed and ready to go, and I sat beneath the protection of a fir tree waiting while Muse peeled himself slowly from his bag like a rotten banana. From day one on this journey, I kept a spare set of heavy wool socks in the secret pouches of my hip strap. And today was their redeeming day for the two thousand miles of portage thus far. Still clinging to the tenets of ultra-light theory, Muse had but two pair of thin wet socks at his disposal, two shirts, and one thin nylon rain jacket. Part of his inability to rise quickly in the morning is because he fears leaving his sleeping bag for the morning freeze.

Meanwhile, I wear all my jackets to bed; thus, I rise in the morning without too much shock, save for the unavoidable suffering of pulling near-frozen, water logged shoes onto my feet.

We took to the trail amidst the snow, which thickened into flurries. Needless to say, the air was rightfully cold, but as opposed to rain, snow did not soak into my clothing and suck the warmth from my body. Muse stopped prematurely, complaining of dangerously frozen feet. As a remedy, he cut sock sized pieces from our emergency blanket, wrapping them around his feet. Further along, his general body became chilled, so I leant him my thermal top, which he wrapped about his neck.

At Lava Spring we stopped beneath the dry shelter of trees and made lunch. The water from Lava Spring bubbled up from beneath the bumbling black lava flow into a sparkling clear pool which fed the Muddy Fork. I drank directly from the spring, seeing no need to filter such purified waters. Tamara and Ryan caught up to us and sat down to smoke some weed.

As we descended in elevation, our snow turned to sleet, which eventually gave way to rain once again. And so went the remainder of our day.

The next day the trail ascended gradually to where we entered the Goat Rocks wilderness. Brief breaks in the clouds showed the orange skyline of the Goat Rocks, and windows of the glacial flanks of Mount Adams. My hopes that the clouds would clear were soon dashed to pieces as we climbed to the ice-bitten detritus slopes of the Goat Rocks; the clouds regrouping for war against us. The trail forked evenly in half just before a sketchy talus slope. Even aided with the guidebook Muse was unsure of which way to go. We chose the northwesterly trending trail, which carved a niche across the crumbling talus slope. Angry, wet wind continued to batter the mountains, and rocks, gathering weight from freezing rain, began tumbling down the talus slope around us. One fist-sized stone passed directly through my legs as I walked. I shuddered to think of the injury it could have caused me. The few wind-twisted trees we passed bore icicles growing sideways from the ice winds. Our trail traversed a knife-edge ridge, which seemed to grow thinner and more precipitous the farther we hiked; coupled with the fact that we were not certain we were on the correct trail at the moment. Glancing down the cliff on either side of me, I could see only a fall into an abyss of roiling clouds. They lay banefully in the rocky chasms below us; they filled and darkened the sky above, and blew in foggy wind over the ridges like native ghost armies. Somewhere in the chasm to my left was Packwood Glacier—on my right, McCall Glacier. And the socked-in trail ahead of me disappeared into the whipping fog, and seemed that it might drop off the edge of a cliff at any moment. It was a miserable hike.

After what seemed an eternity, the trail descended gradually and showed us to a Pacific Crest Trail sign nailed to a tree at which point I felt immensely better.

On our last day out we walked around twenty-five miles to reach our re-supply point at White Pass, the last five miles of which were incredibly nauseating. My hood leaked water into my bandana, which dangerously chilled my head. My feet and gloves were soaked and cold. Tired of wiping snot from my raw, red nose onto my gloves, I could do nothing but watch as it dripped from my nose to the ground. I walked with my head down for miles so the snot would not slime down my lips, and to shelter my face from the sideways rain.

We descended the final ridge to Highway twelve at White Pass, and walked about a quarter mile along the shoulder to White Pass Village. Muse rented a lodge room straight away, and I went to the Kracker Barrel gas station/espresso bar/snack bar to dry out and warm up. The Calabama boys milled about, along with Rig, GQ and Switch, and Girl Scout. We all sat around filling ourselves with coffee and snacks. Rig bought me a twenty-four ounce Budweiser; thanks for the food and new socks I had given him at Shelter Cove.

Rig helped me carry our re-supply box back to our room. We knocked and Muse opened the door, standing in nothing but his briefs pulled up to his chest. "See what I get to put up with?" I said to Rig.

I remember well the hot shower I took that night. The warmth was good, but I felt estranged from the feeling of wetness; I wanted to feel dry. I took my shoes into the shower with me, filling them with water, endlessly pouring out dirt and sand. That night the wind howled through White Pass. Muse and I had socks, packs, and clothes hung over every chair and sill by the blasting heater, drying at long last. When I left the room to go here or there via the outdoor corridors of the Inn, the black wind penetrated through to my soul, reminding me of its presence out there, while I retreated to my safe house of contrived warmth. I thought back to the dripping, seething forest where I failed to start a campfire, the howling cold night at Sheep Lake, the rain murdering my fire in the Mount Adams wilderness. Feelings of such lonesomeness come in the darkness and the cold—when everything seems wet, and chilled, and hopeless—when you balance on your ground cloth at night, fearful to touch the wet ground surrounding.

In the Calabama's lodge room, spirits were high: Teflon, Gouda, Nate, That Guy, Rig, Girl Scout, Muse and myself. Everybody laughed, and nobody complained. Why should we? What would be accomplished?

Tuesday, September 26, 2006

8:09 p.m.

My First Night Alone

We stayed one night at White Pass Village. The various city folk who visited the Kracker Barrel gas station told us that this storm was about to pass, after which we would be blessed with clear skies. Nevertheless, we left White Pass in the afternoon while rain continued to fall on lonesome highway twelve. Some switchbacks took us up into the William O. Douglas wilderness where the trail leveled off in a misty flatland of lily pad ponds and lakes, surrounded by umbrella-like firs and hemlock. The rains petered out as the day grew old, but the sky remained gray.

At day's end we began searching for a flat place to camp, but the forest floor was thick with huckleberry and heather. Game trails crossed the forest floor everywhere I looked. Muse delegated trails for me to explore, in hopes they would lead to campsites, but I revealed to him that the trails were animal trails and would lead to nothing but wetter shoes. Eventually we kicked a level area free of rocks and branches and tied up the tent. The rain had ceased by evening time and I slept peacefully through the night.

In the morning, I rose first from the tent, breaching the morning silence of the forest. The trees had been hung with icicles like ballroom chandeliers of sparkling crystal, and every puddle was frozen over with cobwebbed ice. I stood on the trail and lifted my eyes to the sky—the blue, blue sky! I tried not to get my hopes up, but instinctively I felt the storm had passed. I would feel the sun on my back this day!

We had a mere twenty miles to reach Chinook Pass, where Muse's friend Gloria was scheduled to pick us up and drive us to Seattle. Muse would stay with Gloria in Port Orchard for two days, while I would stay in downtown Seattle with Rachel and Joe. I think Muse and I sorely needed this respite from each other. The trail wandered into Mount Rainier National Park where Muse and I were dumb-struck with our first sudden view of fourteen thousand foot Mount Rainier standing powerfully against the blue sky.

We reached Chinook Pass in the afternoon where Gloria successfully found us sitting on a wall beside the highway and drove us down the pass to a Claim Jumper restaurant in Puyallup, where I picked up the tab.

When Rachel picked me up from Claim Jumper last Friday night she told me that Joe, her boyfriend, had proposed to her. Hallelujah! The next day Joe and Rachel gave me a tour of Seattle, visiting places such as Gas Works Park, the eighteen-foot tall troll under Aurora Bridge, and Alki beach on the peninsula for some scenic views of the Seattle skyline from across the sound.

On Sunday we all woke up late. Joe and Rachel left the house to attend some event having to do with newborn babies. While they were away, I cleaned up the house a bit; I took out the trash, put away dishes, and cleaned the litter box for the three cats.

When Joe and I picked up Muse from Pike's Market, I asked him how he was doing. He said he was tired. After two days off the trail, he was tired. So much so that he slept pretty much the whole drive back to Chinook Pass. He has hardly said a word actually since we picked him up. He says he is tired, but my guess is something else is eating him. The weather in Seattle was perfect during my visit, and when Joe and Rachel drove us back to Chinook Pass on Monday morning, we hiked off into Rainier National Park with more beautiful weather.

At the moment I journal by the light of a campfire near a dirt road in the Blowout Mountain area. I lay here alone, not knowing where the hell Muse is. Around two o'clock today we stopped at a spring so that I could make lunch while Muse took a nap, claiming he was not hungry. After lunch he took the lead with me following close enough behind. After crossing a dirt road, the trail forked, and I did not see which fork Muse took. We have made it a point to wait for each other at junctions to prevent separation. But Muse had not waited this time. After exploring the upper trail a bit, I decided to follow the lower trail. Soon after, I caught up with Popsicle and Moose who said that Muse was maybe three minutes ahead of me. I hiked fast, for three hours, but still did not overtake him. In a silent forest I sat down and waited, thinking I may have passed him somehow. I waited forty minutes; no Muse. I left a note beneath a rock on the trail, in case he was behind me, and continued hiking until reaching this dirt road just before seven p.m.

So, here I am; my first night completely alone on the trail.

Thursday, September 28, 2006
4:34 p.m.

More Tension

I found the first note from Muse after about a mile of hiking the next morning. The note was duct taped to a PCT post and read, "I wasn't here. Time: The moon is over the left peak of Mt. Rainier." Okay. Clearly Muse was going insane. I hiked on. Six miles later, I found another note on which was written the water source information for the day. I hiked into Snoqualmie Pass alone that day. It was a pleasant day, though I felt extremely worn out at times, probably from not eating enough while I was in Seattle. But twenty-nine miles later I reached the Snoqualmie Pass trailhead at six p.m. Another note from Muse said he was going to get a room at the inn with a red roof. I gazed over Snoqualmie Pass and saw a red-roofed building. The inn with a red roof turned out to be booked due to a convention. Muse left a note at the front desk saying that he had gone to the Hyak Lodge.

When I entered the Hyak Lodge, there stood the deep-thinking Muse, searching the reaction on my face for having maliciously and purposefully ditched me. I smiled and told him I had a good time with his notes—kind of like a scavenger hunt.

Muse and I, and the two section-hiking ladies from Florida, Yonder and Daybreak, were the only boarders at the Hyak Lodge. Jim and his wife ran the joint like we were their personal houseguests, and we were the first two thru-hikers they have had since buying the building not long ago.

At dinner we all sat around the dining table like a family: Jim, his wife, the gals from Florida, and the squabbling siblings Muse and I. Dinner cost twelve dollars for a pot roast, salad, and bread with garlic olive oil. After finishing my plate, Jim asked me if I wanted more, which I did. At no extra charge, he brought out a bowl of pasta with roasted zucchini and Italian sausage. I ate all of that too. Then Daybreak shared two quarts of Hagen Daz ice cream with everyone.

The next morning, Jim cooked a breakfast of beer pancakes (using Pabst Blue Ribbon Beer) with sausage, bacon and scrambled eggs. That morning Muse had been speaking to me as if he was going to hike on without me: "I'm gonna hike now." I'm doing this; I'm doing that. The tension between us had reached a new level of intensity— unnecessarily, in my opinion, and I had had enough. When I told him that I would like to speak with him in the other room he said, "I'd rather not." I asked him please, and he reluctantly followed me to the dining room. I asked him what the problem was. "I just need some time alone, man," was his answer. I did not believe it. I probed him further. Then he said he felt like I was using him to finish the trip, and that I did not care for him at all. Surprised, I told him that I thought the last couple weeks of hiking had been good between us. But something happened during our break in Seattle after which he had hardly spoken to me. Muse mentioned his continued frustration that I was not keeping our cook pot clean enough, and that he was sick of the smell of my cigarettes, and other issues. It was a mess. Being a solution-oriented man, I offered to go to Seattle and purchase a guidebook so we could split up, and he would not have to deal with me anymore. "I'm not that cruel," he said. "We can just use a copy machine for the remainder of the guidebook." "That would be fine," I said. Ultimately though, he did not want to split up. I guess I called his bluff. So here we are.

We sorted through our bounce box for the last time today. I separated my belongings into one box to be shipped to my aunt's house in Vancouver. Muse is shipping his half to his parent's house in Texas. We have decided to stay another night in Snoqualmie Pass, as the inn with the red roof now has some vacancy. Popsicle and Moose are here, as are Ryan and Tamara, and Dr. Tart, a hiker I have not met up until now.

I am currently journaling in the lobby as our clothes dry. Muse is watching the Simpsons in our room. I have been smoking all day today and yesterday, from the first pack of cigarettes I have bought since Ashland, Oregon. I had determined to quit smoking after Ashland, which I successfully did up until this recent stress with Muse. We only have less than three hundred miles to Canada, but I may die of frustration before then.

Saturday, September 30, 2006

12:18 p.m.

Not Amused

I am still alive, and hiking once again. Yesterday, we entered the Snoqualmie/Mount Baker wilderness area and had some magnificent views of mountain slopes painted red with sumac—Mount Rainier drifted far away like a fairy castle at the edge of imagination, and the brown crags of Snoqualmie Mountain, Red Mountain, and other rock fists and fingers rose to dizzying heights.

Soiling the surrounding beauty is Muse; he is barely talking to me, and avoids taking breaks with me. I am at a loss of how to neutralize his malice—his foul mood, and do not know how much more of this I can endure. Muse is rude, he does not talk to me, and he acts like he does not even want to be in my presence; yet, he does not want to separate! Perhaps he wants us to stick together so he can continue torturing me. You really get to know someone after walking with them for two thousand miles. Muse has no more control over his moods and emotions than he does the weather. Nor does he handle his spells of depression in a mature way. I have told him several times on the trail to grow up and be a man. "I'll never be a man," is always his response. "I'm a boy."

Last night we camped by the waterfall of Delate creek. Some time during the night, some mice chewed into Muse's food bag. The next morning he declared, "Twenty to thirty percent of my food is gone." I doubted that a mouse or two could eat twenty to thirty percent of his food; more likely it chewed into his bag of crackers, and forever fearful of germs and disease, Muse dumped the rest out. His Sporteyez ultra-light sunglasses with elastic head strap also disappeared during the night. Come morning he asked me if I knew where they were, which I did not. "I always put them five feet from my head! It doesn't make an sense!" Poor guy. His world was caving in. I hated those stupid sunglasses with the elastic strap around his head, creating a bowl-haircut effect. Anyhow, these overnight mettlings seemed to double his foul mood. Later that morning we came to a junction where a hilarious tree had grown in the form of a seated man with a huge erection—a woody, one might say. Someone had even carved a mouth and eyes into the trunk and put glasses on him. I pointed it out to Muse who had no reaction. "You don't find that the least bit funny?" I asked. He stared at me seriously. "I'm just not in a very amused mood at the moment," he said.

Sunday, October 1, 2006
6:27 p.m.

Skykomish

I am at the cozy Cascadia Inn and Restaurant, enjoying dinner by myself. Today was our last day out from our next re-supply point of Skykomish, and I hiked fast all day, leaving Muse far behind. I can no longer slow myself down than can a freight train high-balling down the line. I spin the earth beneath my feet as I walk. About an hour ago now, I emerged from my mountain home and stood along Highway 2—my thumb in the air. I left a note for Muse indicating that I had secured a quick hitch and would be in town. Luckily, I really did score a quick hitch from a man with a thick Russian accent. He knew that I was hiking the PCT and was overjoyed to talk about hiking all the way down to Skykomish. When he dropped me off he handed me two peaches and wished me luck. I walked down the quiet tree-lined streets of Skykomish eating the peaches, which were delicious. Behind the small wooden town the Burlington Northern/Santa Fe rumbled between the mountain peaks. Skykomish is an old rail town, serving as maintenance and fueling station for the Great Northern Railway, which had been extended from Montana to the West Coast in 1893 creating Skykomish. The emblem of the Great Northern, a silhouetted mountain goat atop a rock outcrop, is still seen all over town—in restaurant windows, on cups and dishes, and painted on historic buildings. I like towns proud of their railroad history.

Here at the Cascadia restaurant they have provided me the telephone number for the Dinsmore's: a hiker house somewhere nearby. I borrowed a man's cell phone and spoke with Andrea Dinsmore who said she would come pick me up after dinner.

There is a teenage girl working here in the restaurant who keeps glancing over at me. No doubt I look strange; my white shirt is stained all over, hair retreats in every direction from beneath my green bandana, and feathers still dangle behind my ears. She is playing and replaying a Death Cab for Cutie album in the restaurant. I did not expect to hear Death Cab way out in Skykomish, Washington.

Muse walked in the door just as I finished my ground beef and onion dinner. "Hey, you made it," I said, sounding as amiable as possible. He sat down and raised the menu to his face. "Who'd you get a ride with?" I asked.

"Just...just let me think about what I want to eat!" he snapped. Nothing had changed. I sat out front of the Cascadia and talked with a couple locals who were trading stories about the Arctic Lynx—discussing evidence that the elusive creature did, in fact, live in the surrounding area.

Tuesday, October 3, 2006

2:10 p.m.

The Dinsmore's River Haven

The perfect example of a stock character, Jerry Dinsmore, who is as wide as he is tall, was never without a bent up cigar clenched in one side of his mouth. He wore a CAT baseball style cap everywhere he went and a white v-neck undershirt with a huge cigar burn-hole at the neckline. He obviously did not care how he looked, which precipitated his wearing some awesome outfits. Jerry was retired from a career in big rig repair.

We enjoyed a zero day yesterday at Jerry and Andrea Dinsmore's River Haven. They have a nice house off of a dirt road that connects to Highway 2. Their backyard runs up against the wide Skykomish River, rambling noisily over rocks and stones, on the far side of which are nothing but forests and mountains. A pathetic little dog follows Andrea Dinsmore around everywhere, but mostly Andrea climbs the metal, spiral staircase to the upstairs bedroom where she lingers all day watching television in her bathrobe.

Our first night at the Dinsmores, I scrounged a bag of soup from the hiker box and cooked it in Andrea's impeccably clean kitchen. It felt strange to use the pristine kitchen of perfect strangers—pulling hanging pots down from their ceiling hooks, exploring drawers for silverware—all the while Jerry sits puffing on his cigar in the neighboring room. Before long Jerry joined me in the kitchen, as did Andrea, wrapped up in her bathrobe. The presence of Jerry and his cigar filled the house like only a man can. Jerry has *his* chair by the desk in the front room, on which is *his* ash tray and lighter where he sits and puffs away, critiquing the stupidity on television, and starting each sarcastic statement with a long "Yuup..."

I called to Andrea's dog and it ran over to me, shaking and trembling as if on the verge of implosion.

"Woooow," murmured Andrea with a smoky voice. "She don't let nobody touch her but me. You must be special."

"It must be the feathers in my hair," I said. "You guys have just about the perfect place here: the sound of the river in the backyard—distant freight trains pulling over the pass…"

"Yup," said Jerry, chewing on a cigar. "Cept' you forgot the most important thing," he said managerially.

"Oh, yeah? What else is there?"

"The sound of a big rig coming down the hill—those air brakes clamping down…" He glanced almost fondly at his wife, and she at him. Big rigs had brought them together. Andrea was once a dispatcher. Ahh, romance.

"So, what got you guys into the hiker-house business?"

"Welp," started Jerry. "We just started seeing these hikers all over town and started giving 'em rides here and there." Pause. Rekindle cigar. "I'm a people person!" Jerry exclaimed, smiling through brown teeth.

For the night, Jerry had put Muse and me out in the trailer parked in the driveway, which suited me just fine. Muse hardly said a word to me all day, or the next, but the pall of his negativity was countered somewhat by Jerry Dinsmore, who I followed around in rapt amusement.

Dr. Tart arrived at the Dinsmores on our zero day, as well as Yonder and Daybreak.

When the reclusive Andrea Dinsmore made an appearance downstairs in her bathrobe, I asked her what I could do to help out around the house. She had me move a bunch of boxes from the upstairs deck down into the shed, which I did in short order. "Anything else?" I asked her when I was done. Andrea stared at me with a smirk on her face. "You know," she said. "I have some pheasant wings upstairs in a basket by the fireplace. Why don't you go pick out a couple good feathers for your hair." I did just that.

All the trail talk this past week has been about the difficulties of our next section—the Glacier Peak Wilderness; over a hundred miles of high ridges and deep canyons—true wilderness. Our guidebook introduced this section as being second in difficulty and ruggedness to the High Sierras. Yet, that is not what all the talk is about. Back in 2003, a severe spring storm battered the Glacier Peak wilderness; swelled rivers splintered seven major bridges; landslides erased large sections of trail, and sliced through switchbacks. Due to the remoteness of the Glacier Peak Wilderness, nobody has yet had the means to repair the bridges, reroute around landslides, or clear the current trail of the numerous blow-downs. On Monday afternoon, we sat in the Cascadia Restaurant—Muse, Dr. Tart, Moose, Popsicle, the effervescent Jerry Dinsmore, and myself. Hot Sister, who finished the trail a week ago, had driven up from Seattle to visit the Dinsmore's, and he sat at the table with us, explaining the difficulties of Glacier Peak, meanwhile assuring us that it was "doable." Moose and Popsicle had decided to walk an equestrian trail around the whole section.

That night at the Dinsmore's River Haven, Jerry's friend Bill came over for a visit. Equally as large, Bill rolled in wearing a baseball cap and white goatee on his face. Bill seemed enamored with my wit, and long after Jerry had resigned himself to cigars and television, Bill and I drank beer in the kitchen, debating political issues long into the evening. As is often the case, Bill, who is a Democrat, was shocked to hear of my conservative trappings.

When we finally joined Jerry in the den, I moved towards the front door to smoke outside. "Where you goin'," stated Jerry.

"Oh, I was gonna go smoke this outside," I said, scissoring a cigarette between two fingers.

"You see me smokin' in here don't you?"

"Yeah, but I have a cigarette, and I didn't know if—"

"Go ahead—smoke. I don't care."

"So wait," Bill said to me from the couch. "You're a Conservative, Christian, hiker, and smoker?"

"Yeah, I guess."

"Man, you are a question within an enigma aren't you."

About three hours ago, Jerry Dinsmore and Bill drove Muse and me back up Stevens Pass to the trailhead. "Wanna lead?" Muse asked me. I said sure, and hiked off. I usually hike for two hours then take a break; today I did the same, figuring it would take Muse a half hour at the most to catch up with me, as he usually walks pretty slow on the first day out of towns. I have been sitting around under a tree for an hour now, waiting for Muse to catch up with me. I am wondering if he started hiking behind me at all. A month or two past, Muse accused *me* of being "completely unpredictable." Muse's on-trail breaks, and periodic naps are as predictable as lightning strikes—some days he is extremely tired, the next he is extremely animated, and the boy stops to urinate no less than every ten minutes due to being over-hydrated. For Muse to name me "completely unpredictable" is the most inaccurate statement of all, as my pattern of hiking has been the same since Northern California—I hike for two hours, take a break, hike for two hours, take a break, and so on. I prefer to eat lunch between eleven and one o'clock, and I have my watch alarm set to make sure I am up no later than seven a.m. I say good morning to Muse, every morning—sometimes without response, and I am consistently in a good mood except when Muse's general rotten attitude sinks to that level where I *must* confront him to find out what atrocity I have unwittingly committed. Unpredictable? One could set their watch to the consistency of my day-to-day locomotion.

Wednesday, October 4, 2006
5:34 p.m.

Unlimited Grace

Muse finally showed up yesterday, as I was journaling. I asked him if he was okay and he said he was fine. Then I asked him how he had fallen an hour behind me, when we had only been dropped off at the trailhead two hours prior. He said that he had stopped to shift some things around in his pack, eat, and relax a bit. I sensed something was unusually awry, so I let him hike on with myself following. The day was cold, cloudy, with periodic sprinkles, as we entered the Henry M. Jackson Wilderness.

Lake Janus came into my view. Through the underbrush and hemlocks, I thought I saw Muse walk off the trail to the lakeshore. When I stood on the edge of the lake however, I did not see him anywhere; just a lapping, gray water lake surrounded by hemlock. I sat down for a couple minutes, pondering what to do—then walked on.

I hiked over an hour and found a dry area beneath a tree and sat down. By that time I figured he must be behind me still, and he was. Muse came walking around the corner, acknowledging me not. I attempted conversation, but he gave me short answers while walking on. I yelled to him that I did not know if he was in front of me or behind me, and that he should make sure I know if he leaves the trail for some reason. He responded again with a smart little comment, sufficiently pissing me off. I had been extremely nice to him at the Dinsmore's and before, all through his continued coldness—trying my best to change the candor of our relations. But I had had enough. I raised my voice and told him that his attitude was bullshit. "*You* are creating a dangerous situation," I said. "Here we are, entering one of the most dangerous sections of the trail and you won't even talk to me!"

"You're right," he responded.

"I have been nothing but cordial and nice to you since the Dinsmore's and you've been consistently rude."

"Well, now you know how I have felt for the last three months!" he said. There was some truth to this. I have never been outright rude, but I had given him somewhat of a cold shoulder due to his obsessive-compulsiveness and rotten attitude. Regardless, I told him that it is going to suck to hike the last 180 miles in this condition, and that he needed to start being nice to me so that we could make this enjoyable.

"Even if you don't feel in your heart that you like me," I said, "if you *act* nice, it will eventually change your heart as well."

He stood leaning on his trekking poles. "You're asking me for unlimited grace," he said religiously, as if he has had to forgive me over and over again. I wanted to challenge his perception of grace, but kept quiet. His next answer would determine whether I walked back to Stevens Pass and went home, or continued hiking to Canada. The trail revealed to me that I am a long-suffering man, but my breaking point had arrived, and I would not continue hiking with this precocious, deep-thinking, train-wreck of emotional swings; this ultra-light, ultra-sensitive, ultra-juvenile boy. I had suffered under enough complaining, enough obsessive-compulsiveness, too many bad moods taken out on me, and enough over-reactions over trivial matters.

Rain slowly leaked from the sky.

"Alright," he finally said. "I'll do it."

"Alright," I said.

He told me to go ahead and make camp somewhere; he wanted to sit and take a break. I walked on until seven and found a flat spot below a twisted tree on a bluff, but then decided it was too early and continued on. I hiked until dark, eventually reaching a junction where I sat down against a tree in the darkness and waited in silence. From far off I heard Muse's bear whistle. He must have been worried that I hiked on into the night without stopping, leaving him behind. I answered with my whistle and listened as his grew closer and closer. Finally he arrived. He sat down with his flashlight and took some food out. "I'd like to talk about this some more," he said. I said all right.

Thursday, October 5, 2006

11:28 a.m.

Erased Trails

It is before noon, yet I feel as though I have hiked all day. This morning I came to a junction sign with a detour sign attached. We are in the Henry M. Jackson Wilderness, nearing the Glacier Peak Wilderness where the spring storm of 2003 demolished large portions. Muse and I read the details and decided that the detour sounded just as difficult as sticking to the washed out portions of the PCT. We had heard that hikers had been going through the storm area so we decided to try it.

The difficult part started just a couple hours ago, beginning with some expected tree blow-downs across the trail. This was manageable. Then the trail crossed some streams where the bridges had been torn from their foundations by raging waters and discarded in broken pieces along side the creek. Fording these creeks was also manageable. Then we came to a larger stream where the bridge had also been discarded by raging waters, and lay in the rubble beside the creek like a desiccated and bleach-boned fish. Muse attempted to step across the stream on some rocks, but they were slick with a mud film, and before he even made it half way, he promptly slipped off the stones, almost fell, and dunked both feet in the stream. I walked back up the stream where someone had written, "log crossing" in pen on a log beside the trail. I pushed through the trailside brush, slid down the creek's muddy embankment, and found a log that lay halfway across the stream. I traversed the log easily, then climbed on all fours on exposed rocks to finish fording the creek, safe and dry.

We have stopped for lunch at the moment, having completed our most difficult challenge thus far. We encountered a valley where massive floodwaters had indeed left behind banks of mud, houses of logs, and debris everywhere. The waters had torn up the hillsides and changed the face of the canyon bottom—leaving a wiped-out flood plain of hardscrabble rocks and boulders. With it went a stretch of the PCT. Our switchbacks descended into the canyon, but before delivering us safely to the canyon floor, the trail abruptly ended where torrential waters had washed away the remaining switchbacks, leaving me staring at a twenty-foot drop-off. Muse and I walked back up the trail where hikers before us had beaten a tunnel through the bushes down the muddy slope to the valley below. Having reached the mess of the canyon floor, we wandered around for a while, following some pink ribbons tied to trees, but were unable to find where the PCT continued on the far side. Unfortunately, out of this whole trip so far, this is the one, and only section that Muse has actually lost the guidebook for some days ago, and we had decided not to go back and look for it.

Searching for the trail was not a simple matter of exploring each corner of the washed out canyon. Traversing the flood plain was an arduous, laborious task. Should I decide to explore the opposite bank, I must first find my way down a steep, water-carved and crumbling embankment; then scramble the boulder and log-strewn flood-plain; then find somewhere to safely ford an angry creek; then negotiate more trees and boulders before reaching the other side.

We stood at the edge of the flood plain stretching down from the rilles and cuts in the Glacier Peak volcano looming east, trying to figure which direction the PCT would trend. Muse said that we should go north, which was generally up-canyon.

"What does your trail instinct tell you," he asked me, convinced by this time in my superior sense of direction, though I had become lost two times for which I was given the silent treatment for days. During our hike through the snow-bound Sierras, I had repeatedly located the trail where it re-emerged from beneath the snowfields. I had saved Muse from going the wrong direction north of Aloha Lake. I had saved Muse from going the wrong direction in the Mount Hood Wilderness. I had saved Muse from going the wrong direction in the Mount Washington wilderness as well.

"I think that the trail would continue south down-canyon for a bit; then curve around back to the North." Muse trusted my judgment and we walked south, exploring the dense forest for a while on the far side of the flood plain; crawling over logs, pushing through bushes—my shins were scraped and bleeding. Still we did not find the trail. We backtracked a little bit—Muse and I walking far apart to cover more territory. I came to a high, washed out embankment near the river's edge and decided to scale it. Dirt and mud slipped beneath my feet. I grabbed roots and hoisted myself atop the ridge, and was rewarded for my effort; there was my old friend, the PCT wandering to the south before it curved back north—just as I predicted.

Thursday, October 12, 2006
11:22 a.m.

The Final Showdown

There are a lot of bears in the Glacier Peak Wilderness. I believe I have seen nine in this wilderness alone, and one bear in the Snoqualmie area, bringing my total bear count to thirteen so far on this trip. The trail continued around the west side of Glacier Peak where we encountered numerous trees blown down across the trail—cliff-side switchbacks with twenty-foot segments eroded and cut-away by sliding mud and rocks. We crossed the canyon of another major drainage of Glacier Peak where the wooden bridge had been undermined and discarded down stream. Half of the footbridge still lay across the creek; water ran across the planks where it clung partially submerged, like a wooden ship, battered and half sunk in the ocean.

Our last major ford was the Suiattle River, which roared through another expansive floodplain of boulders and tossed logs. The Suiattle was swift and deep—not at all fordable, leaving us with the task of finding a way across. Muse walked along the bank upstream, while I walked around a curve downstream where I was led to a huge log, stripped of all branches, laying supernaturally perfect across the river. I put one foot in front of the other, watching my step—the roaring waters rushed below me. Having safely crossed the Suiattle, Muse discovered where the trail continued on the far side and before long we crossed a junction sign on which was fixed a notice that we had reached the far end of the detour section. I think Muse and I may have even smiled at each other.

As I had said earlier in an entry, Muse wanted to "talk" more about our issues with each other that first night out from Skykomish— and we did. He had obviously sat down earlier to think about his case and build a tremendous argument against me that would prove me self-centered and depraved once and for all. From where we sat in the darkness of the night forest, he started off by listing three instances where he had given of himself in an unselfish manner, and how I had never reciprocated his generosity. The three examples are the following: he had once purchased for me a book of edible plants used by Native Americans; he had made a compilation CD of music for me; and when I accompanied him on his move from Orange County to San Antonio, he had purchased my return airplane ticket. He listed his three killer pieces of evidence from some dark corner of the forest and awaited my response. "What? I'm not deserving of an answer?" he said to me impatiently.

"No, of course you are. Let me think about this," I said. "Let's start hiking again."

We walked off into the night. Muse asked me another question.

"For my own sanity," he said, "please just tell me—do you really think that we have done an equal amount of work on this trip?"

"No," I said. "You have clearly done more. I've never thought that we have done an equal amount of work. But," I continued, "just because you did more work does not mean it was all necessary work; like putting together an eight-tabbed spreadsheet with macros, incorporating moon phases and meteor showers. It's impressive, but not necessary to walk the PCT."

Then I gave him a response to his first challenge of reciprocation. "As for your first question," I said, "just let me say that I am truly appreciative of the things you have done for me." I continued my answer by comparing our friendship with that of another friend of mine who has also been very unselfish with his money towards me. I explained to Muse that despite the fiscal generosity of this friend, my relationship with this person could never reach a deeper level due to the fact that our personalities are very different—he is often angry and emotional, where I am calm and passive. I also said I would love to sit down with this friend one day and thank him for his generosity, but also implore him to be more of an actual friend, meaning, someone with whom I can talk about deep things or stupid things, and someone who I know is not going to get angry and have a foul attitude.

"The truth is," I said as we climbed a ridge under a full moon, "I was turned off by you very early in our trip, due to the fact that you demonstrate three constant dispositions; you are either stressed out, in a bad mood, or being obsessive/compulsive over some trivial issue."

I talked for a while—explaining to Muse, as I had countless times before, that we choose our own reactions in life—whether we laugh at a situation or stress over a situation. I told him that it is easy to be morose and depressed, but consistent joy is the challenge in life. We owe it to people around us to be in a good mood—it is our moral duty. Society would not work if everyone acted out their emotions constantly. "It sounds trite—to be happy all the time—but it is more important than you think."

"But some of the most beautiful music and poetry comes from a state of depression," Muse countered.

"That's true," I said. "But you are not writing any music or poetry out here that I have seen. There are times in life to be sad, to be depressed—it's inevitable. But a mature person deals with their depression objectively; the immature person takes out their depression on those around them. To be depressed does not mean you are some deep and thoughtful person. I went through that depression phase in life, when I wore all black, listened to depressing music, and pondered on all the unfairness in the world. But I grew out of it; it's an immature phase that many people go through."

There was a pause at the end of which Muse said, "Wow, that really hurts. But I can see that you're being completely honest about everything. Wow. So, have you tried to tell me this all along and I just blew you off?"

"Yeah, I'd tell you here and there," I said. "But not in such a thorough way as I am now."

"Man, you've pointed out some things about me that my parents have also pointed out."

I raised a curious brow when he said that. Nevertheless, it felt good to lay it all on the table and let Muse do whatever he wanted with it. Was this a final admission a victory for me? No, I was just happy to have restored civil communication between us as we entered the difficult, detoured section of Glacier Peak.

Our last night before reaching Stehekin, we camped in a deep, cold forest of hemlock, spruce, fir, pine, and red cedar. We rose early, hiked at a fast pace, and reached the dirt road at the Stehekin River on a sunny afternoon. During the summer months and into fall, the Stehekin resort, ten miles down the dirt road, sends a shuttle four times daily, dropping off tourists at various trailheads along the way. The shuttle's last stop is High Bridge, where Muse and I sat on some roadside logs in front of the ranger station, waiting to be ferried to the Stehekin resort located alongside the blue-green tourmaline waters of Lake Chelan. Lucky for us, we arrived on the last day the shuttle ran for the season. Chelan is a Salish Indian name meaning both "lake" and "blue water." The impressive lake is fifty miles long, and 1, 486 feet at its deepest point.

When Muse and I darkened the doorway of the Stehekin restaurant, we spied a bearded young man with drab clothing seated by himself at a table. We had traveled over 2,500 miles, but had not yet seen, nor met Hannibal. He turned out to be another solid guy. We sat with Hannibal and discussed the problem of acquiring our re-supply boxes on a holiday weekend. The post office was closed and Monday was Columbus Day, leaving Tuesday as the next day the post office would be open. But Hannibal had already been in contact with the postmaster who said she would make a special trip to open the post office for us.

On Saturday night Muse and I found ourselves at the Purple Point campground, as the resort rooms were booked due to a wedding. After the sun set, I zipped myself up in my bag beneath the forest trees, and closed my eyes. Wooden boats floating on Lake Chelan knocked gently at the dock not far below. Far off in the distance, some kind of waterfowl honked. I could not sleep; not from the sounds of the lake, but from thoughts that raced through my mind—excited thoughts. Tomorrow we would enter the North Cascades National Park to complete our final seventy miles to the Canadian border. Seventy miles equals three days, equals…the end of my journey: Mexico to Canada. I thought of our very first stop at Warner Springs so long ago, yet so poignant the memory of when I came limping into the Warner Springs Ranch office with six blisters, shin splints, an aching left knee, and a torn ligament in my right foot.

I walked down to the lake and dangled my legs from the edge of the gurgling, burping dock. The night was warm, and a gentle breeze moved spiritually over the tarp of black water that filled every canyon, and surrounded each mountain fin and flank. The broad lake seemed to hold all of my memories somehow, and staring across the water, I thought of and remembered much. The last five days in the Glacier Peak Wilderness had been difficult—the terrain inconsistent and dangerous. My food supply had been woefully insufficient and I had rationed, suffering through hunger and want, and filling my maw with huckleberries from passing bushes. The pressures, pains, and hungers are wonderful in the sharpening of a person—teaching one to thoroughly appreciate—appreciate a solid meal, a warm shower, and generosity; a clean bed, a chair, a dry pair of shoes. I will never again take for granted a warm day and blue sky.

Tuesday, October 17, 2006

3:13 p.m.

The North Cascades

In the deep hours after midnight, a wind picked up over Lake Chelan, knocking the wood boats a bit louder, and silencing the distant waterfowl. I was awakened by the trembling air; rain was coming. A wall of clouds swept in over the lake, and the temperature dropped. I gathered up my belongings and walked down to a concrete enclosure on the bank of Lake Chelan. An hour later the rain came.

The North Cascades are different than I had expected. The PCT trends along the dry, eastern side of the Cascade divide, which seemingly lies in obscurity from any hint of civilized interest, protected from many storms by Mount Baker, Mount Shuksan, and the Picket Range to the west. Our stony trail was flanked on both sides by dry ridges ascending to saw toothed peaks of shale, granite, and whatever else. The open ground all about was covered in scrub huckleberry, brown heather, and dried grasses. Clumps of rugged forest run the valleys and flanks of the range—firs, white pine, mountain ash. Gone were the deep wet forests I traversed in Oregon and southern Washington. This land was raw—dominated by rock in the form of flatiron ridges, fans, and angry jagged peaks.

We entered the North Cascades in a trickling rain, but the next day the storm had passed. The remaining clouds thinned and faded to opalescence, then disappeared into cold blue skies for the remainder of our trip. Some intangibility about the North Cascades—the same intangible feeling I experience in the High Desert—inspired in me notions of eternity and ancientness, purity and fragile dominance. I felt as though the North Cascades had given birth to every mountain range stretching north and south—like this was the center of all beginning, the ebullient fountain of all mountains. The North Cascades are a wonderful place to complete my journey, for at trails end there is no wall, no finish line—no huge to city put away the thought of wilderness. From the prominence points of the North Cascades one realizes that they have walked into the middle, into the center, the cynosure of everything wild and alone. From my ridge top views were mountains upon mountains flowing south and north in a lonesome parade that did not sing songs of beginnings and ends; finish lines and final exhalations. If the mountains bore any resounding exclamation, it is the pronouncement that my journey has just begun—the mental, physical, and spiritual journey of life is dredged from the depths of one's mind by the timeless mountain views. One casts the fishing line of their gaze so far, the string of sight unravels to the end of its spindle, and that spindle is connected to the deep parts of the mind, and every wish and dream that we keep in dark places is sudden tugged to the forefront of one's mind; and we smile. Dreams do come true. Dreams are the blueprints for how we build our lives.

Muse and I leap-frogged with Hannibal and Dr. Tart the last couple days. When we had fifty miles left to Manning Park, Muse declared that he was going to hike the fifty miles in one day by getting up at two a.m. and hiking by moonlight until the sun rose wherein he would finish in the afternoon. I told him I was not interested in walking fifty miles, starting at two a.m., but despite my opting out, Muse maintained that he was going to do it. The impropriety of walking 2,600 miles with someone, then attaining the finish line apart from one another simply to finish one day early would dawn on the deep-thinking Muse, once his impulsiveness abated; thus, I predicted his change of mind on the whole matter, as I have successfully done countless times before on this journey.

On Monday afternoon, he built a campfire where we had lunch, and burned everything that was considered expendable. He burned a brand new pair of wool socks, gave away another pair, and generally did away with all extra bags, food and toilet paper to save on weight. Next, Muse recommended that I read up on the guidebook, seeing that I would be without access to it very soon. I uselessly wrote down the names of the major passes still ahead and handed the guidebook back to him. Needless to say, later that day, as we headed towards Glacier Pass, he decided against the fifty miles and vocally lamented having burned and given away the socks.

Our last night we camped at the top of forested Woody Pass. As has been my custom throughout Washington, I found a tight grove of trees, flattened out the bedding of pine needles beneath, and made myself at home. Lying there I could touch tree trunks on either side of me, and another behind my head. In my pine grove, I am protected from any sudden downpours, and feel less exposed to creatures of the night. Soon after we had bedded down, Dr. Tart and Hannibal breached the pass and joined us in our grove.

The forest that night was shafted with the pale light of the frozen moon. Somewhere nearby, a heavy animal ran through the trees coming closer, then fading, then silence; on this went. I raised my head once when it sounded near and saw a shadow pass in the moonlight through a window of trunks. Possibly a moose, deer, elk—who knows.

On Wednesday morning, we rose at five a.m. with cold, snow-patched mountains, and hiked off in the light of the moon. Around ten a.m. Dr. Tart and Hannibal, Muse and myself counted down the final four switchbacks to the Northern Terminus trail marker. Done! We took pictures all around, drank some wine, then continued down the trail eight miles further to the Manning Park Lodge to enjoy the restaurant and a good night's rest.

Saturday, October 21, 2006
7:18 a.m.

The Final Insult

I just arrived in Sacramento from Seattle via train—a twenty-hour clink down the hobo rails. I spent a good amount of time on the observation deck reading "Into the Wild."

From the Lodge in Manning Park, Muse and I took a Greyhound bus to Vancouver where my aunt Marianne picked us up and lodged us in their home in Delta, just south of Vancouver, British Columbia. My uncle Herb is an amateur pilot and is also one of few harpsichord and organ repairmen in the area. Herb showed Muse and me the harpsichord that he was working on in the basement.

Before Muse left the house the next day, he asked me the following question: "Hey Mojave. Could I get the memory card from your camera so I can put all the pictures together when I get home?"

"Well, I still need it," I said. "I'm gonna be visiting family and friends on the way home and I will still need the memory card." Muse turned from me and said nothing else. Later that morning, my aunt drove him to the bus station and he was gone.

Several days later I was visiting with my cousin Shannon who drove me around Vancouver with her two sons. We pulled over in a park on the North side of Vancouver for a group photo in front of the Vancouver skyline, but when I turned my camera on, I discovered that the memory card was gone. Thank you, Muse. Have a safe trip home.

Along the canal that runs through Delta, I picked wild blackberries, and brought them to the house for everyone to enjoy. My parents had mailed a box of civilian clothes to Delta, but they have not yet arrived; probably stuck in some customs office. I am still wearing my stained white Patagonia shirt, and green nylon shorts. I bought new shoes though, after finally throwing away the New Balance trail running shoes I had bought in Redding, and wore all the way to Canada. It was a parting of such sweet sorrow.

My cousins Warren and Shannon came over on Saturday for Saturday waffles—a tradition that I could quickly get used to. Shannon is married to an Anglican priest and has two well-behaved boys, Adam and Jacob. Warren also has two children, Rosy and Paul.

On Saturday, Shannon treated the boys and me to sushi in downtown Vancouver. Like a shell-shocked soldier just returned from a long tour of duty, I watched from the car window the hordes of people walking up and down the city streets. They appeared clean, and well-fed. Saturday night I spent at Shannon's, and went to church with her family the next morning where we sang some old-time hymns that I had not heard in many years. Shannon has a beautiful voice and sings loudest in the congregation.

On Sunday afternoon Shannon and her family went to the memorial service for her father-in-law who had recently passed on. I spent the day alone in Shannon's house. I emailed, smoked in the backyard, ate a banana, watched television. When they returned, we all went out for Chinese food. A lady whose name I forget drove me downtown around 8:30 and dropped me off in front of the Commodore Theatre for the Mew concert that I had bought a ticket for long ago in Ashland, Oregon. Mew played well, though they were not the headlining band. The singer entered the bar area after the concert where I confronted him. I shook his hand. "Hi, I walked from Mexico to see you guys."

He leaned forward a bit, as if he was not sure he heard me correctly. "You're from Mexico?" he asked.

"No, no," I yelled over the music. "I'm from California." The music made it impossible to carry on a conversation. I held up my camera and took a picture of him and me together, then left the concert to take a midnight bus back to Delta.

On Monday, Herb took me up in his Piper where we flew from Point Roberts to San Juan Island—landing on a grass airstrip. The day was warm and drowsy as we walked around the docks and observed the old buildings.

I spent four days in Vancouver, but my package of clothes did not come in the mail. On Tuesday morning Marianne delivered me back to the Greyhound Station where I was bound for Seattle. My package arrived at their house that afternoon. She forwarded it to Sacramento.

At eight p.m. on Tuesday the Greyhound bus hissed into the station in north Seattle, not far from Broadway, and dumped me onto the street. I stood in my nylon shorts, jacket, and same pack on my back twenty seven hundred miles later. I was here to stay with Joe for several days, Rachel's fiance, but at 8:00 pm he was bartending over in Alki Beach.

I walked up the street to the huge REI store where I remembered Ridge Walker said he was employed. Sure enough, he was there, helping a customer, then helping me—attempting to find a bus route that would take me to Alki Beach past eight p.m. Failing to do so, he invited me to stay at his house for the night; tomorrow I would take a bus to downtown. Ridge Walker lives with no less than a million young people crammed into an old house. I bought a six-pack of beer as a house warming gift, but he stuck them in the fridge and implored me instead to help finish off a leftover keg of beer from a recent party. I did my best.

After treating Ridge Walker, to breakfast the next morning I boarded a bus on its way to downtown, and stepped of at Pike's Market where Joe eventually picked me up. Joe worked most of the time while I was there, and Rachel was down in Orange County visiting her parents; thus, my several days in Seattle I spent wandering the streets from the downtown mall, to Pike's Market, to Pioneer Square, and so on—unable to stop walking. A seminal moment came in Pioneer Square where the bums, panhandling change from passersby, quietly watched as I walked through their midst, as if recognizing the badges of a wanderer.

On Friday morning, I rose at eight a.m., packed my stuff, and tramped the downtown streets of Seattle to the Amtrak station where I purchased a ticket to Sacramento. Sleep on the train was hard to come by because the man sitting next to me, who at every stop exited the train to smoke pot, I found sleeping and sprawled across his seat and mine. Defeated, I resigned myself to sleeping on the downstairs luggage racks, which were not quite long enough to stretch out, but were flat and away from people. I may have slept if the bathroom door, which was right across from my luggage rack, had not slammed shut every time someone entered and exited the bathroom throughout the night. At 6:30 a.m. people began congregating downstairs where I layed with the luggage. The train pulled into Sacramento in a cold dawn halo and poured me in steam and oil fumes into old town. I know Sacramento well, from having worked here for several months. I hoisted my pack and walked towards Sacramento's China-town where I knew of a Denny's. And here I sit with coffee, journal, and breakfast, waiting until Dani and Sam pick me up later.

Afterword

From atop the Flamingo Hotel in Las Vegas, anemones of fireworks boomed and bloomed overhead—reining in the new year of 2008. On Las Vegas Boulevard I stood with three friends, and a million other people, jostling shoulders and complaining of the cold wind. The Mojave Desert can get very cold in the wintertime; I have seen snow fall on the streets of Las Vegas.

I walked around recognizing, but not bothered by the cold. I wore jeans, running shoes, a long sleeve wool shirt, nylon Golite jacket with collar zipped high—the same jacket that accompanied me through the coldest stretches of the PCT. I thought back to my second day on the trail, when the sky was still beleaguered with late winter clouds and drizzle. I had simply tied a bandana around my neck, which amazingly seemed to warm my whole body. Standing on Las Vegas Boulevard, I pulled a bandana from my pocket and did the same.

It remains to this day a common occurrence: I am seated outside with a group of friends somewhere—them complaining of the cold while I feel perfectly contented. Hiking the Pacific Crest Trail has given me a larger measuring stick with which to measure hot and cold, distance, and people—even insects. What was "cold" before, I now measure against the experience of six days of wet feet, rain, sleet and snow. A problem person at work I now measure against five months of managing an obsessive-compulsive personality.

Speaking of Muse…

I finally returned home on November 1st of 2006. I waited about two weeks before sending him a polite email, hoping he had made it home all right, and inquiring as to the status of our photos. I made no mention of his stealing the memory card from my camera. To my email, I received no response. I called his parent's house in Texas a week later and left a message with his mother; still he did not call back. I called one more time and caught him in the same room with his mother. She handed the receiver to Muse.

"Hey, how's it goin?" I asked.

"Fine."

"Yeah, well, I was just wondering what's going on with the pictures?"

"You should've gotten them already. I mailed them out a week ago."

"Oh, okay. I guess they're just no quite here yet."

Silence.

"Well," I continued through his cold silence, "I guess I'll talk to you later."

"Bye."

"Bye."

It seemed pretty clear to me that Muse did not want to have anything to do with me. Oh well, I had other concerns: Meadow. We had agreed back in June that I would call her after my journey was done. But when the trip was actually over, I hesitated to do so; instead I cowardly met up with her friend Robin for sushi.

"So, how's Meadow?" I finally asked towards the end of dinner, as if Meadow had suddenly sprung to my mind.

"She's good," said Robin. "She's been busy moving to a new place and I haven't really talked to her lately."

This wasn't the information I was looking for, so I just came out and asked the question.

"So, does she have a new boyfriend?"

Robin sighed and looked away. "Joel, I didn't want to be the one to tell you…"

My heart sank. I reached for my glass of Coke, nearly knocking it over.

Nevertheless, I did call her several nights later, as I paced up and down the sidewalk in front of the Gypsy Den coffee shop. Ring, ring, ring. "Hi, this is Meadow, leave a message." I left a message. No call back, ever. The PCT giveth, and the PCT taketh away. Regrets? None. Such is the life of a Wanderlust.

Upon my return to city life, I re-enrolled in college instead of going back to my previous job. I had had eighteen units left to graduate when I quit school back in 2000 to work full time at my previous job of six years, so I figured I would take this opportunity to finally finish. Now

I am the "new guy" on campus—the 31-year-old guy who sits in the front row of class constantly asking and answering questions.

I took a part time job at the Lakeview and Rancho senior centers of Irvine. Initially, I was hired simply as a facility operations person where my responsibility was to set up rooms for different events. It was just the kind of job I wanted while I finished school—repetitive, brainless, and devoid of any major responsibility. Soon after my employment one of the head supervisors learned of my PCT hike. She is an outdoorsy person and had actually done some trail angel work along the PCT sometime in a past year. She moved me into the senior fitness center monitoring the senior's work-outs and conducting orientations for new members. Now they want me to start developing programs around the fitness center, and so on. I call this "responsibility creep," where an adept employee is given more and more responsibility without raises or promotions. Well, I have received several raises actually, but so have the other workers bearing my same title of Leader II, but their responsibilities have remained the same. I consider it a compliment however and do not complain. In fact, hiking the PCT has heightened my aversion to complaining. I make a conscious effort not to complain at work, or anywhere else. Like I said, hiking the PCT gives one a larger measuring rod with which to measure life's inconveniences.

To this day, over a year after my completion of the trail, when I step out of my house on a perfectly warm and sunny Southern California day, I think back to the miserable cold of Washington and give thanks to God for a warm day. And I do not imagine that I will ever take another warm day for granted again.

Several weeks ago Muse called me. I was filming a school project when he called.

"Hey, how's it going?" he asked amiably.

"Good, how are you? I heard you were off hiking in New Zealand?"

"Yeah, I just got back," he said. "But my liquid funds are finally running low, so it's time to get a job again. I hear you're going to hike the Appalachian Trail?"

"Yeah," I said. "If I can save up enough money, I'd like to hike it from North to South."

"When will you start?"

"Probably around late June, early July of '08."

"That's cool. I remember Dude said that it's better to hike the AT from North to South."

"Oh?"

"Anyhow, we should get some chai tea or something…"

"Yeah, let me give you a call back. I'm filming a school project at the moment."

"Alright."

It is true, the Appalachian Trail is my next major goal. I would like to say that I am vigorously planning for the hike, but I'm not. I bought the AT trail guide which is currently lost amongst the garbage in my car; beyond that, my plan is to do as little planning as possible: one bounce box to mail forward along the way, no re-supply boxes, no eight-tabbed spreadsheets, and no trail partner. This time, I go solo.

Before I put a cork in this bottle, I would definitely like to thank some people who helped us along the way: first and foremost, my loving parents for all their prayers, and for the handling of our twenty-seven resupply boxes that cluttered the extra bedroom of their home. I am sure my mother was happy to see them slowly disappear week after week so that she could vacuum each newly revealed portion of the floor. Thanks to Pam, Paul, and Maddie for driving us down to Campo, and for lunch at Highway 173. Thanks to Nate Hines for tirelessly picking us up from the trail around Tehachapi, particularly at three a.m. from Jawbone Canyon. Thanks to Andrew and Anju for dinner in Idyllwild, and for making our pictures available on the Internet. Thanks to John Tran for driving us home from Lancaster. Thanks to Ron Nipper for driving us back to Kennedy Meadows. Thanks to Dave Ervin for the Budweiser at Vermillion Valley, and thanks to his wife Dianne who made a care package for me that Dave forgot to deliver. Thanks to Sam and Dani Bader for picking us up from Donner Pass, and for spending the night with us out of Belden, and for housing me again on my way home. Thanks to Bryce Lighthall for the pick-up from Old Station, and for the new earphones. Thanks to Gloria for the pick-up from Chinook Pass. Thanks to Rachel, Joe, and August for the stay in Seattle, both times. Thanks to uncle Herb and aunt Marianne for the time spent in Vancouver, and thanks to my cousin Shannon for sushi and the stay in her home. Thanks to Scott Usher for the stay in San Francisco, and to Drew Glassell for the final ride back home. And of course, a special thanks to Muse for all of his tireless and meticulous planning before and during our adventure together. I could barely do it with you, but I could not have done it at all without you.